FROM THE WRITER'S NOTEBOOK

Around New Zealand with 80 authors

LYDIA MONIN

Published by Reed Books, a division of Reed Publishing (NZ) Ltd, 39 Rawene Road, Birkenhead, Auckland 10. Associated companies, branches and representatives throughout the world.

ISBN-13: 978 0 7900 1108 0
ISBN-10: 0 7900 1108 5

A cataloguing-in-publication record for this title is available from the National Library of New Zealand.

First published 2006

Design by Jason Anscomb
Maps by Outline Draughting

Printed in China

Contents

THIS, TO SOME EXTENT, IS A spurious exercise. The only real 'debt' on this book is to the authors whose work graces the pages and who have portayed my country with such perception and affection. However, this work would not have been possible without the following who accompanied me either directly or indirectly on the journey:

For everything, Andrew; for their help, advice and 'The Esplanade', Mum and Dad; for their help, advice and their library, Peter and Paul; for 'Glannau Llwchwr', Lyn and Len; for answering my queries and providing documents, David Page, Peter and Jill Grenfell, Jinty Rorke, Esmé Richards, Richard Greenaway, Jenny Penman, Robert McGregor, Katherine Milburn, Don Stafford, Paul Clements, Thomas H. Pauly, Teresa Scally, Clarice Stasz, Nick Tolan, John Chibnall, Rod Burke, John Leigh, Stuart Park, Kim Wilkinson, Lynne Huddleston, Pat Mock, Jan Giles, Tom Heyes, Wendy Pettigrew, Anna Wilkinson, Marianne Foster, Jo Massey, Warren Feeney and numerous other staff members from a variety of museums, hotels, clubs, schools, visitor centres, libraries, newspapers and city councils as well as the New Zealand Historic Places Trust; for their invaluable resources, Room 315 of the New York Public Library, Trinity College Library, British Library, British Newspaper Library, Auckland City Library, National Library of New Zealand, Alexander Turnbull Library, Dunedin City Library, Hocken Library and Archives New Zealand.

Many thanks to the following for permission to reproduce copyrighted material: from 'New Zealand's windy city', Jan Morris, by permission of Jan Morris; from *Future Indefinite*, Noël Coward, by permission of Methuen Publishing Ltd © The Estate of Noël Coward; from *The Letters of Rupert Brooke*, edited by Geoffrey Keynes, by permission of Faber and Faber Ltd; from *A Visit to New Zealand*, J.B. Priestley (© Estate of J.B. Priestley 1974) by permission of PFD (www.pfd.co.uk) on behalf of the Estate of J.B. Priestley.

Arrival

Mark Twain was surprised to discover that New Zealand wasn't linked to Australia by a bridge. He believed, like most of his compatriots, that New Zealand lay very close to 'Australia or Asia, or somewhere'. According to Twain, people liked to *think* they knew where New Zealand was in the same way they liked to *think* they knew where 'Hertzegovina' was, how to pronounce 'pariah' and how to use the word 'unique' correctly. 'There are but four or five people in the world who possess this knowledge, and these make their living out of it,' he wrote. Twain learned the true position of New Zealand from a Yale University professor he met on a steamer sailing the Great Lakes. The author quizzed the academic further. 'When he was done,' Twain wrote, 'I was lost in wonder and admiration, and said to myself, he knows everything; in the domain of human knowledge he is king.'

Much has been written about New Zealand since the Europeans arrived; its cannibals, fertile lands, climate and remarkable beauty were a source of great fascination. In March 1914 the British *Bookman* commented that New Zealand was becoming so well known that 'people on this side of the world are even forming the habit of "running down" there for a little fishing or mountaineering, or to study the unique social conditions of the Dominion'. But since the earliest days of settlement visiting New Zealand from the northern hemisphere has largely been the preserve of the privileged. Despite an emerging post-war travel boom, James Michener's feature about the country in *Holiday* magazine in early 1951 was prefaced with: 'It's 7000 miles away and chances are you'll never visit it, but you should know something about the land many travellers call the most beautiful on earth.'

A wealth of literature about New Zealand has existed for at least a century and a half, yet for much of that time the average northern hemisphere resident wasn't interested in reading it. The country was small, inaccessible and a long way from the world's most powerful states. A lack of knowledge engendered many curious ideas. Sir Arthur Conan

Doyle wrote in the 1920s that the average Briton thought New Zealand was one solid island but that a trip across the wild Cook Strait would quickly sort out the misunderstanding. In the 1960s British travel writer Jan Morris wrote that Americans had a notion they could find geysers in Wellington's suburbs and Maori in 'grass aprons' on the city's outskirts, while the English would probably associate the city with a joke about the entire Royal Navy being accommodated in its harbour. Few foreigners would be able to describe New Zealand's capital city in any detail, Morris claimed, or even be sure whether it was in the North or South Island.

British writer Thomas Babington Macaulay best encapsulated the enduring perception of the almost incomprehensible distance between New Zealand and Europe in 1840. In *On Ranke's History of the Popes* he wrote the Roman Catholic Church 'may still exist in undiminished vigour when some traveller from New Zealand shall, in the midst of a vast solitude, take his stand on a broken arch of London Bridge to sketch the ruins of St. Paul's'. Macaulay's image of a solitary traveller sitting in a London wasteland inspired a Doré engraving entitled *The New Zealander*. Anthony Trollope drew on Macaulay's idea when he titled his commentary on English society, politics and culture, *The New Zealander*.

During the Cold War an idea was developed that New Zealand was so isolated it could survive a global catastrophe like nuclear war. In John Wyndham's 1955 book set in Eastern Canada, *The Chrysalids*, New Zealanders rescue a group of people in a post-holocaust world. Like Wyndham's other famous novels *The Day of the Triffids* and *The Kraken Wakes*, *The Chrysalids*, which some critics say is his best novel, is a story of survival. The narrator, David, lives in the community of Waknuk, which is beset by genetic mutation. Anyone born with a deformity is deemed offensive and unacceptable to God so newborn babies with abnormalities are killed. David, who is able to communicate telepathically with a group of other young people who share his dangerous secret, has to flee Waknuk with a cousin and Petra, his younger sister. Petra makes telepathic contact with a woman halfway around the world from a place with two parts, surrounded by sea and where 'you can see the sun shining on it for miles and miles and it's all blue'. Most of its people are telepathic but they are not persecuted for it. After the holocaust, 'Sealand', which hasn't been as badly affected as other places, is cut off from the rest of the world and sinks 'back almost to barbarism', before the strain of 'thought-shape makers' becomes more powerful and sophisticated. Sealanders rebuild flying machines, establish contact with other thought-shape makers and try to contact and rescue whoever they can. They represent an evolving sector of humanity.

In Aldous Huxley's *Ape and Essence*, published in 1948, the 'New Zealand Rediscovery Expedition' arrives by ship in Los Angeles more than a century after a devastating nuclear war. It's February 2108 and New Zealand has escaped the effects of the war because 'it was too remote to be worth anybody's while to obliterate'. It continued to exist in isolation while its people waited for the radioactivity blighting the rest of the world to abate. After the expedition arrives in the United States, its leader, Auckland University's Dr Alfred Poole (nicknamed 'Stagnant Poole' by his students and young colleagues) becomes separated from the other New Zealanders and falls in love with a local woman, Loola. Eventually the New Zealanders return home and Dr Poole and Loola escape to the desert. *Ape and Essence*, one of four science fiction novels by Huxley including *Brave New World*, was written while the author was living in California.

The New Zealanders in *Ape and Essence* represent a decent, civilised society in contrast with the nightmarish, depraved and misogynistic world they discover. Deformed babies are violently murdered on 'Belial Day' (although the rules are slightly more flexible than in *The Chrysalids* as it's legal to have up to three pairs of nipples and seven toes and fingers), women who give birth to deformed babies are punished, there is state-controlled mating, the Devil is worshipped, graves are robbed and culture is of no value. New Zealand is portrayed as 'nothing very exciting or spectacular, of course. No Parthenons or Sistine Chapels, no Newtons or Mozarts or Shakespeares; but also no Ezzelinos, no Napoleons or Hitlers or Jay Goulds, no Inquisitions or NKVD's, no purges, pogroms or lynchings. No heights or abysses, but plenty of milk for the kids, and a reasonably high average IQ, and everything, in a quiet provincial way, thoroughly cosy and sensible and humane.'

Utopian ideas about New Zealand weren't confined to works of fiction. When George Bernard Shaw set sail for New Zealand in February 1934 the American press reported that he was on his way to see 'the only country in the British Empire where white men and natives have lived for a century on terms of perfect equality and friendship'.

Many of these perceptions are partially true. New Zealand *is* a long way from Europe and America and it wouldn't have been devastated in the first phase of nuclear conflict. It could be argued that, in general, Maori and the British have enjoyed better relations than many other indigenous peoples and their colonisers. New Zealand has introduced some admirable welfare legislation such as milk in schools and old-age pensions, and it was the first country in the world to give women the vote. But perception is often, at the very least, an exaggeration of the truth. The real New Zealand doesn't have perfect race relations, and it wasn't the idealised, uncomplicated, nuclear bombproof society of Wyndham and Huxley's novels. Interestingly, in his 1957 post-holocaust novel *On the Beach*, British-born Australian novelist Nevil Shute reveals a far more pessimistic view of how his country and neighbouring New Zealand would fare after nuclear war. Their inhabitants survive only until the radiation inevitably spreads south from the northern hemisphere.

What writers *actually* experienced when they visited New Zealand as opposed to what they *thought* they would experience makes for fascinating reading. Standing in the rain in New Zealand's capital and holding a live kiwi, Jan Morris remembered her 'misty preconceptions of Wellington, and decided that the truth far surpassed the fancy'. When

Arthur Conan Doyle had to sail through Cook Strait he experienced the particularly turbulent stretch of water separating the North Island from the South and Twain, of course, found no bridge over the Tasman Sea.

Playwright and composer Noël Coward told a reporter that he avoided reading up on New Zealand before arriving in the country. 'Descriptions and even photographs create impressions which are far from the reality. I have found it best to do one's study after, and not before.' As Coward suggests, the gap between perception and reality can be rather large. But Charles Dickens' Mr Booley would argue that the value of travellers capturing images of distant lands for people who couldn't travel was also immense. In *Some Account of an Extraordinary Traveller*, Mr Booley appears to have abandoned his routine life one day at the age of 65 to visit many far-flung nations including New Zealand. But the story ends with the revelation that Booley has been visiting panoramas in London. 'Some of the best results of actual travel are suggested by such means to those whose lot it is to stay at home. New worlds open out to them, beyond their little worlds, and widen their range of reflection, information, sympathy, and interest. The more man knows of man, the better for the common brotherhood among us all,' said Booley.

After Twain heard all about New Zealand, he tested the Yale professor's knowledge about 'Hertzegovina, and pariah, and unique', but the academic started to generalise and looked embarrassed. Twain asked him why he was so knowledgeable about just one topic. The stranger replied that a professor from Wellington once visited him at home. College etiquette required him to invite the caller to dinner and the event had to begin with a speech honouring the guest's country. The professor realised he knew nothing about New Zealand except that it was linked to 'Australia, Asia or somewhere' by a bridge. He asked his wife to keep the guest busy while he ran to another professor's house to ask him to host the dinner and save the university's reputation — but the second academic also knew little about New Zealand. Several other professors in the faculty were consulted and they were all equally ignorant. Finally, the men devised a plan: they could attend the dinner without embarrassment if their wives entertained the visitor while they all studied New Zealand furiously for the next eight and a half hours. At the dinner that night the Yale professors talked confidently about New Zealand for some time, before noticing their guest had become quiet. When questioned, the Wellington academic confessed *he* was the embarrassed one. Although he'd lived in New Zealand for 18 years and had been a professor for five, he realised he knew 'almost nothing' about his country. 'I have learned 50 times,' he told them, 'yes, a hundred times more about New Zealand in these two hours at this table than I ever knew before in all the eighteen years put together.'

TALES OF THE ANGLER'S BRAVADO

His was a world of gunslingers, desperadoes, virtuous women and wild, untamed landscapes. He was the biggest, 'baddest' writer of them all. Zane Grey was in town. It was high summer 1926, and he rode into the 'beautiful little hamlet' Russell by boat across a bay which 'resembled that of Avalon, having a crescent-shaped beach and a line of quaint white houses'. He wasn't wearing a 'sombrero, chaps, spurs and guns', much to the disappointment of the children. Born Pearl Zane Gray, the western author later dropped his feminine-sounding first name (thought to have been bestowed upon him by his mother in honour of Queen Victoria who liked wearing pearl grey clothes), began using his middle name and changed the 'a' in Gray to an 'e'.

Although Grey's works weren't critically acclaimed, his popularity was such that his book sales were counted in tens of millions during his lifetime. The author noticed that copies of *Riders of the Purple Sage*, *The Light of Western Stars* and his myriad of other western blockbusters were everywhere he went in New Zealand, even in remote houses in the bush. They were well-thumbed and made him realize 'the appalling responsibility of a novelist who in these modern days of materialism dares to foster idealism and love of nature, chivalry in men and chastity in women. Yet how potent the knowledge for renewed hope and endurance!'

Grey spent a couple of days in Russell discussing fishing with anglers and boatmen. The more he listened to tales about the hooking of great fish that broke free or had to be cut away after hours of battling, the more convinced he became that the area was an untapped fishing haven. Grey spent two months in the Bay of Islands with his fishing companion Captain Laurie Mitchell and a large entourage that included a cook and her assistant sons, a secretary, an American film photographer and a New Zealand photographer supplied by the government that also provided two servants. Grey and Mitchell had two boatmen each. Grey wrote about his adventures in *Tales of the Angler's Eldorado, New Zealand*, published in 1926. His exploits were reported in detail by local newspapers and he brought international recognition to the Bay of Islands.

The excitement surrounding Grey's presence in the Bay of Islands that summer, even though he spent little time in Russell, had a marked effect on the town.

> The presence of Mr Zane Grey and the accompanying strong contingent of overseas sportsmen has had much to do with the degree in which even the casual holiday-maker, whose personal ambition travels little further than throwing a line over the wharf to await the juvenile snapper and kahawai occasionally caught there, yet discourses learnedly of marlin and broadbill, or mako and thresher. It is not that Russell sees much, or, indeed anything, of the majority of these visitors. They keep to their camps at the entrance or the outer islands, but word of their exploits travels fast.
>
> *Auckland Weekly News*, 4 March 1926

It was early on a clear and still summer's morning, four days before Christmas 1835, when a sailing ship with three masts and ten guns appeared near the mouth of the Bay of Islands. The HMS *Beagle*, which had been ponderously circumnavigating the world for four years, was becalmed for several hours but finally anchored in the early afternoon. It was captained by Robert FitzRoy, who would later become governor of New Zealand, and carried on board a keen young naturalist. After more than three wretched weeks at sea since leaving Tahiti, Charles Darwin was eager to explore his new surroundings. From the anchorage the 26-year-old could see houses scattered along the water's edge, three whaling ships at anchor and the occasional canoe crossing the bay. Only a single Maori canoe came alongside and the *Beagle*'s arrival was quiet compared with the 'joyful and boisterous welcome' it had received at Tahiti. A small church with rows of arched glass windows was being built in one corner of the bay. 'Placing a church at the head quarters of iniquity, at such a notorious place as Kororadika [Kororareka], is certainly a bold trial,' Darwin and FitzRoy later wrote in 'A letter, containing remarks on the moral state of Tahiti, New Zealand, &c.' in the *South African Christian Recorder*. The crew of the *Beagle* had arrived at a place they described as 'the very strong hold of vice'. Others knew it as at the 'Hellhole of the Pacific'.

AMERICAN WESTERN WRITER ZANE GREY, 1926. S.C. SMITH COLLECTION, ALEXANDER TURNBULL LIBRARY, WELLINGTON, NEW ZEALAND. G-48159-1/2.

Darwin had dreamed of travelling to remote lands since he was a schoolboy reading the pocket book *Wonders of the World,* which described such glories as Mt Vesuvius, the Andes, the Geysers, Niagara Falls and the Great Wall of China. He 'disputed with other boys about the veracity of some of the statements' and wrote in his autobiography that the book 'first gave me a wish to travel in remote countries, which was ultimately fulfilled by the voyage of the *Beagle*'. Darwin read that Captain FitzRoy was willing to give up part of his cabin for a naturalist to join the expedition without pay. But events conspired to prevent Darwin joining the voyage: his father objected to the trip and persuaded him to refuse the position, until his uncle Josiah Wedgwood intervened. And then there was his nose. He later found out it was a clear sign that he wasn't up to a long sea voyage.

> Afterwards on becoming very intimate with Fitz-Roy I heard that I had run a very narrow risk of being rejected, on account of the shape of my nose! He was an ardent disciple of Lavater, and was convinced that he could judge a man's character by the outline of his features; and he doubted whether any one with my nose could possess sufficient energy and determination for the voyage. But I think he was afterwards well satisfied that my nose had spoken falsely.

Kororareka was in the heart of the Bay of Islands, an area of attractive mainland beaches with a scattering of pretty islands, numerous coves and clear blue waters. Yet Darwin found the village repulsive. The place now known as Russell, about one hundred and ninety kilometres north of Auckland, was a thriving whaling port where Maori and European sailors regularly traded food, alcohol, girls, timber and firearms. Darwin saw 'filthy hovels' and he was shocked to see English and Maori alike living in squalor. He wanted to civilise the place and gave money to the church that was being built. He compared Maori unfavourably with the Tahitian.

> He may, perhaps be superior in energy, but in every other respect his character is of a much lower order. One glance at their respective expressions, brings conviction to the mind that one is a savage, the other a civilized man … No doubt the extraordinary manner in which tattooing is here practised, gives a disagreeable expression to their countenances … But, besides this, there is a twinkling in the eye, which cannot indicate anything but cunning and ferocity.

Rum shops lined the beach at Kororareka in Darwin's time and Londoner Joel Samuel Polack had recently built the country's first commercial brewery. Polack, a Jewish immigrant, had lived for a year as a trader at Hokianga, further north on the west coast, before moving to Kororareka and getting involved in the flax, timber and brewing industries. He bought nine acres of land from Maori and built a house at the northern end of the beach. He returned to England in 1837 and promoted the colony in two well-received books about his adventures, *New Zealand: Being a Narrative of Travels and Adventures During a Residence in that Country Between the Years 1831 and 1837* and *Manners and Customs of the New Zealanders*. 'The cause that has induced me to present to the public a narrative of a few of my adventures in that country is principally to excite attention towards it by a statement of plain, unvarnished facts,' Polack explained. He advocated colonisation before a House of Lords select committee in London in 1838 and he believed that Maori would only survive through systematic, rather than ad hoc, settlement.

Polack was interested in the numerous rules of tapu and the many beliefs that governed Maori daily life. He saw a group of Maori carrying bags of flour and biscuit from a boat into his shop when one of the bags ripped open spilling biscuit. The broken bag was carried by an 'inferior chief' and a 'slave man' standing nearby bent down to pick up the bread. Polack offered him the bread for his trouble, but the 'chief carrier' intervened and said the slave should be given something else, because if he ate something that had been carried on the chief's back he would die.

After auctioning some of his New Zealand land in London, Polack returned to the country in 1842. In his absence a treaty was signed at Waitangi, north of Paihia, British

CHRIST CHURCH, RUSSELL. Special Collections, Auckland City Libraries (N.Z.), 4-6152

sovereignty was proclaimed, and New Zealand's first capital was established a few kilometres south of Kororareka at Okiato. Less than a year later the seat of government was transferred to Auckland and Kororareka spiralled into decline. Its name, so long in ill repute, was gradually dropped in favour of Russell, while the site of the first capital was known as 'Old' Russell or by its former name Okiato. In July 1844 Nga Puhi leader Hone Heke's second-in-command cut down the flagstaff on Maiki Hill, near Kororareka. Originally a gift from Heke for flying a Maori flag, a Union Jack had been attached to it instead. The following year Heke cut down the new flagpole and felled yet another later the same month. Maori attacked the village and the flagstaff was cut down for the fourth time. Kororareka was razed by a powder-magazine explosion and Polack's house and records were burnt so he moved his business to Auckland and stayed there until 1850 when he left for California, never to return.

The crew of a nineteenth century whaling ship, having 'passed with the utmost rapidity through all the stages of drunkenness' lay 'like logs, in the full blaze of the sun, on the beach,' wrote Frank T. Bullen in his 1898 work *The Cruise of the Cachalot.* The *Cachalot*'s crew had been given a day off for the first time since leaving Honolulu, with ten shillings to spend in Russell. Bullen, first mate on the *Cachalot* during a three-year whaling expedition around the world from New Bedford, Massachusetts, wrote that the crew had been ashore at other places but 'that was not looked upon in the same light as a day's freedom in a town where liquor might be procured, and the questionable privilege of getting drunk taken advantage of'. To the 'ordinary sailor-man', Bullen wrote, 'the place presented no other forms of amusement besides drinking, and I was grieved to see almost the whole crowd, including the Kanakas [Pacific Islanders], emerge from the grog-shop plentifully supplied with bottles, and, seating themselves on the beach, commence their carouse. The natives evinced the greatest eagerness to get drunk, swallowing down the horrible "square gin" as if it were water.' Most were prostrate on the beach less than an hour after going ashore so the captain suggested they be brought back to the ship 'as they were only exposed to robbery by the few prowling Maories [*sic*] that loafed about the beach — a curious contrast to the stately fellows met with in other parts of New Zealand,' wrote Bullen.

Russell had lost its vitality, Bullen thought. 'The whole place seemed a maritime sleepy hollow, the dwellers in which had lost all interest in life.' He thought it was a pity that when the whaling population dwindled the former capital of New Zealand didn't have any vibrant industries of its own to fall back on. 'Remembering, as I did, the beauty, the energy, and prosperity of the great New Zealand ports, some of them with not a tithe of the natural advantages of Russell, I felt amazed, almost indignant, at its dead-and-alive appearance.'

Bullen had a tough childhood before becoming a sailor. By the age of seven or eight he was roaming the streets of London in search of food. He left school at nine and worked at a variety of lowly jobs before going to sea a few years later, in a ship commanded by an uncle who beat him. By the time he joined the *Cachalot* he was an 18-year-old with six years' sailing experience, but neither he nor his crewmates knew they were signing on to a whaler. They didn't know what the ship was called, where it was going, how long they'd be away, or how much they'd be paid. In 1882 Bullen came ashore for good and by the turn of the century he was a full-time writer. His books were full of romanticised adventures. He wrote 'as if he were talking' and his only revision involved checking for omissions and punctuation. But his work drew praise from Rudyard Kipling. In a letter accompanying the 1899 edition of *The Cruise of the Cachalot*, Kipling called the work 'immense'. He had 'never read anything that equals it in its deep-sea wonder and mystery', nor did he think any other book had 'so completely covered the whole business of whale fishing, and at the same time given such real and new sea pictures'. Bullen loved reading Kipling before he became a writer and offered him the material for *The Cruise of the Cachalot*. After Kipling refused, he asked whether the eminent author would write an introduction. Kipling declined again, saying that if his name was in the book his critics might attack Bullen, but he advised the budding author to get his manuscript typed and agreed to read it. According to his 1915 obituary in *The Times*, by the age of 40 Bullen was on 'a flood tide of prosperity' and was 'enjoying a keen demand for his books, stories and articles'.

In the 1830s, missionaries battling to convert the local Maori lived across the harbour in a small village about one and a half nautical miles southwest of Kororareka. Paihia lay in a sheltered inlet, protected from the Pacific Ocean by the peninsula on which Kororareka was situated. The village, known as 'Heaven', bore a striking contrast to the disreputable settlement and beach it faced, otherwise known as 'Hell'. Paihia was home to teachers, blacksmiths and carpenters and it had a printing press that was producing Maori translations of parts of the Bible. Darwin admired the missionaries' whitewashed cottages with their gardens of honeysuckle, jasmine and sweetbrier that outshone the 'hovels' of Maori servants and labourers. Augustus Earle, an artist who had travelled to New Zealand

and lived among Maori before Darwin's trip, criticised the missionaries' attitude towards New Zealand's indigenous inhabitants in his book *A Narrative of a Nine Months' Residence in New Zealand in 1827.* Earle's book was sent to the Williams brothers a few weeks after publication who then put up a vigorous defence in a series of letters to church superiors. Earle had also been on the *Beagle* voyage with Darwin before ill-health forced him to leave the ship, but a copy of the *Narrative* remained on board. Darwin concluded that Earle's claims were unjustified. He vented his annoyance in a letter to his sister Caroline from his cabin after a meal of pork and potatoes the day after Boxing Day, 1835. 'We are quite indignant with Earle's book, beside extreme injustice it shows ingratitude. Those very missionaries, who are accused of coldness, I know without doubt that they always treated him with far more civility, than his open licentiousness could have given reason to expect.'

CHARLES DARWIN C.1875 (PHOTOGRAPHER UNKNOWN). ALEXANDER TURNBULL LIBRARY, WELLINGTON, NEW ZEALAND. F-38711-1/2.

On Christmas Day Darwin attended a part-English, part-Maori service at the Paihia chapel, a lath and plaster building which has since been replaced several times, most recently by a stone church. In his diary entry for the twenty-fifth he wrote that his party hadn't heard of any 'recent acts of cannibalism', and that charred human bones found near a fireplace on a small island near the anchorage could have been there for several years. 'It is probable that the moral state of the people will rapidly improve,' he predicted. Tales of cannibalism in the South Seas were well known in Europe by the time of Darwin's visit. French Enlightenment writer and philosopher Voltaire mentioned New Zealand in his eighteenth century musings on the subject. Voltaire wrote of humans eating one another in several of his works. In his famous 1759 'conte philosophique' *Candide*, and in his *Dictionnaire Philosophique* published in 1764, he explored the idea that cannibalism may have been motivated by a need for food rather than lust. In another of his contes, *Les Oreilles du comte de Chesterfield* (*Lord Chesterfield's Ears*), published in 1775, M. Grou, who had voyaged around the world with Banks and Solander, joined a conversation with two other philosophers. He said he had often been asked, 'whether all the inhabitants of that large country called New Zealand, who are to this day the most barbarous of the barbarous, were baptized in the Catholic Faith? I have answered, I knew nothing about it, but that the thing might nevertheless be; that the Jews who were still greater barbarians than the New Zealanders, had two baptisms instead of one. I allude to their baptism of justice, and their baptism of dwelling.'

Grou declared that no other religion he had seen on his travels compared with the island of Otaheite (Tahiti). The island was 'much more civilized than New Zealand' and 'in some respects is far preferable to either France or England'.

The cannibalism shocked and disgusted the missionaries in the Bay of Islands, but it inspired one of the great American authors, Herman Melville. In *Moby Dick*, Melville's sailor Ishmael needs a bed for the night in a strange town. An inn's landlord offers him a bed that he has to share with a harpooner, Queequeg, who has just returned from the South Seas and is in town trying to sell 'four heads strung on a string, for all the airth like a string of inions'. When 'the infernal head-peddler' Queequeg returns, Ishmael glimpses his tattoos.

Although Queequeg comes from Kokovoko ('an island far away to the West and South. It is not down on any map; true places never are'), Geoffrey Sanborn of Bard College argued in *American Literature* that Melville based Queequeg on George Lillie Craik's 1830 depiction of Tupai Cupa in *The New Zealanders.* The book tells the story of the touching friendship between British merchant ship captain Richard Reynolds and Tupai Cupa (Te Pehi Kupe), a Maori chief who travelled with Reynolds to England after boarding his ship in 1824 and saying in broken English that he wanted to go to Europe and 'see King Georgy'. Like Te Pehi Kupe, Queequeg was heavily tattooed.

> Such a face! It was of a dark, purplish, yellow colour, here and there stuck over with large blackish looking squares. Yes, it's just as I thought, he's a terrible bedfellow; he's been in a fight, got dreadfully cut, and here he is, just from the surgeon. But at that moment he chanced to turn his face so towards the light, that I plainly saw they could not be sticking-plasters at all, those black squares on his cheeks. They were stains of some sort or other. At first I knew not what to make of this; but soon an inkling of the truth occurred to me. I remembered a story of a white man — a whaleman too — who, falling among the cannibals, had been tattooed by them. I concluded that this harpooner, in the course of his distant voyages, must have met with a similar adventure.

'The most important thing [Melville] took from *The New Zealanders* was the atmosphere of romance that suffuses the relationship between Te Pehi Kupe and Reynolds,' Sanborn argued. After getting over his initial horror that Queequeg was a tattooed cannibal, Ishmael starts to warm to his companion. 'For all his tattooings he was on the whole a clean, comely looking cannibal. What's all this fuss I have been making about, thought I to myself — the man's a human being just as I am: he has just as much reason to fear me, as I have to be afraid of him. Better sleep with a sober cannibal than a drunken Christian.'

Meville drew on his own adventures when he wrote *Moby Dick* and other sea tales. In 1841 he left New Bedford on the *Acushnet* for a whaling voyage to the South Pacific, which he and a friend later deserted in the Marquesas Islands in what is now French Polynesia. Seeking refuge in an area inhabited by the supposed cannibals, the Typees, Melville escaped the island a few weeks later on the *Lucy Ann,* a whaler that had been used extensively in Sydney-New Zealand trade and had often carried Maori artifacts and tattooed heads to Sydney. Melville swapped the company of rumoured cannibals for drunken and mutinous sailors and when the ship landed at Papeete he refused to work. He was arrested and tried but was allowed to escape after his ship departed. After a spell on Moorea he was picked up by another whaler that took him to the Hawaiian Islands before he joined a US frigate bound for Boston, where he was finally discharged more than three years after leaving home. Melville's adventures gave him material for several novels. *Typee: A Peep at Polynesian Life* was published in 1846 and the sequel, *Omoo*, in which the *Lucy Ann* became the *Julia*, soon followed. *Moby Dick*, Melville's famous whaling story, was published a few years later in 1851.

In *Manners and Customs* Polack wrote that Maori preserved a tattooed head of their enemy by removing it from the body and then extracting the brain, eyes, and tongue. Next, the scull was 'carefully cleansed from any putrefying remains; the inside is filled with dressed flax, and the skin hanging from the neck is closed up, being drawn together like a closed purse, it is then demi-cooked by the steaming process peculiar to the people, and the fat carefully wiped off, it is then exposed to the strong rays of the sun, and at night to the smoke of a wood fire, which is sufficient to preserve it for many years, with an occasional airing, as a preservative from damp.' By the end of this process, Polack explained, the head of a man could shrink to that of a ten-year-old boy's. Preserved heads were placed on poles in the village and produced on gala days and for important visitors.

A bloody event at Te Hue Bay, on the western side of another Bay of Islands peninsula to the east of Russell, inspired a work by French author Alexandre Dumas (Père). French explorer Captain Marc Joseph Marion du Fresne arrived in the Bay of Islands in March 1772. The *Mascarin* and the *Marquis de Castries* anchored to the west of Moturua Island, one of a chain of islands spread over some 13 nautical miles northeast between Russell and Cape Brett, beyond which lies the vast South Pacific Ocean. Marion du Fresne required a prolonged stay in the Bay of Islands to repair his storm-damaged ship, so the French established one camp on Moturua Island and another on the mainland close by, for cutting spars. He and his men enjoyed a friendly reception from the Maori and the two groups traded and socialised. But several weeks later Marion du Fresne and more than twenty of his crew were murdered. It's not clear what led to the massacre, but misunderstandings were rife and it's possible the French may have angered Maori by fishing in sacred waters or violating tapu in some other way. The remainder of the French party retaliated by attacking the Maori and razing three villages. Before they left they buried a bottle claiming New Zealand for the French. The bottle has never been found.

In the mid-nineteenth century, Dumas, the author of *Le Comte de Monte-Cristo* and *Les Trois Mousquetaires,* read about Marion du Fresne's death in *Nouveau Voyage à la Mer du Sud*, written by Crozet, the second-in-command. Dumas was collecting material concerning disasters at sea for his work *Drames de la Mer* and decided to include Marion du Fresne's story.

Dumas' *Le Capitaine Marion* was translated into English by a New Zealander who built up one of the largest collection of works by and about Dumas outside Paris. Frank Wild Reed, brother of the publisher Alfred Hamish Reed, developed a passion for Dumas after reading *The Queen's Necklace* (*Le Collier de la Reine*) in 1886, just before his family immigrated to New Zealand from England. When Reed wanted to read the books that hadn't been translated into English he learned French and translated them himself. His collection of more than 3300 volumes is now housed in the Auckland City Library.

Alexandre Dumas also worked on publishing the journal of a surgeon who served on whaling ships in and around New Zealand waters in the 1830s and 40s. Dumas rewrote and edited Felix Maynard's journal, published as *Les Baleiniers* (*The Whalers*). The work came out serially in *La France* and then in book form in 1859 and Reed's English translation followed in 1937. Reed had also translated the first four volumes of *Le Journal de Madame Giovanni,* another journal reworked and edited by Dumas, but didn't publish it because it contained many inaccuracies and he didn't think it would sell. *The Journal of Madame Giovanni* is the account of a woman who travelled to New Zealand, Australia, the Pacific Islands, California and Mexico between 1843 and 1853 with her Italian merchant husband.

British novelist Eric Linklater met the 'self-made scholar' Frank Reed in the Northland town of Whangarei ('a little place but prosperous, both port and market town') during a lecture tour in 1951, and was given a general bibliography of almost 500 pages. The New Zealander's enthusiasm for Dumas, he wrote in *A Year of Space: A Chapter in Autobiography*, 'had not grown weary, the spell was still upon him'.

> It is an impertinence, I suppose, to say of any man that he is happy; but when, at seventy-odd years of age, a lively and ardent mind is discovered behind the

placid mien of a lifelong scholar — when an old man talks with the exuberance of youth about a subject to which he has been faithful for half a century — why, there is some reason for suspecting happiness.

French explorer Jules Sébastien César Dumont d'Urville was inspired to write a novel about New Zealand after just two weeks in the Bay of Islands. Dumont d'Urville was second-in-command on Duperrey's 1822–25 voyage of discovery on the *Coquille*, which stopped at the Bay of Islands from 3 to 17 April 1824. He wrote the first draft of his novel, *Les Zélandais: Histoire Australienne*, on the homeward journey. The manuscript wasn't published until Carol Legge translated *The New Zealanders: a story of Austral lands* into English for Victoria University Press in 1992. Legge noted that according to Monsieur Lesson, the *Coquille*'s pharmacist, Dumont d'Urville had second thoughts about publishing the book because he was concerned about the public mixing up his scientific work and his fiction. In his introduction Dumont d'Urville claims the author is a convict who was shipwrecked in New Zealand and it appears to be an attempt to distance himself from the work of fiction.

The original manuscript, in Dumont d'Urville's wife's handwriting, is kept in the Archives Nationales fond Marine in Paris. Legge describes the work as an 'ethnographic novel' that blends fact and fiction. Set in Northland, the novel is about the rivalry between two chiefs. Dumont d'Urville is sympathetic to Maori and their culture, soon to experience massive upheaval caused by the arrival of Europeans. Like many French people at the time, Dumont d'Urville was influenced in his perceptions of New Zealand and the du Fresne episode. He went to New Zealand expecting Maori to be hostile and untrustworthy but although he found intertribal warfare he was surprised and impressed by their character and nobility. Dumont d'Urville later returned to New Zealand on two further voyages.

✶

In the waters of the South Pacific off the northernmost tip of the North Island, one of America's most famous writers got caught up in a two-week storm after abandoning his plan to visit New Zealand. Jack London embarked on a round-the-world cruise on the *Snark* in 1907. 'In a general way we know that we shall wander through the South Seas, take in Samoa, New Zealand, Tasmania, Australia, New Guinea, Borneo, and Sumatra, and go on up through the Philippines to Japan,' he wrote in *The Cruise of the Snark*. Although London's experiences in the South Seas inspired many literary works, the *Snark* expedition was a disastrous voyage with incompetent crew members, a leaky boat, spoiled food, a succession of sacked captains, sickness and a brief mid-trip return to California to sort out financial affairs. The voyage ended with London in a Sydney hospital, suffering from a mysterious condition that caused his skin to peel off. He underwent months of treatment in Australia for a range of ailments including a double fistula and malaria. While convalescing he wrote about visiting New Zealand before going back to the United States, but he never made it. 'Too bad! He'd have loved it,' was the reaction of Sonoma State University history professor Dr Clarice Stasz, referring to London's appreciation of wild landscapes. Stasz also believes he would have written about Maori in the same way he wrote about other indigenous peoples in the Pacific Islands.

In 1909 London returned to California on the Scots collier *Tymeric* via Pitcairn Island, Ecuador, Panama, New Orleans and Arizona. London's wife Charmian said the *Tymeric*'s captain inspired the stories *Samuel* and *The Sea Farmer* but London also alluded to the *Tymeric* journey in other works. In an article about small boat sailing in *Yachting Monthly* in August 1912 he wrote,

> I remember labouring in a fourteen days' gale off the coast of New Zealand. We were a tramp collier, rusty and battered, with six thousand tons of coal in our hold. Life lines were stretched fore and aft; and on our weather side, attached to smokestack guys and rigging, were huge rope-nettings, hung there for the purpose of breaking the force of the seas and so saving our mess-room doors. But the doors were smashed and the mess-rooms washed out just the same. And yet, out of it all, arose but the one feeling, namely, of monotony.

In 'The Hussy,' a story in *Cosmopolitan Magazine* in December 1916, the words of his character Julian Jones suggest he took further inspiration from the trip.

> Ever been in Ecuador? Then take my advice — and don't. Though I take that back, for you and me might be hitting it for there together if you can rustle up the faith in me and the backbone in yourself for the trip. Well, anyway, it ain't so many years ago that I came ambling in there on a rusty, foul-bottomed, tramp collier from Australia, forty-three days from land to land. Seven knots was her speed when everything favoured, and we'd had a two weeks' gale to the north'ard of New Zealand, and broke our engines down for two days off Pitcairn Island.

Jack London never set foot in New Zealand but one of his rivals for the title of world's best-selling author most certainly did. Zane Grey was encouraged to visit New Zealand by English sportsman Alma Baker and the New Zealand government, which wanted to publicise the country's deep-sea game fishing and to rejuvenate Lake Taupo's reputation for good trout fishing. Grey avoided the popular fishing base of Deep Water Cove Camp, the popular starting point for anglers targeting the waters adjacent to Cape Brett, the furthest mainland peninsula east from Russell. He headed instead for the largest island in the Bay of Islands, around eight and a half nautical miles northeast of Russell, called Urupukapuka, owned by Charles F. Baker. The island was 'large, irregular, with a range of golden grassy hills fringed by dark green thickets and copses, indented by many coves, and surrounded by channels of aquamarine water, so clear that the white sand shone through'.

Grey and Mitchell entered the largest bay, where 'a beach of golden sand and coloured seashells stretched in graceful crescent shape' and 'a soft rippling surge washed the strand, and multitudes of fish, some of them mullet, splashed and darkened the shallow waters'. He saw numerous pohutukawa trees (the 'New Zealand Christmas tree') in crimson bloom. The men set up camp on the other side of the bay, where the hillside was covered in tree ferns and cabbage and tea trees. Grey named the site 'Camp of the Larks' because larks sang until after dark and woke him again at dawn. He was reminded of Shakespeare's sonnet 'Hark! Hark! The lark at heaven's gate sings'. He described the scene at the top of the hill near the camp. 'The summit was a grassy ridge and afforded a most extraordinary view of islands and channels and bays, the mainland with its distant purple ranges, and the blue band of the sea. It was all so wonderful, and its striking feature was the difference from any other place I had ever seen. Seven thousand miles from California! What a long way to come, to camp out and to fish, and to invite my soul in strange environment!'

From their base at Urupukapuka Grey and his companions explored the waters near the camp and around Cape Brett, the nearby Piercy Island and Bird Rock. They ventured further north to the Cavalli Islands and Whangaroa Harbour and sailed for several hours south to the Poor Knights Islands, northeast of Whangarei. Grey and Mitchell broke world records as they pulled marlin, broadbill, kahawai, mako, snapper and yellowtail kingfish from the ocean. They photographed the most impressive fish, some more than twice their height. Grey wrote with admiration about the enormous fish he sought to overpower, as if each kill was the result of a noble battle. When he wasn't fishing he observed gulls and gannets, quail, blackbirds, skylark and albatrosses. He listened to the song of the tui, larks and the thrush.

Grey caught the first broadbill swordfish on rod and reel in New Zealand waters. 'To make a long story short,' he wrote, 'I fought him with all the strength I had, and with all the play the great tackle would stand. Toward the end of the fight he sounded even deeper, and this time he quit down there. I knew it, but did not tell the boatmen.' Grey worked hard to bring the fish to the surface. 'How familiar the heaving chest, the wet face, arms, neck, breast, the aching back and blistered hands! Could it really be that I had caught a broadbill, way out in New Zealand? At last I had him up so that we could see the gleaming pale colour, then the massive shape, the long fierce-looking sword. What the boatmen said I could never remember, but it was a medley of whirling words.' The excited fishermen sailed four miles to the Cape to show off their 400 pound catch to a cluster of boats there. Then they went back to camp just before sunset and took pictures. The boat crew took the fish to Russell to exhibit and for the village to feast on. Late at night people were still peering at the catch with torches.

On another day Captain Mitchell caught a 976 pound black marlin, the world record for a fish caught on rod and line. It was twelve feet and eight inches (3.86 m) in length, with a girth of six feet and two inches (1.87 m), and had to be taken to Russell and cut into three pieces to be weighed. Its stomach contained two large kahawai and nine large red snapper and it took nearly four hours to land.

Grey brought international recognition to the Bay of Islands. 'It hardly seems an exaggeration to claim that New Zealand waters contain the greatest game fish in the world. It would take a volume to do justice to New Zealand waters. I saw 100 Marlin in one day; I hooked 12 and caught five in one day,' Zane Grey was quoted as saying in *The Times* of London the following year.

Urupukapuka became a world famous fishing resort thanks to the writer and his entourage. When Grey returned to the Bay of Islands in 1927 a new fishing club bearing his name had been established on the spot the author christened 'Camp of the Larks'. It was reported in the *Auckland Weekly News* that a Wellington syndicate bought the island from Charles F. Baker and established The Zane Grey Sporting Club Ltd. Urupukapuka was one of a group of islands acquired by the Crown as reserves in the 1970s and 80s. It is now administered by the Department of Conservation, although the Zane Grey Resort at Otehei Bay is still run as a commercial venture, offering visitors accommodation and other facilities.

Remnants of the Zane Grey fishing camp can still be seen at the bay and considerable development on the island is planned over the next few years. New owners want to rekindle the glory days of the resort, when Urupukapuka was a more sought after destination than Russell. A building known as 'the Zane Grey cabin' will be retained and there are plans to create an information centre and museum displaying Maori artefacts as well as Zane Grey memorabilia. A Zane Grey Fishing Club has also recently been established and its members will fish in the Bay of Islands and Taupo. Regular ferries run to Otehei Bay from Paihia, now a tourist centre and the main departure for cruises around the Bay of Islands.

Not far from the *Beagle*'s anchorage between the heroic missionaries of Paihia and the lawless inhabitants of Kororareka, Charles Darwin found a small settlement that seemed thoroughly English. He was invited by William Williams to visit the missionary settlement of Waimate, 21 kilometres west of Paihia and roughly half way between the east and west coasts of Northland. James Busby, who had been appointed the British Resident of New Zealand and was charged with protecting 'well disposed settlers and traders' but was given no resources to do the job, offered to take Darwin through 'a creek, where I should see a pretty waterfall'. The 'creek' was probably the stretch of the Waitangi River from its mouth near Busby's residence at Waitangi, just north of Paihia, to Haruru Falls, (originally called the Waitangi Falls) a few kilometres upstream. The Treaty of Waitangi was signed on 6 February 1840 outside Busby's house, which is now a tourist attraction and known as 'Treaty House'.

When Busby asked a neighbouring chief to recommend a guide for the inland excursion, the chief, 'a light active man, dressed in a dirty blanket, and with his face completely tattooed', offered to go himself. He asked how many pounds Darwin would give him but was happy with the offer of two dollars. Darwin wanted 'a very small bundle' carried so the chief brought along a 'slave'. As the boat was launched a second chief clambered aboard for the ride. 'I never saw a more horrid and ferocious expression than this man had,' wrote Darwin. 'It immediately struck me I had somewhere seen his likeness: it will be found in Retzch's outlines to Schiller's ballad of Fridolin, where two men are pushing Robert into the burning iron furnace. It is the man who has his arm on Robert's breast. Physiognomy here spoke the truth; this chief had been a notorious murderer, and was an arrant coward to boot.' When the boat landed, probably at the foot of the Haruru Falls, the party continued on foot and Darwin 'could not help admiring the cool impudence of the hoary old villain, whom we left lying in the boat, when he shouted to Mr Bushby, "Do not you stay long, I shall be tired of waiting here."'

The men walked several kilometres along a 'well beaten path, bordered on each side by the tall fern, which covers the whole country'. They followed a similar course to today's road between Waitangi and Puketona, skirting the path of the Waitangi River. They came to a small village with a few 'hovels' and some potato plants, probably near the present site of Puketona, about seven kilometres from the falls. The chief and his 'slave' pressed noses with the locals, a customary Maori greeting Darwin found intriguing:

> The women, on our first approach, began uttering something in a most dolorous voice; they then squatted themselves down and held up their faces; my companion standing over them, one after another, placed the bridge of his nose at right angles to theirs, and commenced pressing. This lasted rather longer than a cordial shake of the hand with us, and as we vary the force of the grasp of the hand in shaking, so do they in pressing. During the process they uttered comfortable little grunts, very much in the same manner as two pigs do, when rubbing against each other.

As they continued their walk, the chief talked incessantly to Darwin, who didn't understand a word. When he thought a reply was needed the young naturalist threw one of the three Maori words he knew into the conversation: 'good,' 'bad' and 'yes'.

> The path led through the same undulating country, the whole uniformly clothed as before with fern. On our right hand we had a serpentine river, the banks of which were fringed with trees, and here and there on the hillsides there was a clump of wood. The whole scene, in spite of its green colour, had rather a desolate aspect. The sight of so much fern impresses the mind with an idea of sterility: this, however, is not correct; for wherever the fern grows thick and breast-high, the land by tillage becomes productive.

After 'so many miles of an uninhabited useless country', they reached Waimate, with its 'exceedingly pleasant' houses belonging to the missionaries Williams, Davies and Clarke. The Clarke house, now 'Te Waimate Mission House', still stands, essentially as Darwin would have seen it, because later alterations were reversed in the 1960s. Darwin saw crops of wheat, barley, an array of fruits and vegetables including asparagus, cucumbers, rhubarb, apples, pears, figs, peaches, apricots, grapes, olives, and gooseberries, a variety of flowers, a water mill, animals and a blacksmith's forge. Maori labourers and servant girls whose 'clean, tidy, and healthy appearance, like that of the dairy-maids in England, formed a wonderful contrast with the women of the filthy hovels in Kororadika'. In this little oasis FitzRoy and Darwin could indulge in English pastimes like cricket and tea drinking. A decade after Darwin's visit the quaint village with its manicured gardens was severely damaged when occupied by British troops. Over time the mission buildings disappeared. The dam for the mill-pond remains but what was the country's first water-driven flour mill was destroyed in the latter half of the nineteenth century.

On another inland excursion with James Busby, Darwin entered the Kawakawa River south of Paihia, travelled the short distance along the river to the village of Kawakawa, and then went on foot to the village of Waiomio. 'Following one of the arms of the bay,' he wrote, 'we enjoyed a pleasant row, and passed through pretty scenery, until we came to a village, beyond which the boat could not pass. From here a chief, 'at this time rather notorious from having lately hung one of his wives and a slave for adultery', and a party of men volunteered to walk with Darwin's group the rest of the way to Waiomio. They passed through another village on a hillside, where the daughter of a chief, 'who was still a heathen', had died five days earlier. 'The hovel in which she had expired had been burnt to the ground: her body being enclosed between two small canoes, was placed upright on the ground, and protected by an enclosure bearing wooden images of their gods, and the whole was painted bright red, so as to be conspicuous from afar. Her gown was fastened to the coffin, and her hair being cut off was cast at its foot.' Darwin described the gruesome grieving process that ensued. 'The relatives of the family had torn the flesh of their arms, bodies, and faces, so that they were covered with clotted blood; and the old women looked most filthy, disgusting objects. On the following day some of the officers visited this place, and found the women still howling and cutting themselves.'

The party continued on to Waiomio, the site of 'some singular masses of limestone, resembling ruined castles. These rocks have long served for burial places, and in consequence are held too sacred to be approached. One of the young men, however, cried out, "Let us all be brave," and ran on ahead; but when within a hundred yards, the whole party thought better of it, and stopped short. With perfect indifference, however, they allowed us to examine the whole place.' Before leaving the village the visitors were each given a basket of roasted sweet potato to eat on the road.

When Darwin sailed from the Bay of Islands on 30 December he was glad to leave the country. 'It is not a pleasant place. Amongst the natives there is absent that charming simplicity which is found in Tahiti; and the greater part of the English are the very refuse of society. Neither is the country itself attractive. I look back but to one bright spot, and that is Waimate, with its Christian inhabitants.'

Although he didn't enjoy his stay in New Zealand Darwin's voyage on the *Beagle* was pivotal in his career. He collected insects, shells, fish, rocks and a gecko, about which he wrote detailed notes. Extracts from his journal were sent home as letters. On his return his *Journal of Researches into the Natural History and Geology of the countries visited during the voyage round the world of H.M.S. Beagle* was published, and the critical and commercial success of his 'first literary child' delighted Darwin. The *Beagle* voyage 'has been by far the most important event in my life, and has determined my whole career, he wrote in his autobiography. 'Everything about which I thought or read was made to bear directly on what I had seen or was likely to see; and this habit of mind was continued during the five years of the voyage. I feel sure that it was this training which has enabled me to do whatever I have done in science.'

In the decades after Darwin's visit Russell underwent a transformation. The supply port for whalers disappeared, the capital moved to Auckland and tourists and fishermen replaced the violent drunken criminals and disreputable traders. Russell is now a quaint, picturesque, historic town. The church Darwin noticed as he arrived on the *Beagle* still stands as New Zealand's oldest and the notebook listing Darwin's donation to its construction can be seen at the Russell Museum in York Street not far from Kororareka Bay. The museum also has memorabilia from another famous author who brought a new kind of fame to the Bay of Islands in a happier time. Its Zane Grey collection comprises a set of binoculars, a camera, a telescope, a tent from Taupo, a jacket given to a New Zealand friend and autographed photos.

Zane Grey was very popular when he first arrived in New Zealand, but the adoration didn't last. He became embroiled in controversy after writing articles for the *New Zealand Herald* criticising the country's fishermen for using a three-pronged hook, which he considered crude. In *Tales of the Angler's Eldorado* he wrote that giant swordfish hooked in the stomach or throat with a triple hook were liable to break free whereas the single hook through the fish's mouth allowed the fisherman to engage in a 'leaping fight'. He claimed a swordfish with a triple hook in its gullet could eventually be hauled in — either dead or as good as — by someone as inexperienced as a 'ten-year-old child'.

Grey also claimed local fishermen were using the wrong tackle if they wanted to fight a fish rather than follow it until it was so exhausted it had to surface to be gaffed or harpooned. He advised placing reel and line guides on top of the rod not below it so the angler could brace his feet on the boat and pull hard. In response to Grey's criticism, Mr G.A. Buddle of Auckland wrote, 'It would be more sportsmanlike, to my mind, if Mr Grey would give his reasons for these attacks on his brother sportsmen — constructive criticism is a help and is appreciated by all, mere denunciation is not.' He agreed the use of treble hooks was 'unsatisfactory' but not 'unsportsmanlike' and suggested Grey simply wanted to break world records for the size and number of fish caught while other anglers just wanted to enjoy the sport of fishing.

The *New Zealand Observer* commented that Grey might think New Zealanders' tackle was inadequate, but that New Zealanders thought his tackle was not 'in accordance with our ethics of sportsmanship' and ran a page of cartoons satirising Grey and his substantial angling equipment.

> New Zealanders could easily have put up records such as those of Zane Grey had they been content to use tackle which would drown any fish and thus enable them to get it aboard the launch in a short space of time. Deep-sea anglers have in the past taken great pride in landing big fish with light tackle. They fish according to the strict customs of British fishermen and these customs are kept according to Cocker by the new arrivals from the Old Country who have learned to play the game in the good old school of sportsmen, the best school in the world. Zane Grey may be able to land a lot of swordfish but he is attempting to teach his grandmother to suck eggs when he lectures Britishers on sportsmanship.

The following year an Australian newspaper listed the things the author did that 'annoyed New Zealanders, Australians and Englishmen alike'. When the American caught a swordfish he announced 'through a megaphone in grandiloquent tones, "Mr Zane Grey has caught another swordfish; weight 273lbs," as the case might be. Then there would be run to the mast head a pennant with "swordfish" printed on it.' An Australian who regarded this practice as 'swank', the article continued, 'announced, when he caught a swordfish, that it weighed 6000 pounds and in the place of the pennant ran up to the mast head his pyjama pants instead'.

'THE ETIQUETTE OF SWORD FISHING' (Artist unknown). Alexander Turnbull Library, Wellington, New Zealand. N-P 1077-3.

In *Eldorado* Grey wrote that he had been so keen to convert anglers to his way of fishing he sent a boat to Deep Water Cove to bring back Mr Andreas, 'the champion of the Camp Brett anglers', but the invitation was refused. Grey cancelled his agreement to write further newspaper articles. Instead, his companions Captain Mitchell and Alma Baker wrote long pieces defending the American methods, 'the most significant points of which the newspapers refused to print,' argued Grey, who also claimed to have been misquoted.

Just before Grey left New Zealand the Bay of Islands Swordfish and Mako Shark Club sent a circular to its members asking their opinion of the single versus the treble hook. Grey was critical that the circular was only sent to members and omitted the argument about having the reel on top of the rod. He took great offence at the downturn in his popularity. 'My visit to New Zealand was prompted by Alma Baker and the New Zealand government, who wanted me to come and fish and write for the benefit of the sport — to make it known to anglers all over the world. The importance of this and the zest and thrill with which it inspired me quite blinded me to the possibility that there might be New Zealanders who would not want me to do anything of the kind.'

In 'Big Game Fishing in New Zealand Seas' in *Natural History*, Grey wrote that his first New Zealand trip was 'in the nature of a pioneer expedition' and he expected criticism and opposition, but that he had converted some New Zealand anglers to American methods and that his and Captain Mitchell's record-breaking catches, 'surely never surpassed in the angling history of the world', justified the trip.

The arguments that Grey started in the Bay of Islands rumbled on for several years. The author caused further controversy with his suggestion in a British fishing magazine that most swordfish in New Zealand were harpooned. In 1930, when the new owner of Great Mercury Island off the Coromandel Peninsula prevented Grey from setting up camp there, he wrote that it 'was more of the poison I am continually compelled to swallow from the jealous anglers who frequent Cape Brett'. In 1932 a fishing magazine revealed that Grey believed he was justified in his criticism of the methods used, but was sorry he was misunderstood and that he didn't mean to attack the sportsmanship of New Zealand fishermen. Grey was reacting to the persistence of an Aucklander who had been writing to him, but it seems at the time he was also planning another trip to New Zealand.

Another visiting American could sympathise with Grey. Psychologist David Ausubel travelled to New Zealand on a Fulbright Scholarship in 1957. In his controversial 1960 book *The Fern and the Tiki: An American View of New Zealand*, he claimed the typical New Zealander had an 'acute sensitivity to and exaggerated defensiveness about any criticism, explicit or implied, from an overseas visitor'. Ausubel wrote that negative opinions about social problems like race relations and education expressed through media interviews soon resulted in 'much emotional comment and resentful name-calling'. Although New Zealanders appeared calm, they were suffering from repressed anger brought about by an authoritarian education was his theory. It wasn't welcomed.

Grey was also criticised for the cost of his trip to both the Bay of Islands and Taupo in the central North Island. 'An impression appears to have gained currency that the Government is meeting the expense of Mr Grey's fishing activities at the Bay of Islands and Taupo,' an Auckland newspaper reported. The article confirmed that the government had given Grey use of the railways and of the launch at Taupo, but that the visitor was paying for everything else. The New Zealand government and the author were also going to exchange film and photographs of the trip. 'The expense that the small facilities accorded Mr Grey will total is infinitesimal, compared with the advertisement that New Zealand fishing resorts will obtain,' it was added. In the end Grey's party spent £4000 in New Zealand and the government obtained valuable international publicity for the region. But by the time Grey and his entourage left the Bay of Islands and moved south towards Auckland on his way to Taupo, it was clear some New Zealanders no longer welcomed the presence of a famous author and his many tales of great angling adventures in the abundant waters of a small Pacific nation.

A BONFIRE WITH THE VANITIES

IT SHOULD HAVE BEEN A ROUTINE departure from Auckland for the *Janet Nicoll* on the evening of Saturday 19 April 1890. The sea was smooth and the small black cargo steamer had almost cleared the harbour when the explosion happened. Red, blue and green flames shot high above the ship's deck into the dark autumn sky. A man stood in front of the brightly coloured flames, stunned and unaware he was inhaling chemical vapours. 'Let no man say I am unscientific: when I ran, on the alert, out of my stateroom, and found the main cabin incarnadined with the glow of the last scene of a pantomime, I stopped dead: "What is this?" said I. "This ship is on fire, I see that; but why a pantomime?"' What had transfixed Robert Louis Stevenson and almost destroyed the *Janet Nicoll* that night were exploding fireworks, purchased by the author's sailing companion in Auckland.

Twenty-four hours earlier, Stevenson, his wife Fanny, his stepson Lloyd Osbourne and Jack Buckland, the man to blame for the near-disaster, arrived in Auckland after a rough, week-long crossing from Sydney during which Stevenson was confined to his cabin. The Auckland stopover was part of a recuperative cruise for the author. The previous year he had visited Samoa, found the environment good for his delicate health, and bought land on which to set up home. He and Fanny travelled to Sydney in order to settle some affairs before returning to Samoa. But owing to the author's ill health and the relief he found at sea, they looked for a vessel on which they could cruise for several months. Despite a seaman's strike Fanny discovered a small fore-and-aft rigged steamer called the *Janet Nicoll* that was able to go to sea because its Melanesian crew were not union members. Two officers deserted the ship in Auckland complaining about the recruitment of non-union men they claimed didn't know how to sail. They said it was a 'terribly anxious' time as the mistakes of the seasick crew had to be continually corrected.

Auckland is built on a narrow isthmus between the Pacific Ocean and the Tasman Sea, amid extinct volcanoes and numerous islands. Stevenson and his wife ate and slept at the Star Hotel on the corner of Swanson and Albert Street. The site of the hotel, on which a high-rise building now stands, is a short walk from the harbour. Buckland and Osbourne were to meet the Stevensons in the morning with a shopping list. Buckland was a trader on whom Stevenson and Osbourne's character Tom Hadden in *The Wrecker* was based. Known as 'Tin Jack' (the island term for 'Mr Jack'), he had a reputation for liking a good practical joke and for blowing his money on drunken binges.

ROBERT LOUIS STEVENSON C.1894 (PHOTOGRAPHER UNKNOWN). ALEXANDER TURNBULL LIBRARY, WELLINGTON, NEW ZEALAND. F-15876-1/2.

The next day Stevenson visited Wildman's bookshop in the Victoria Arcade, an elegant building close to the harbour that used to occupy a full block on Queen Street, between Shortland and Fort streets. The bookshop owner recognised Stevenson as the eminent author of such works as *Treasure Island* and *The Strange Case of Dr Jekyll and Mr Hyde*, but he was one of only a few people who did. After an hour's shopping and strolling Stevenson was so tired he retired to his bunk on the *Janet Nicoll*. Fanny bought clothes as gifts and Tin Jack and Fanny's son went to a chemist to buy fireworks for entertainment. The fireworks included four and a half kilograms of 'calcium fire' to add colour to the pyrotechnics, which concerned Lloyd, who asked the chemist whether it was safe to carry on board ship. They were assured it was as harmless 'as a packet of sugar' and not even a lighted match would set it off. Then the chemist asked Buckland whether he wanted the fireworks with or without 'fumes'. 'The thrifty trader thought that he might as well get all he could for the money expended, therefore took it with fumes,' wrote Fanny Stevenson in *The Cruise of the "Janet Nichol" Among the South Sea Islands.* Tin Jack also bought cartridges, grease paints, a false nose and a wig.

The fireworks were loaded into the *Janet Nicoll* along with various other parcels. The packages had no distinguishable marks so Lloyd piled them all up, along with a couple of hundred pistol cartridges, on his bunk in the cabin he shared with Tin Jack. The trader could distribute them later. The parcels included a pistol belonging to Stevenson, which Tin Jack had taken ashore for repairs.

The *Janet Nicoll* set sail at about eight o'clock in the evening with the same non-union crew of seamen as well as two replacement officers and a stray cat. A couple of hours later, Stevenson lay in his quarters, Tin Jack and Lloyd drank coffee in another passenger's cabin, and Fanny ate bread and butter in the saloon. The 'calcium fire' proved a little more volatile than sugar. It ignited, triggering the rest of the fireworks. The panicked helmsman ran from his post and the captain, who initially thought the engineer was letting off steam, was left to save his ship without knowing what had caused the blaze.

Fanny ran into her cabin, grabbed a heavy red blanket and managed to hand it to the captain through a haze of choking fumes. Armed with the blanket, a rug and a hose the captain doused the flames and saved the *Janet Nicoll*, her illustrious passenger and his family but he took days to recover from the effects of the fumes.

A literary disaster was also narrowly averted. In the confusion Fanny noticed two sailors about to throw a blazing trunk containing Stevenson's manuscripts overboard. She stopped them just in time. Lloyd lost most of his clothes and many of the Stevensons' photographs were destroyed. Tin Jack lost only his fireworks. Many 'small necessaries that conduce to comfort on shipboard' were lost and Fanny worried about her husband suffering a haemorrhage. 'If he does I shall feel inclined to do something very desperate to the chemist, who for the sake of a few shillings, put us all in such deadly peril.'

The danger of shipwreck was on Sir Arthur Conan Doyle's mind as the *Maheno* approached Auckland from Sydney in dense fog in December 1920. Lying in his cabin he was subjected to a constant, depressing commentary from the bunk above him as the foghorn sounded intermittently. The chatterer was Carlyle Smythe, the agent who organised Conan Doyle's lecture tour in New Zealand and who was described by his illustrious client as 'a small, alert competent gentleman', and 'a musician, a scholar, and a man of many varied experiences'. As they neared the Three Kings Islands, a small rocky cluster some fifty kilometres northwest of the northern tip of New Zealand, Smythe mentioned the story of the *Elingamite*, a trans-Tasman steamer that was wrecked on one the islands with the loss of 45 lives. Smythe told Conan Doyle that the tragedy, in which survivors kept themselves alive by catching fish with improvised lines made from ladies' stay laces, happened on 'just such a morning as this'. As the ship approached the Hauraki Gulf, the stretch of water between Auckland and the Coromandel Peninsula dotted with numerous small islands, Smythe continued,

> You can't anchor here, and there is no use stopping her, for the currents run hard and she would drift on to one of the ledges which would rip the side out of her. (Whoo-ee! repeated the foghorn). The islands are perpendicular with deep

> water up to the rocks, so you never know they are there until you hit them, and then, of course, there is no reef to hold you up. (Whoo-ee!) Close by here is the place where the *Wairarapa* went down with all hands a few years ago. It was just such a day as this when she struck the Great Barrier …

Conan Doyle went up on deck and spent the rest of the morning with the captain as he navigated the ship through the fog and the rocky islands over an 'oily lead-coloured sea'. He wrote about the 'strange results when one stares intently over such a sea, for after a time one feels that it all slopes upwards, and that one is standing deep in a saucer with the rim far above one'.

A much bigger ship, the *Niagara*, from Vancouver, just beat the *Maheno* into Auckland. By the time the port authorities had finished with the *Niagara* it was too late for the *Maheno*'s passengers to disembark. Conan Doyle spent his first night in Auckland on board ship, sad to disappoint fans who had been waiting on the quay to greet him for 12 hours.

The author visited New Zealand at the height of his career, having created one of the most famous literary characters, Sherlock Holmes. The former doctor's business-like approach to writing made him the highest paid writer in the world in the 1920s. But he wasn't touring the antipodes to talk about his novels; he was promoting spiritualism. Conan Doyle became a spiritualist in the late 1880s but didn't proselytize for the cause until the First World War, when he became convinced of life after death. In 1914 his wife's brother, Malcolm Leckie, was killed, and the following year a girl the Conan Doyles were looking after began to write messages in what they believed was Leckie's handwriting. After Conan Doyle put a question to 'Leckie' about a private conversation they'd had, he claimed to have received an answer no one else could have known. Just as his famous detective used deductive reasoning to solve crimes, Conan Doyle deduced from his experiences that there was life after death. The famous author was mocked for his spiritualist views and his works on the subject were not widely published. His friend Harry Houdini thought the author extremely gullible, but Conan Doyle retaliated by describing the escapologist as 'the greatest medium-baiter of modern times'.

A big, affable man, Conan Doyle had accepted an invitation to lecture in Australasia, for which he would not receive a fee. He told a reporter in Auckland that he came against the greatest personal interest possible and at his own great loss. But he had only agreed to the tour on condition that his travel costs were met as well as those of his wife and three young children. He addressed 25 meetings and 50,000 people during the tour. It also gave him material for *The Wanderings of a Spiritualist*, published in 1921.

Conan Doyle dismissed criticism that he only became a spiritualist after he lost his son Kingsley during the Great War (he said he heard the voice of his dead son at a Southsea, Hampshire séance) and claimed to have studied the subject for many years. However, a world 'which was distraught with sorrow' made him realise his psychic studies 'were of immense practical importance and could no longer be regarded as a mere intellectual hobby or fascinating pursuit of a novel research'. He claimed 'the relief afforded by posthumous messages taught him how great a solace it would be to a tortured world if it could share in the knowledge which had become clear to himself'. This was why he embarked on extensive lecture tours throughout Australia, New Zealand, America, and Canada. Arriving in Auckland he said, 'I had found in England that my lectures had brought great consolation to those who had been bereaved in the war, and I felt that, Australia and New Zealand having made such sacrifices for the Imperial cause, if I could possibly carry the consolation to the people there it was my duty to do so.' Conan Doyle said that in researching the history of the Great War (he wrote about the war in articles and several books including the six-volume *The British Campaign in France and Flanders*) he had discovered that the New Zealand Infantry Division had the 'finest record of the British Army in France for the proportion of killed and wounded to prisoners taken'.

In a bright sunny Auckland harbour on the morning of 15 March 1934, journalists and members of the public excitedly awaited the appearance of famous playwright George Bernard Shaw. 'Certain citizens,' it was reported, 'advocate his being debarred from entry into our earthly paradise, as being anti-social and a menace,' and Shaw, who had been in the Soviet Union, wrote that the country had recently passed 'a law prohibiting the landing of any person who has recently visited Russia'. But a welcoming party of government officials and around thirty fans and reporters met Shaw on his arrival. The Auckland scribes wondered whether he would talk to them. He was known for his acerbic wit, memorable one-liners and passionate socialist views. But he also had a reputation for being a difficult, temperamental man who would rudely cast aside or ignore fans and newspapermen alike. Their concerns were soon dispelled. Shaw emerged from a doorway on deck into the late summer sunlight. He began his performance with some poses for a 'talking picture camera'.

> With mock solemnity, he rehearsed the incident of walking up to the camera. Head down and hands behind back, he walked slowly along, and then, looking up smartly and smiling broadly, said: 'Oh good morning ladies and gentlemen. I suppose you have seen at least fifty million pictures of me. You want to see the 'animal' walk about and you want to hear the 'animal' talk. On this occasion you want to hear me say exactly the same things you have heard about fifty thousand times. I am not going to say them. I have only seen a little of New Zealand so far, but it is a very bright morning, and it looks at its best. I don't know whether

> I am looking my best. Such as I am, here I am. Now, here I am full face (turning around). Now, side face (again turning). This is the intellectual portion of my brow, and here is my back! Now, ladies and gentlemen, you have had as much of me as I could reasonably expect you to stand. I may have the pleasure of seeing some of you. I hope I shall. Good morning.'

Shaw and his wife travelled extensively, especially between 1931 and 1936. Shaw said he had come to New Zealand for a month's holiday, to see the scenery and for some sunshine. The couple journeyed to New Zealand without staff but in comfort. Their requirements included two staterooms with the beds to be placed away from portholes and doors. They liked to eat alone at their own table rather than the captain's, reading silently as they did at home. Both read prolifically on the voyage, donating the finished texts to the ship's library. Among 23 books given by the Shaws to the RMS *Rangitane* were two volumes of *War Memoirs of David Lloyd George*, Hitler's *Mein Kampf* (although Shaw would later say he only dipped briefly into the work), biographies of De Valera, Napoleon, Sydney Smith, and Cecil Rhodes, and some novels and books about New Zealand. A *Rangitane* officer told a reporter Shaw read 'all the way through his meals, and, it seemed, during the greater part of each day. His best exercise came after his morning swim in the ship's baths — this without fail at about seven o'clock — and after it he made good entertainment for the others on board by going through a system of exercises on his back.' After his exercises Shaw would look on deck for a woman he could impress with his celebrity, put his deckchair beside hers and ask whether she minded him working on his new play silently. With a new friend to protect him from interruption he could get on with his work. If he had not been writing he 'would have gone over the side', the *Auckland Star* reported.

Dockers cheered as the couple walked down the gangway and a smiling Shaw devoted more than an hour and a half to answering questions from journalists and fans and posing for photographs. A man who offered 'hearty greetings from the Friends of the Soviet Union' handed him a copy of the *Moscow News*. 'I have been in Russia. It is a very remarkable place. Now I want to see if New Zealand is any better,' came Shaw's response. He stressed that he and his wife were looking forward to a quiet, relaxing holiday in New Zealand but for the next four weeks Shaw was subjected to a torrent of questions. He told the crowd at Auckland harbour that despite their fear of communism it was better for New Zealand and Australia that China and Russia were communist because they would represent a far bigger threat as large capitalist powers. Shaw said he was 'really one of the makers of New Zealand', adding that he was surprised the country introduced a Fabian programme at a time when England was taking no notice of the Fabians like himself who 'took Socialism off the barricades and made it entirely respectable'. He talked of his friendship with New Zealand politician, writer and renowned orator, William Pember

Reeves. Reeves had been influenced by Fabian socialists like Shaw and was the leading ideologist of what became the Liberal Party in the late nineteenth century. Both were witty and got on well.

In answer to a question about the chance of Nazism spreading to Britain, Shaw said, 'Nobody has attempted to answer Herr Hitler's point that there is no responsibility under majority rule and that he and Mussolini and Kemal and Pilsudski are the only really responsible rulers in Europe.' He said world peace would only be secured when 'the Powers are convinced, by poison gas or otherwise, that war is a crudity they can no longer afford'. Shaw also criticised New Zealand's dependency on the 'Home' market. He advocated self-sufficiency and diversification and then New Zealand wouldn't care about Britain importing cheap foodstuffs from elsewhere:

> 'What you have to do in these islands is to eat your own butter and see that everybody in New Zealand has plenty of butter to his bread. When you have reached this point, stop producing butter and produce something else.'
>
> **A voice:** 'What?'
> **Mr Shaw:** 'Start producing brains, perhaps.'
> **A voice:** 'They take all the bright brains from New Zealand.'
> **Mr Shaw:** 'Do as Russia does and don't let them go.'

'Auckland considers herself to be the cream of New Zealand, so does New Zealand consider herself to be the cream of the British empire' was British writer Anthony Trollope's impression of the city of around 25,000 when he visited in 1872. Even though Dunedin was the biggest city in the country at that time, 'because of its age, and old history, and early dealings with the Maoris, I regard Auckland as being the representative city of New Zealand,' he wrote. Aucklanders thought they had the 'most perfect climate in the world'.

> The mean temperature of the coldest month at London is 37°, which is only five degrees above freezing, whereas at Auckland it is 51°, which enables growth to continue throughout the whole year. Of the hottest month the mean temperature at Auckland is only 68°, which, — says the Aucklander, — neither hinders a European from working, nor debilitates his constitution. All good things have been given to this happy land, and, when the Maori has melted, here will be the navel of the earth.

The author of numerous works of fiction such as the Barset and the Palliser novels, Trollope also wrote several volumes of travel literature. He travelled all over Europe and used many foreign cities as settings for his novels. His younger son, Fred, went to Australia to pursue a career as a farmer and after a brief return to Britain in the late 1860s resolved to settle in Australia for good. Trollope and his wife decided to visit him and the author wanted to write about his journey. He knew a publisher would only pay him half the amount he would usually get for a work of fiction and he would be lucky to cover his expenses on the road. Trollope wrote the two-volume *Australia and New Zealand* while travelling and brought it back to England all but completed in late 1872. It was published the following year. He thought it was a better book than the one he had written 11 years before on the United States, but not as good as his work about the West Indies in 1859. He was surprised the book did as well as it did. 'Feeling that these volumes on Australia were dull and long, I was surprised to find that they had an extensive sale. There were, I think, 2000 copies circulated of the first expensive edition; and then the book was divided into four little volumes, which were published separately, and which again had a considerable circulation.'

When Arthur Conan Doyle reached the Grand Hotel on his first morning in Auckland, six men calling themselves the city's leading photographers challenged him to produce the negatives of the spirit photographs he was to show during his lectures. Conan Doyle refused, explaining that the photographers who originally captured the images held the negatives. 'My experience at Sydney had shown me that such challenges came from people who had no knowledge of psychic conditions, and who did not realise that it is the circumstances under which a photograph is taken, and the witnesses who guarantee such circumstances, which are the real factors that matter, and not the negative which may be so easily misunderstood by those who have not studied the processes by which such things are produced,' he wrote in *The Wanderings of a Spiritualist*. His refusal to meet the photographers' challenge by way of a letter in which he maintained it was 'absurd to submit such results to the judgement of gentlemen who have no psychic experience' and that in every case he explained to the audience 'what is the guarantee of the photograph' so that they could make up their own minds, resulted in a 'long tirade of abuse' in the newspapers.

Victor R. Millard wrote in the *New Zealand Herald* that on behalf of the 'six principal studios of the city' he regretted Conan Doyle's refusal of their request, an action 'we consider to be contrary to his professed intention to enlighten the world'. He said he had offered Sir Arthur 'every assistance to justify his claim, my studio, camera, plates etc., are at his entire disposal' and that Conan Doyle was:

> ... a man who by force of character succeeds in dominating the minds of the people and nations, is banqueted, decorated, and worshipped as a God-man by

> the spiritual communities wherever he treads. If there is an atom of truth in his power to photograph the spirit, let him prove it in one of our city studios, and present the results to our city library. This would be at least something in return for the few hundreds of pounds he will relieve the city of, and justify his power, which we emphatically deny.

In what Conan Doyle described as a 'comic jumble' a local miller worked his criticism of the author into an advertisement for his produce. Conan Doyle warned Aucklanders to discourage such activities in case they ruined the 'beautiful impression' the visitor gets of the city. 'I hope I was the only victim, and that every stranger within her gates is not held up to ridicule for the purpose of calling attention to Mr Blank's desiccated corn.' A conjurer in Auckland, 'Carter the Great', offered £1000 to charity to match anything Sir Arthur Conan Doyle could do. Carter the Great's alleged speciality was to make a huge lion disappear and reappear at will. 'As I could do nothing, it seemed easy money. In any case, the argument that because you can imitate a thing therefore the thing does not exist, is one which it takes the ingenuity of Mr Maskelyne to explain,' Conan Doyle wrote. Underneath the announcement for Conan Doyle's performances in the *New Zealand Herald* was an advertisement for a show by an 'ex-medium' who claimed that the author only knew the spirit world indirectly and he promised an 'even more revealing' message.

SIR ARTHUR CONAN DOYLE. Library of Congress, Prints & Photographs Division, LC-USZ62-78587.

Conan Doyle had his critics in Auckland but on two successive nights in the Town Hall he attracted even larger and more adoring audiences than he had in Sydney. 'All the newspaper ragging and offensive advertisements had produced (as is natural among a generous people) a more kindly feeling for the stranger, and I had a reception I can never forget,' he wrote. The Town Hall, designed in the style of Imperial Baroque, still stands in the centre of the city's commercial centre with its clock tower pointing towards the harbour. More than 3000 packed the hall on the first night and several hundred were turned away.

Conan Doyle 'appeared to make a profound impression' reported the *New Zealand Herald*. He told his audience he was qualified to lecture on spiritualism because he had studied it for 34 years, he was a medical doctor, he knew a little about detective work (at which the audience laughed) and was a 'pretty good judge of evidence' as he once proved the innocence of a man sentenced to seven years' jail. The hall was packed again on the second night, during which Conan Doyle explained that mediums exuded a substance called psychoplasm, which could take human form and be temporarily inhabited by a spirit. He said cameras had captured the substance on film and scientists had studied it. Despite his bizarre claims, Conan Doyle endeared himself to the audience with his enormous sincerity and conviction. 'He is kindliness himself,' an Auckland scribe wrote about the author, who had an imposing physique and a smile 'that breaks down all barriers'.

Noël Coward began a three-week goodwill tour of New Zealand to broadcast and raise patriotic funds in Auckland in January 1941. But he got the impression he wasn't going to be a popular attraction. 'I was both relieved and a little dunched to observe that my arrival in New Zealand had apparently caused little stir among the population,' the playwright, composer and actor wrote in *Future Indefinite*, the second part of his three-part autobiography, published in 1954. It wasn't an elegant start to his stay in New Zealand's biggest city. Getting ready to go ashore from the *Mariposa* in Auckland harbour, he finished breakfast, took a bath and was shaving when there was a knock on his cabin door. Believing it to be the steward, Coward called for the man to come in. Mr Stephens, a representative of the prime minister, was met by the illustrious, yet stark naked, playwright. Coward apologised and grabbed his dressing gown while Stephens conveyed the prime minister's greetings and told the author the Auckland mayor and three reporters were waiting on deck. Fully clothed, Coward met the mayor and posed for photographs 'on gangways waving archly to imaginary crowds', before being ushered ashore and driven to his hotel.

Coward travelled extensively with Stephens and described him as 'really a nice young man, but desperately jocular. He invariably greeted me every morning with "Good morrow, kind sir. How are we this merry morn?" He alluded to any hotel proprietor as Mine Host and referred to any female, regardless of age or size, as Girlie.' Coward's escort was probably Frank Burcon Stephens, who joined the Internal Affairs Department in the mid-1930s and later became Assistant Under-Secretary of Internal Affairs.

Coward had just completed a similar tour of Australia, which required 1400 handshakes a day. He regarded a lunch with the governor-general, a civic reception in the Town Hall and an evening broadcast as a light itinerary for his first day in Auckland. His New Zealand-born accompanist, Sefton Daly, 'giggled sympathetically at my astonishment and reminded me that New Zealand was less dashing and go-ahead than Australia and that I must be prepared for a slower tempo'. Coward feared his visit wasn't going to be particularly successful but his concerns were unfounded and the Town Hall on Queen Street was packed for the civic reception after which Aucklanders filled the streets to see him drive away. Coward gave two concerts for the troops, followed by a public performance under a string of amber-coloured lights, all to full and appreciative audiences. 'Seldom has an audience in the Town Hall demonstrated more enthusiasm' than at Coward's concert, one newspaper reported.

Coward's popularity almost caused a tragedy. He returned to Auckland for a couple of days to wait for a flight to Canton Island after his official New Zealand tour had ended. On a Saturday night he was the guest at the now demolished State Theatre in Symonds Street and the cinema manager announced to the packed theatre that Coward was in the audience. During the interval he was hounded by autograph hunters. At the end of the movie it took 20 minutes for him to get from the lobby onto the pavement and into the car. A hysterical mother handed her baby to Coward through the car window shouting 'Kiss my little girlie, go on, kiss her!' The vehicle moved as Coward was holding the baby's head, while the mother had her legs. 'With commendable presence of mind,' he wrote, 'I struck the mother sharply on the head with my left hand and yanked the child into the car with me before its back was broken. There was a great deal of shrieking, the car stopped, and I handed back girlie unhurt and unkissed. She had, however, utilised her brief moment of perilous reflected glory by wetting me to the skin.'

Conan Doyle was impressed with New Zealand's detectives and police force. He followed two murder trials in Auckland and complimented the work of the detective sergeant assigned to the cases. In Sydney, Conan Doyle had regaled an audience with stories about being mistaken for the detective he created. 'You beast,' wrote one old lady after Conan Doyle killed off his much-loved character to release himself from the commitment of Sherlock Holmes to write other things. Although he was best known for Holmes, Conan Doyle considered his historical novels to be his best works of fiction. After he had resuscitated the famous sleuth and sent him into the country to live an unassuming life as a beekeeper, a few women wrote to offer themselves as housekeepers for Holmes. One insisted she was especially well qualified as she could 'segregate the Queen'. A boatman claimed Holmes must have been badly injured when he was thrown over the cliff, as 'he never wrote quite the same afterwards'. Conan Doyle received correspondence for Holmes, care of himself, and even now letters are still sent to Holmes' fictitious Baker Street address.

The Sherlock Holmes creator was staying, as many celebrities did, in Auckland's fashionable Grand Hotel. A plush establishment built in 1889 to receive the Earl and Countess Onslow, it had vaulted ceilings, crystal chandeliers, red carpet, marble statues and a commanding view of the city. It stood on Princes Street, a few blocks back from the harbour where the land rises steeply. The hotel had a dramatic history. A fire in 1901, which killed three children, a maid and a guest from Wellington, gutted the building. It's thought someone left a gas heater burning in a bathroom and the spiral staircase acted as a chimney feeding the flames. The injured were treated in the nearby Northern Club. The building was rebuilt along the same lines and the spiral staircase winding around an open-shaft lift remained a feature. The hotel became important in the Auckland social scene once more, catering for glitzy receptions and grand dinners. Today only the façade of the hotel remains.

THE GRAND HOTEL IN AUCKLAND, 1902. Special Collections, Auckland City Libraries (N.Z.), 1-W1053.

Two women from the countryside were such dedicated Arthur Conan Doyle fans they travelled about one hundred and fifty kilometres to hear his lecture and visit him at his hotel. One claimed her son, who had been killed at Gallipoli, had given her a detailed account of events before and after a shell struck him. Then she showed the author a small silver box containing what looked like a small cube of sandstone wrapped in white silk. The woman claimed she and her family were holding a séance when the object appeared with a message that it was from her son's grave. 'If it was, indeed, an apport,' noted Conan Doyle, 'it is surely one of the most remarkable for distance and for purpose recorded of any private circle.'

Conan Doyle struck up a friendship with another writer staying at the Grand Hotel, American Harry Moors. A well-known businessman in Samoa, Moors wrote a book about his friendship with Robert Louis Stevenson called *With Stevenson in Samoa*, in which he described meeting the author for the first time in December 1889:

> He appeared to be about thirty years of age, although really nine years older, of fair and somewhat sallow complexion, and about five feet ten inches in height. He wore a slight, scraggy moustache, and his hair hung down about his neck after the fashion of artists ... He was not a handsome man, and yet there was something irresistibly attractive about him. The genius that was in him seemed to shine out of his face. I was struck at once by his keen, inquiring eyes. Brown in colour, they were strangely bright, and seemed to penetrate you like the eyes of a mesmerist. His feet were bare, and I remember that he was dressed in a thin calico shirt and a light pair of flannel trousers, with a little white yachting cap — one of those cheese-cutter things — on his head.

Moors told Conan Doyle that he visited a group of spiritualists in Sydney, none of whom could have known who he was, and that one of them said, 'Above your head I see a man, an artist, long hair, brown eyes, and I get the name of Stephens.' Conan Doyle concluded that if Moors 'was indeed unknown, this would seem fairly evidential'.

In December 1913, 26-year-old Rupert Brooke wrote from the Grand Hotel to the young actress Cathleen Nesbitt with whom he was romantically involved, saying that he had visited the Public Library and had read in the *Daily Telegraph* that she was to star in *Quality Street.* The public school and Cambridge-educated writer variously described as an 'English Adonis' and 'the handsomest man in England' read the London newspaper in what is now the Wellesley Wing of the Auckland City Art Gallery. It stands on the corner of Wellesley and Kitchener streets, a short walk from the Grand Hotel, where shelves of books and long tables have been replaced by benches and an exhibition of European painting. Brooke also wrote to Reginald Berkeley, a young English friend he spent time with in Suva and promised to give advice to. He advised him on writing and urged him to 'be kind to life: and do not bruise her with the bludgeon of the *a priori*. Poor dirty woman, she responds to sympathy. Sympathetic imagination with everybody and everything is the artist's one duty.'

Georgian poet Brooke sailed first class (even thought he was short of money) from Fiji to Auckland on the RMS *Niagara*, in company with the 1913 All Blacks. Brooke, unaware he was close to the end of his life, is remembered chiefly as a war poet, but at the time he sailed to New Zealand he had already been publishing poetry for several years and 'The Old Vicarage, Grantchester' is his most well-known work after his war sonnets. He was commissioned to write a series of travel articles for the *Westminster Gazette* and he journeyed to the United States, Canada, New Zealand and the South Sea Islands. The previous year he suffered an acute nervous breakdown, probably due in part to his love for two women.

Brooke planned to sail from Auckland to Tahiti but he missed his connection and couldn't leave New Zealand until early January 1914. He found it strange that December in Auckland was midsummer and he could eat large strawberries every day. 'It feels curiously perverse, like some frightful vice out of Havelock Ellis. I blush and eat secretively.' The former president of the Cambridge University Fabian Society wrote that New Zealand was 'a sort of Fabian England, very upper middle class and gentle and happy (after Canada), no poor and the Government owning hotels and running charabancs. All the women smoke, and dress very badly, and nobody drinks. Everybody seems rather ugly — but perhaps that's compared with the South Seas.'

George Bernard Shaw mingled with the Governor of the Reserve Bank of New Zealand Leslie Lefeaux and other dignitaries at a lavish reception at the Grand Hotel on his first evening in Auckland. He repeated some of the political points he made in the harbour and said New Zealand should get rid of her 'old cob-webby parliament' and students should study Trotsky's *History of the Revolution* rather than 'useless knowledge' about 'a past era'. The Shaws' Auckland trip involved a 'continual whirl of people and entertaining and sightseeing and journalists'. They drank tea with the Prime Minister George William Forbes and lunched with Governor-General Viscount Bledisloe. The 'old elf in the zip-fastened jersey', as he was described in one newspaper, thought his five days in Auckland ('bright, clean, sunny and happy; all gay bungalows with brilliant little gardens — a garden city') so exhausting he refused to travel to any more cities except Wellington, his departure point. He later relented and travelled as far south as Christchurch.

✶

Mark Twain attracted huge audiences in November 1895 in two inner city halls that no longer exist, City Hall in Queen Street and the Opera House in Wellesley Street. His performances were part of a world lecture tour promoted as Mark Twain 'At Home'. More than 2000 people paid two to four shillings per head to hear him on the first two nights at City Hall before he moved to the Opera House for the third night. The *New Zealand Herald* reported that although those who were familiar with his work were concerned the performances would be a let-down, the first two evenings showed 'conclusively that, however high the expectations of his audiences ... this prince of American humourists is quite able to satisfy them'. The *New Zealand Observer and Free Lance* didn't agree, printing a critical review of his lectures a few days after Twain had left Auckland. 'However great Mark Twain may be as a humorous writer, he is by no means a success as a humorous lecturer. Immense audiences assembled to hear him in Auckland, but Mark was scarcely more entertaining than a speaker at an average Sunday school bun scuffle.' The same paper had earlier reported that Twain was so famous, a New Zealand schoolboy said in a class exercise that Twain was responsible for the independence of the United States and 'as Mark is the hero of the hour just now, we won't attempt to confute the boy small boy who had conceived so big a notion of the American humourist'.

Vikram Seth was welcomed with music when he met a group of around fifty fans at the Carlton Hotel, on the corner of Mayoral Drive and Vincent Street in the central city, in 2000. A lone violinist played 'The Trout' in honour of the work around which Seth crafted his book *An Equal Music*. Hearing the music Seth interrupted his interview with a newspaper reporter to ask 'Isn't that "The Trout"?' Later in the interview Seth talked of his love of music. 'I can't concentrate on anything else when there's music playing. I can't play it while I'm working. If it's bad I'm annoyed. If it's good I can't stop listening.' Seth's fans, wrote the reporter, treated him 'almost like a lover — or a son'.

> 'Oh,' says the woman in the front row, when he says he has no children. 'After writing a love story like that! What a shame!' Adroitly, Seth moves on. As he says later, 'There's no need to be brusque.'

From Mt Eden's 'grassy crater-summit', wrote Mark Twain after he had been on several drives around Auckland, 'one's eye ranges over a grand sweep and variety of scenery — forests clothed in luxuriant foliage, rolling green fields, conflagrations of flowers, receding and dimming stretches of green plain, broken by lofty and symmetrical old craters — then the blue bays twinkling and sparkling away into the dreamy distances where the mountains loom spiritual in their veils of haze'. Auckland was one of Mark Twain's more leisurely stops around New Zealand. He planned a weekend trip to Rotorua between performances but after learning that the train would take ten and a half hours to 'go about 200 & odd miles', he decided the trip would be too tiring. He told one Auckland correspondent 'travelling and lecturing are like oil and water; they don't mix'.

Auckland is spread over a volcanic field and one of the best views of the city can be seen from Mt Eden, the highest volcano on the isthmus. Many authors have written about the panoramic scene from the 200 metre-high summit. 'The crater is round as a punch bowl,' wrote historian and novelist James Anthony Froude after walking to the volcano on his second day in the city. 'On the mainland, all across the isthmus, rise grass-covered craters, which seem as if at any moment they might open fire again. At Mount Eden, on the skirts of the city, the slag lies in a heap at the bottom of the bowl, as if it had cooled but a few years ago. The country round is littered with ash and scoria which were vomited out of Mount Eden and its companions, and half the city stands on rock which was once fluid lava.'

'I have never seen a more magnificent view than that from Mount Eden,' declared Arthur Conan Doyle. 'Below lay the most marvellous medley of light blue water and light green land mottled with darker foliage. We could see not only the whole vista of the wonderful winding harbour, and the seas upon the east of the island, but we could look across and see the firths which connected with the seas of the west.' To Conan Doyle the only comparable view was the one of Edinburgh from Arthur's Seat, another extinct volcano, except that the Scottish capital was often obscured by smoke. The air was so clear in Auckland he could see Great Barrier Island, the Hauraki Gulf island he had passed on the way into the Auckland harbour as his agent so morbidly talked of shipwreck.

Residential areas cover the extensive lower slopes of Mt Eden, and it was in the streets around this key Auckland landmark that German-Jewish poet Karl Wolfskehl lived in exile during the Second World War. A flat in the suburb of Mt Eden was Wolfskehl's first proper New Zealand home after he came to Auckland in 1938, then a city of a quarter of a million people. Aged 68, he'd fled Germany five years earlier after the Reichstag fire and wanted to get as far away from his homeland as possible. Some say that one of his poems written in 1934 inspired the would-be assassins of Hitler. Wolfskehl became a respected figure among the New Zealand literary establishment and developed friendships with writers like R.A.K. Mason, A.R.D. Fairburn (who dedicated his *Poems 1929–1941* to Wolfskehl) and Frank Sargeson. Sargeson used to visit the German poet regularly with a backpack of home grown tomatoes — until one day without explanation he stopped coming. Sargeson later wrote that Wolfskehl's European heritage and knowledge was becoming oppressive and was affecting his identity as a New Zealand writer. 'There were times with Karl Wolfskehl when I could feel myself overpowered, weighted down by so much civilisation,' wrote Sargeson in *More Than Enough*.

Wolfskehl's flat in Esplanade Road in Mt Eden was in a brightly painted, typical wooden New Zealand house with a corrugated iron roof. 'The room where Wolfskehl passed his time and received his guests seems especially tiny in my memory, perhaps because the man who occupied it was excessively large,' wrote Paul Hoffman in *Landfall* in March 1989. Subtropical plants, a variety of birds and majestic old trees surrounded the house. Wolfskehl identified with the fig tree, or Feigenbaum, in his Mt Eden garden, which had also been transplanted far from its Mediterranean origins. In his poem 'Fig Tree' he explores the theme of living in exile so far from home:

> You suffer not alone. We are both stranded.
> Say: do we flourish? Do we live? Who knows!
> To wither in the scantiest sand of homeland
> What kinder lot! Is it not so, my tree?

Wolfskehl later moved from Mt Eden to the North Shore, on the corner of Bracken Avenue, now a doctor's surgery, close to Takapuna Beach. He died in Auckland a decade after his arrival and his grave in the Jewish section of West Auckland's Waikumete Cemetery is covered with a granite slab on which are inscribed the words 'Exul Poeta'.

In 1991 another exiled writer in Auckland, Chinese poet Yang Lian, wrote a poem about Grafton Bridge in the central city, known locally as 'Suicide Bridge'. The bridge runs off Grafton Road, where Yang Lian lived from 1989 to 1993. The poem begins:

> as you cross the cemetery beneath the bridge closes in
> pine trees raise suspicious faces
> an ocean of the dead like iron, giving off a fishy smell

Yang Lian belongs to a group of Chinese writers known as the 'Misty Poets'. Born in Switzerland to diplomat parents, he grew up in Beijing during the Cultural Revolution. Like many of his generation he underwent 're-education', was sent to the countryside and was made to work as a gravedigger. He began writing poetry in the late 1970s and with the help of another Misty Poet, Gu Cheng, he joined a group associated with the underground literary publication *Jintian* (Today). Both he and Gu Cheng were visiting scholars at the University of Auckland when the Tiananmen Square massacre occurred in June 1989. They stayed on in Auckland and helped to organise protests, and Yang later became a New Zealand citizen. He wrote 'Grafton Bridge' while he was a writer in residence in Berlin in 1991. In the *New Zealand Herald* he explained '137 Grafton Rd is a very important address for me in my life ... Grafton Bridge is just next to the road, on the way from my home to Auckland University. During the very first difficult period of exile life, I remember very clearly the view from the bridge: it was the view of that time and the situation.' Yang Lian revealed more of his thoughts on Auckland in *Ghostspeak,* a meditation on writing in exile:

'Every day you climb the stairs you think: this is exile. Feel every step carefully. Miss a step and the whole world comes tumbling down on you.'

Thirty-five minutes by ferry from Auckland, in the Hauraki Gulf, stands a beautiful island with an international reputation for picturesque beaches, award-winning vineyards and Tuscan-like landscapes. But in China in the 1990s Waiheke Island became known as the site of a gruesome act. Yang Lian's fellow Misty Poet Gu Cheng committed a murder-suicide there in 1993, a few months after completing a strange autobiographical novel, *Ying'er* (Little Ying), named after a woman he had an affair with.

Gu Cheng and his wife, Xie Ye, both in their thirties, moved to Waiheke in 1988 after arriving in New Zealand the previous year. Gu Cheng, who wore a 'thinking cap' made from the bottom of a trouser leg, embraced the idea of a simple life on an island paradise, but the couple, who had a young baby, struggled to pay the bills. The marriage became strained and Gu Cheng invited a student admirer of his, Li Ying, to leave China and live with them. Xie Ye agreed and offered to divorce Gu Cheng if he wanted, but he preferred to live with two women. Li Ying eventually left after trying unsuccessfully to persuade Gu Cheng to divorce his wife. Xie Ye began her own writing career and in 1992 the couple accepted an invitation to write and teach in Germany. On their return Xie Ye asked for a divorce so she could live with her lover, a Chinese man from Berlin who was coming out to New Zealand. In October 1993 Gu Cheng murdered Xie Ye with an axe on the path outside his sister's Ostend house and then hanged himself from a nearby tree. The Auckland coroner found Gu Cheng suffered from the 'eternal triangle syndrome'.

The tragic events on Waiheke Island inspired a Hong Kong feature film, a contemporary dance work, an opera — and a macabre tourist tour. For a while New Zealand's Chinese language newspapers offered tours of 'Gu Cheng Island'. Li Ying defended her reputation in her own book *Heartbroken on Waiheke*.

The New Zealand government offered to arrange and sponsor a trip for J.B. Priestley after he told the country's high commissioner in London that he wanted to visit the country because 'I had never been there, after going to so many places, and that I felt some sympathy with New Zealand because I disliked the Common Market and deeply resented being herded into it.' The English playwright and novelist wanted to use his 1973 trip to write and the book he eventually produced had 'elements of the pot-boiler' according to his biographer, Vincent Brome. But Priestley described *A Visit to New Zealand* as 'a reasonably honest and fairly intimate account of a visit, where we went, and what I thought and what I felt during this journey so far from home'.

Priestley got a poor review when he visited Auckland University. He had lunch with the Students Association, followed by an open discussion session. He later received an article by Helen Davis in the student paper *Happenings,* from which he quoted in *A Visit to New Zealand:*

> JBP entered quietly, a small grey-suited man with deep seamed and tucked bags under his eyes, radiating that self-assurance peculiar to a vanishing breed of Englishman; an arrogance beyond arrogance by virtue of being entirely unconscious. He sat down in the middle of the room and, at his suggestion, the students gathered around, most at a respectful distance. One young man sat himself down beside the visitor and played, rather disconcertingly, with his bare toes throughout the proceedings ...

Priestley claimed Davis had a colonial chip-on-the-shoulder and that even if he was conceited and vain, he wasn't arrogant, he wasn't Lord Curzon or Kipling, and he was anti-establishment. Priestley began and ended his trip in Auckland. On his first morning in the city he bought two notebooks but only filled the first four pages of one, preferring to rely on his memory. His lack of notes later proved problematic as even with the help of a map he struggled to remember the names of smaller places he had stopped in. He was unhappy about the Auckland city centre hotel he'd been booked into as there was building work going on (it was like a 'giant blacksmith's') and he was equally unhappy with his accommodation in Parnell on his return six weeks later, as he felt cut off from the city and never really felt he got to know it. Parnell, the city's oldest suburb, is located between the harbour and the Domain a short drive from the centre of Auckland. Priestley thought Auckland lacked a defined character unlike Dunedin or Christchurch.

It was in Auckland that Ngugi Wa Thiong'o became the first African writer to be honoured by a New Zealand university. Ngugi Wa Thiong'o lived in exile for 22 years after he was imprisoned without trial by the Kenyan government in 1977 after writing a controversial novel and play. In jail the vocal critic of corruption and injustice wrote a novel on toilet paper, *Caitaani Mutharabaini* (*Devil on the Cross*). Amnesty International helped to secure his release the following year. In 1982, while he was promoting *Caitaani Mutharabaini* in Britain, he was threatened with arrest if he returned to his home country. Ngugi's 1984 Robb Lectures at Auckland University resulted in the book *Decolonising the Mind.* According to its author the work 'has had a worldwide impact on postcolonial theories and has been translated into several world languages'. Professor Ngugi was awarded an honorary doctorate in African literature by the same university in July 2005. When he returned for the ceremony he commented on the political situation in Zimbabwe and said although sport and politics were linked he saw no reason why the New Zealand cricket team, the

Black Caps, shouldn't tour Zimbabwe. The previous year he finally travelled back to Kenya. He and his wife were welcomed by thousands, but were later brutally attacked.

In November 1984 novelist Patrick White was invited to Auckland to award media peace prizes at the War Memorial Museum, which sits in the Domain, one of the city's oldest parks. White was born in England but became an Australian citizen. In his speech 'Peace and Other Matters', which is included in a 1989 compilation *Patrick White Speaks*, he applauded the stand of New Zealand's Labour Government and many of the country's conservatives against the entry of nuclear ships. Invoking the devastating effects of the Hiroshima and Nagasaki bombs, he reminded his listeners that what happened during the Second World War was only a 'trial run for the desolation World War III will inflict on our planet if we, the people of the world, allow megalomaniac leaders to force it on us — the Reagans, the Thatchers, the Mitterands heading the list — with many lesser stars seduced by the idea of power and perks accruing from a superwar'. He dismissed the politician's argument that uranium could be made safe. He said the Nuclear Disarmament Party in Australia had recently been formed and that he hoped New Zealand and its neighbour would support each other.

Not far from the University of Auckland, on the same street as the Grand Hotel, is a majestic gentleman's club that has hosted many literary greats since it was founded in 1869. The four-storey, ivy-covered Victorian building of the Northern Club stands on Princes Street a short walk up the hill from the harbour. There is no memorabilia, no commemorative plaque or painting in the club today to remind its current members of its illustrious literary visitors. But it was here that a banquet was held in 'superb style' in Trollope's honour before he departed from New Zealand. More than forty men sat around tables decorated with colourful flowers for a dinner chaired by Chief Justice Sir George Alfred Arney and vice-chaired by Captain Daveney. When toasting Trollope's health, Arney alluded to the influence and importance of literature in colonial communities — and to the fact that people in newer countries like New Zealand read more books than the English. Trollope, whose novels sold out in Auckland's bookshops during his New Zealand visit, agreed and said he hadn't expected to receive as much attention as he did in the colonies because he thought that the work of establishing new homes and cultivating the land wouldn't leave much time for books. But 'all through the wide extent of Australia, and in every house in New Zealand he had been in, he had not only found some of his own works, but many of the works of Thackeray, Dickens, and other authors of eminence in all the walks of literature,' reported the *Daily Southern Cross.*

An Auckland newspaper, capitalising on the popularity of Dickens' works, got into trouble a few years before Trollope's visit. With his publishing partners Edward and Frederic Chapman, Dickens sued the proprietors of the *Weekly News* for £1000 for printing instalments of *Our Mutual Friend* in breach of copyright. The case was heard in May 1866 in the Northern District Supreme Court of New Zealand but was later dropped after the paper stopped printing the instalments and Dickens' lawyer was advised the company didn't have the money to pay damages and costs of more than £50. In 1864 Dickens had encountered a similar problem with the *Melbourne Weekly Leader*. He had written to his solicitor Frederic Ouvry in July 1865 'Here is a New Zealand vagabond playing the old nefarious game with "Our Mutual Friend"... Terrify him, terrify him, terrify him!'

On a morning in 1951 Eric Linklater was having breakfast in the Northern Club, and listening to two elderly men disagree about the quality of Mark Twain's lectures in New Zealand. Linklater was on a lecture tour of his own and found the remarks discouraging but appropriate in the Victorian atmosphere of the club. It was a place where there was disapproval that the prime minister had been shouted down by rowdy watersiders at a meeting the previous evening and where 'the dignity of the furniture had been mollified by long use, the cutlery was solid and expensive, and on the walls hung steel engravings of the great Queen's Diamond Jubilee,' wrote Linklater. 'After flying fast and noisily across the circumference of the world it was very pleasant to rest for a day or two in a place so calm, so sturdily confined and comfortingly static.' Linklater combined several hours' writing each day with lecturing. He was working on *Our Men in Korea,* as he travelled around the country with documents and notes. He lectured about the Korean War to several branches of the New Zealand Officer's Club. At one meeting a soldier quoted approvingly a line Linklater had once written about 'New Zealanders who looked like Cromwell's Ironsides, and fought with pride and a professional severity'.

'A staring, unbeautiful building, but internally of ascertained excellence,' was James Anthony Froude's impression of the Northern Club. A controversial writer (his autobiographical work *The Nemesis of Faith* was publicly burned by the senior tutor of Exeter College, Oxford), Froude visited Australia and New Zealand in 1884–85 and his resulting book *Oceana; or, England and Her Colonies* was published in 1886. Although he also wrote fiction, Froude was best known as a historian. At the Northern Club he was swamped by reporters' questions, 'as if at the pistol's mouth, about confederation, about the Egyptian war, about the quarrel with Russia, the House of Commons vote, the New South Wales contingent, &c. First, and above all, what did we think of New Zealand.' Having only been ashore two hours Froude asked for time to answer the questions. Outside the dining room on a 'large and airy verandah' he made his plans to see the 'hot lakes' district.

The *Observer* later printed a conversation between a *Star* reporter and Froude, a friend and biographer of Thomas Carlyle, a Victorian author who commended Cromwell's actions in Ireland.

Froude: Well, my little man, and who are you?

W.J.: I am a member of the fourth estate.

Froude: A juvenile journalist I presume?

W.J.: You have hit the mark sir, as you did in your noble prince, Henry VIII.

Froude: What! And do I behold a colonial who has read my history? Delightful! my little coxy-waxy.

W.J.: But, sir, allow me, as a critic, to remark that you have scarcely done justice to Ireland.

Froude: Indeed, sir! Possibly you are from the north of the Green Isle?

W.J.: Right you are, James Anthony.

Froude: Well, sir, since I am so favoured, what hast thou to say touching my "Life of Carlyle"?

W.J.: I did not know Carlyle; he was no friend of mine.

Froude: Then you never interviewed him?

W.J.: Not I, indeed.

Froude: What journal did you say you represented?

W.J.: Not any in particular. I'm the "star" of sensation and the terror of the Armed Constabulary — a man to be feared and respected.

Froude: You are a Fenian; I can see it by the cast of your eyes. Get thee behind me, Satan!

W.J.: Sir — sir, you mistake my calling; I shall yet be recognised as the historian of New Zealand, from chief Te Ta Tito to the fall of King Jacob.

Froude: What do you drink, sir?

W.J.: Seldom anything stronger or more operative than Epsom salts.

Rudyard Kipling spent a night in the Northern Club in late October 1891 after travelling north from Rotorua to Cambridge and before leaving for Wellington. He told a newspaper reporter he thought Auckland was 'perhaps the most beautiful' city he had ever seen, and he would later pay homage to it in his poem 'The Song of the Cities'.

Last, loneliest, loveliest, exquisite, apart —
On us, on us the unswerving season smiles,
Who wonder 'mid our fern why men depart
To seek the Happy Isles!

Kipling, the first British writer to win the Nobel Prize for Literature, was enormously popular during his lifetime, but in recent years the imperialist themes running through his work have made him less fashionable. There were several reasons why Kipling decided to leave England for a while. The tanned man with light gold glasses, and short, thinning hair, whose 'physique and mannerisms were those of a rapid thinker and worker', suffered a breakdown from overwork in 1890 and felt the need for some relaxation. He had been writing prolifically in London and was under considerable pressure and was also suffering recurring bouts of malaria. And then there was Miss Carrie Balestier. They were unofficially engaged but it was a complicated relationship and Kipling needed time away.

The attraction of the South Seas as an escape was the presence of another leading author. 'I had had some notion of sailing from Auckland to visit Robert Louis Stevenson at Samoa, for he had done me the honour to write me about some of my tales; and moreover I was Eminent Past Master R.L.S.,' Kipling wrote in *Something of Myself for My Friends Known and Unknown*, his posthumously published autobiography that was written some forty-five years after his New Zealand visit. Robert Louis Stevenson was an admirer of Kipling's work and had exchanged letters with Henry James in which the esteemed authors praised the young writer's work. Stevenson thought Kipling 'too clever to live'. James remarked that in leaving England Kipling was 'carrying literary genius out of the country with him in his pocket'. Despite his best efforts to secure passage to see Stevenson in Samoa Kipling failed to get a boat. 'Auckland,' he wrote, 'seemed the end of organised travel; for the captain of a fruit-boat, which might or might not go to Samoa at some time or other, was so devotedly drunk that I decided to turn south, and work back to India.'

Another famous British author — although he wasn't famous then — also had a futile search for Robert Louis Stevenson in Samoa. It would be another 14 years before the publication of the first volume of the work John Galsworthy is best known for, *The Forsyte Saga*. Galsworthy, an Oxford graduate who trained as a lawyer, had been restless and infatuated with a woman. His father thought a journey on the high seas would becalm the young man and further his knowledge of navigation and maritime law. But his father's plan failed and travel made Galsworthy even more restless and more determined not to follow a legal career. 'I always want to get inside beautiful things and feel more in touch with them; and somehow one can never get far enough ...' he wrote in one letter. Galsworthy even entertained the idea of gold digging in Australia before he eventually became a writer.

With his close friend Ted Sanderson, Galsworthy left England in November 1892 on a voyage to Australia, New Zealand and the South Seas. After arriving in Australia they found they couldn't get to Samoa from Sydney to meet Stevenson so they sailed to New Caledonia and Fiji instead. Galsworthy wrote to his mother from Fiji about his plan to sail to Auckland, saying, 'the further one goes the more one hears of the beauty of the country there'. He arrived in Auckland in early 1893 and then set off to explore 'the hot lakes and the curious but infernal regions of the North Island'. On his return to the city he said, '... the scenery amounted to a maximum of the marvellous and a minimum of beauty'.

Galsworthy sailed back to England on the *Torrens*, where he met and befriended the ship's first mate Joseph Conrad, who was working on his first novel. Conrad became an enduring influence on Galsworthy's writing career.

Robert Louis Stevenson's desire to travel to the South Seas was partially inspired by a New Zealander. One summer evening in Edinburgh in 1875 he met William Seed who was consulting his father about lighthouse engineering. Seed talked about Samoa, where he'd worked for the New Zealand government, and the 24-year-old Stevenson was so enchanted by the tales of the South Seas he questioned his father's visitor late into the night. He wrote about the encounter to his friend Mrs Frances Sitwell.

> Awfully nice man here tonight. Public servant — New Zealand. Telling us all about the South Sea Islands till I was sick with desire to go there: beautiful places, green for ever; perfect climate; perfect shapes of men and women, with red flowers in their hair; and nothing to do but to study oratory and etiquette, sit in the sun, and pick up the fruits as they fall. Navigator's Island is the place; absolute balm for the weary.

The following year Stevenson was so preoccupied with Seed's stories that he started work on a novel about Navigators' Islands (the former name for the Samoan islands) that was never finished. Seed's visit was still in his memory 15 years later when he wrote to a friend,

> Let me tell you this: In '74 or 5 there came to stay with my father and mother a certain Mr Seed, a prime minister or something of New Zealand. He spotted what my complaint was; told me that I had no business to stay in Europe; that I should find all I cared for, and all that was good for me, in the Navigator Islands; sat up till four in the morning persuading me, demolishing my scruples. And I resisted: I refused to go so far from my father and mother. O, it was virtuous, and O, wasn't it silly! But my father, who was always my dearest, got to his grave without that pang; and now in 1890, I (or what is left of me) go at last to the Navigator Islands. God go with us! It is but a Pisgah sight when all is said; I go there only to grow old and die; but when you come, you will see it is a fair place for the purpose.

When Stevenson visited in Auckland in 1893 he met the former Governor of New Zealand Sir George Grey to discuss Samoan affairs. After settling in Samoa Stevenson became involved in local politics. Grey was governor of New Zealand from 1845–53 and again from 1861–68 and he later held positions as an MP, the superintendent of the Auckland province and New Zealand premier. In 1862 Grey bought Kawau Island, in the northwest of the Hauraki Gulf, and lived there until 1888. He converted the ten-room home of the local copper mine manager into a 20-room building now known as Mansion House. He created a large library, which he later gifted to the city of Auckland.

Grey met James Anthony Froude at the Northern Club and invited him to Kawau Island. It's just over an hour by ferry today but took most of a day on a 'delightful' voyage by steamer to get there in Froude's time. They stopped at Waiwera, 'an ambitious little watering-place with a hot spring of its own', on the east coast of the mainland. They touched at a few more places and at around five o'clock in the afternoon 'we turned our head at last towards the harbour at Kawau and saw the white front of Sir George's house at the bottom of a steeply wooded inlet, the hills rising behind it, the soft still sea, and the tiny islands on its skirts like patches of old forest left behind when the water had cut them off from the land, as beautiful as eye could rest on'. Froude explored and sailed and talked politics, history and literature with Grey. 'The week which we had passed at Kawau was one of the most interesting which I remember in my life,' he wrote.

Anthony Trollope met Sir George Grey on Kawau Island in 1872 when he was turning the wilderness into a garden. Trollope tried to refrain from writing about governors who were alive because he had 'received kind hospitality' from many and he thought 'a writer for the public should not praise when he feels himself to be deterred by friendship from censure'. However, he made an exception for Grey, whom he thought 'certainly managed to endear himself in a wonderful way to a population with whom it was his duty to be constantly fighting. There can be no doubt of Sir George Grey's popularity among the Maoris.'

In late 1891 Henry Morton Stanley, the journalist and explorer who famously searched for and found Dr Livingstone, met Grey in Auckland during an Australasian lecture tour. Stanley described the statesman as having 'a grand, quiet face, and a pair of round blue eyes beaming with kindness, and the light of wisdom'. Grey showed him letters at the Public Library he had received from Livingstone while he was governor of Cape Colony.

> It was a keen pleasure to read these old letters, which breathed of work, loyalty of soul, human duties, imperial objects, and moral obligations, and then to look up at the face of the venerable statesman to whom they were addressed, and trace the benevolence, breadth of mind, and intelligence which elicited the spontaneous, free expression of their hopes from these travellers and pioneers.

The North Shore suburb of Birkenhead is only four kilometres northwest of the Auckland city centre, but before the opening of the Auckland Harbour Bridge in 1959 the only way to get there by road would have been a journey of some twenty kilometres through West Auckland. So Arthur Conan Doyle would probably have taken the passenger ferry to Birkenhead to meet 'the most remarkable personality in Auckland'. Clement Wragge was a 'tall, thin figure, clad in black, with a face like a sadder and thinner Bernard Shaw, dim, dreamy eyes, heavily pouched, with a blue turban surmounting all'. He lived in a 'charming' bungalow nestled among a variety of trees and plants on Awanui Street, overlooking Little Shoal Bay where he had settled on the North Shore in 1910 with his wife, 'a charming Brahmin lady from India, who was one of the most gracious personalities I have met in my wanderings', wrote Conan Doyle. There he built his house and founded the Wragge Institute & Museum and the Waiata Tropical Gardens and earned an income by lecturing and encouraging tourists to see his gardens and visit his fortune-telling wife.

Wragge was a widely travelled, eccentric, English meteorologist and a man described by Conan Doyle as a dreamer and a mystic but yet a 'very practical advisor on all matters of ocean and air'. The author was intrigued by the theory that Maori originally came from Hawaii and wanted to know what prevailing winds they would have encountered on their journey. Wragge used a chart to show how they would have met a northwesterly trade wind, then the Doldrums through which they would have had to paddle, then the southeasterly trades that would have blown them towards New Zealand. Conan Doyle believed the British Empire had treated the Maori well and that New Zealand had no 'natural sin upon its conscience as regards the natives'. He developed a theory that Maori had Celtic influences in 'their appearance, their character and their language' and that there were traces of Japanese in their language, with the combinations of letters like Rangi, Muru and Tiki.

> Is it possible that one Celtic branch, far away in the mists of time, wandered east while their racial brethren wandered west, so that part reached Corea while the others reached Ireland? Then, after getting a tincture of Japanese terms and word endings, they continued their migration, taking to the seas, and finally subduing the darker races who inhabited the Polynesian Islands, so making their way to New Zealand. This wild imagining would at least cover the observed facts. It is impossible to look at some of the Maori faces without realising that they are of European stock.

The woman who bought Wragge's old home in 2005 told a newspaper reporter she felt the meteorologist was speaking to her when she first looked around the property. She felt she was destined to own it, which she did after convincing her husband to make the move from Mt Eden. Arthur Conan Doyle would surely have approved.

When he found out Anthony Trollope was coming to New Zealand, the man known as the 'Father of Auckland' invited the author to stay at his house. Sir John Logan Campbell, businessman and politician, was friendly with Trollope's older brother Thomas Adolphus, so he invited Anthony to stay in the house he had built, 'Logan Bank' in Jermyn Street. Neither the house nor the street on which it stood still exist, as Jermyn Street disappeared into Anzac Avenue, a road that runs close to the harbour, during the First World War. Campbell recalled in his memoirs that Trollope had a small room where he wrote a certain amount every morning in private without interruption 'as if he were making bricks by a machine'. In his posthumous autobiography Trollope described his daily writing routine. He worked from 5.30 to 8.30 a.m. so that he could finish before dressing for breakfast. He began by reading his previous day's work for half an hour. Then he placed his watch on his desk and wrote 250 words every 15 minutes.

> All those I think who have lived as literary men, — working daily as literary labourers, — will agree with me that three hours a day will produce as much as a man ought to write. But then he should so have trained himself that he shall be able to work continuously during those three hours, — so have tutored his mind that it shall not be necessary for him to sit nibbling his pen, and gazing at the wall before him, till he shall have found the words with which he wants to express his ideas.

Campbell greatly enjoyed Auckland's climate and landscape and built a house that faced the sea and offered a wonderful view of nearby islands. He thought Trollope neither talked about nor wrote about scenery with enough emotion. The author also incurred Campbell's wrath for running out on his hotel bills in Rotorua. Campbell's biographer, Russell Stone, wrote that the Aucklander 'felt he had acquired as guest not a literary lion, but a fifty-seven-year-old tourist with a "big gruff voice" of uninspired ordinariness'. When Trollope stayed overnight in Auckland three years later en route to San Francisco, Campbell booked him into the Northern Club to avoid hosting him again.

Mark Twain wrote that 'the highest class white men who lived among the Maoris in the earliest time had a high opinion of them and a strong affection for them'. He regarded Campbell as being one of these men. He was a 'close friend of several chiefs, and has many pleasant things to say of their fidelity, their magnanimity, and their generosity,' wrote Twain. 'Also of their quaint notions about the white man's queer civilization, and their equally quaint comments upon it. One of them thought the missionary had got everything wrong end first and upside down. "Why, he wants us to stop worshipping and supplicating the evil gods, and go to worshipping and supplicating the Good One! There is no sense in that. A good god is not going to do us any harm."'

Kauri gum was a major export at the end of the nineteenth century; but Campbell told Twain that when he had shipped a load to England 50 years earlier no one knew what to do with it, so it was eventually sold as a material to light fires. There were up to 1.8 million acres of gum fields scattered between the lower Waikato and the Coromandel Peninsula right up to the northernmost tip of the North Island. Twain, who visited the kauri gum establishment of American firm Arnold, Cheney & Co. in Auckland, wrote that about 8000 tons of gum was coming into the city each year and that it was worth $300 to $1000 per ton. It was mostly being shipped to America.

> It is in lumps, and is hard and smooth, and looks like amber — the light-coloured like new amber, and the dark brown like rich old amber. And it has the pleasant feel of amber, too. Some of the light-coloured samples were a tolerably fair counterfeit of uncut South African diamonds, they were so perfectly smooth and polished and transparent. It is manufactured into varnish; a varnish, which answers for copal varnish and is cheaper.

Trollope was taken to see a kauri forest in the Waitakere Ranges in West Auckland. The area was milled so extensively in the late nineteenth and early twentieth centuries most of the large kauri were destroyed, although a stand in what is now known as Cascade Kauri Park can still be seen. A woodsman showed Trollope a tree he was about to fell. It stood 15 metres tall and was almost three metres in diameter.

> These trees are fast disappearing. Our friend the woodman told us that the one to which he took us, — and than which he assured us that we could find none larger in the forest, — was soon to fall beneath his axe. When we met him he was triumphing over a huge monster that he had felled, and was splitting it up into shingles for roofing houses. The wood as it comes to pieces is yellow and resinous with gum, and on that account, — so he told us, — was super-excellent for shingles. The trees are never cut down for their gum, which seems to be useless till time has given it a certain consistency. Very soon there will not be a kauri tree left to cut down in the neighbourhood of Auckland.

Kauri trees featured in the bizarre world conjured up by Jules Verne in *Voyage au centre de la terre* published in 1864 (appearing in English as *A Journey to the Centre of the Earth, A Journey to the Interior of the Earth* and *A Trip to the Center of the Earth*). Verne, a celebrated storyteller and science fiction pioneer, created an underground world in an extinct volcano in Iceland, in which his characters Axel and his uncle Professor Liedenbrock discover a weird forest.

> Then I observed, mingled together in confusion, trees of countries far apart on the surface of the globe. The oak and the palm were growing side by side, the Australian eucalyptus leaned against the Norwegian pine, the birch-tree of the north mingled its foliage with New Zealand kauris. It was enough to distract the most ingenious classifier of terrestrial botany.

The province of Auckland had gold, it had kauri gum and it was also becoming an agricultural region. The city, which by the turn of the century would be New Zealand's largest, was emerging as a commercial centre.

> It is a land very happy in its climate; — very happy in its promises. The poor Maori who is now the source of all Auckland poetry, must first melt; and then, if her coal-fields can be made productive, — for she has coal-fields, — and if the iron which is washed to her shore among the sands of the sea, can be wrought into steel, I see no reason why Auckland should not rival London.

A PARADISE DISCOVERED – A PARADISE LOST

On the last day of May in 1886 a tourist party of Maori and Pakeha noticed something strange on Lake Tarawera. They thought they saw a fully manned, ceremonial war canoe, something not seen on the lake for half a century, gliding towards them. As it came closer, the canoe disappeared and Maori believed the phantom sighting was an omen of disaster. A few days later another party noticed an unusual rise in the level of the lake. In the early hours of 10 June 1886, Mt Tarawera erupted and its three vents vomited millions of tons of ash and rock as far as ten kilometres away. Earthquakes shook the North Island and Aucklanders, a couple of hundred kilometres to the north, thought they heard cannon fire. Over 150 people were killed, buildings collapsed, surrounding villages were buried, roads and bridges were destroyed and daylight was shrouded by black ash.

The Mt Tarawera eruption also completely destroyed a natural phenomenon so remarkable that many writers proclaimed it indescribable. The magnificence of the Pink and White Terraces had attracted many writers to the central North Island, pens poised, ready to capture the splendour of two grand staircase-like silica structures on the shores of Lake Rotomahana. They were regarded as the eighth wonder of the world. *The Times* of London reported the devastation of 'one of the loveliest spots on earth', adding that 'the terrible news of the disaster that has overwhelmed that wondrous district, and in one short night transformed its every varying beauties into a scene of weird desolation, will be read with lively feelings of regret in many nooks of far distant Europe'. The newspaper reprinted James Anthony Froude's 'striking' description of the terraces as a reminder of what had been lost forever. In 1885 in *Oceana; or, England and Her Colonies* Froude had described the summit of the pink terraces:

> We could stand on the brim and gaze as through an opening in the earth into an azure infinity beyond. Down and down, fainter and softer as they receded, the white crystals projected from the rocky walls over the abyss, but they seemed to dissolve not into darkness but into light. The hue of the water was something which I had never seen, and shall never see again this side of eternity. Not the violet, not the harebell, nearest in its tint of heaven of all Nature's flowers, not turquoise, not sapphire, not the unfathomable ether itself, could convey to one who has not looked on it a sense of that supernatural loveliness.

Anthony Trollope set off from Auckland on a fortnight's tour around the centre of the North Island in September 1872. The Pink and White Terraces were the highlight of any such journey but the whole region was a wonderland of lakes, hot pools and geysers. It was quite an undertaking and the only way to get there at the time of Trollope's visit was on horseback and by foot. It began with a 20-hour voyage on the steamer, the *Southern Cross* from Auckland to the coastal town of Tauranga about one hundred and sixty kilometres southeast where he was joined by his guide. Captain Gilbert Mair was a Paheka soldier who was awarded the New Zealand Cross for his courage and leadership in the New Zealand Wars. He was often asked by the government to accompany eminent visitors through the 'hot lakes' district, as he knew local Maori and the terrain well. Mair found his charge to be 'a typical and jovial John Bull in appearance, with his breeches and gaiters, very stout and hearty, downright in manners and brusque. A fine type of an Englishman, an excellent rider and judge of horseflesh, and he never tired of relating stories of the hunting field. And he hated snobs and society snobbishness with a deadly hatred.' With two assistants the pair began a week-long trek on horseback.

ANTHONY TROLLOPE, FROM 'AN AUTOBIOGRAPHY', 1946. ALEXANDER TURNBULL LIBRARY, WELLINGTON, NEW ZEALAND. BK-509FRONTIS.

George Bernard Shaw slipped on a bright red woman's bathing suit and plunged into the surf at Mt Maunganui on a late summer Sunday in 1934. 'The Mount' as the holiday resort is known, is a town that stands at the foot of an extinct volcano at the head of a peninsula just across the harbour from Tauranga. The beach at the Mount is still popular with holidaymakers and surfers. The breakers were strong when Shaw visited; so strong that the life saving team had cancelled a practice rescue. But the eccentric visiting playwright was undaunted and in his borrowed costume Shaw plunged into the ocean. 'It was evident that Mr Shaw was suffering a severe buffeting, and some spectators were concerned for his safety, but Mr Shaw showed amazing vitality and thoroughly enjoyed his battle with the elements,' a local correspondent noted.

Moturiki Island is a tiny piece of land just off the southeastern end of the beach connected to the shore by a man-made walkway. At its head is a blowhole from which Shaw enjoyed the view. He could look back to the beach and out to the Pacific Ocean and offshore islands. 'Though no resident showed the temerity to ask his opinion of the Mount,' reported the *Bay of Plenty Times*, 'it is understood that he admired the Mount even as much as the Mount admires a daring surfer.' Shaw thought it was 'one of the best ocean beaches he had seen in any part of the world'.

✶

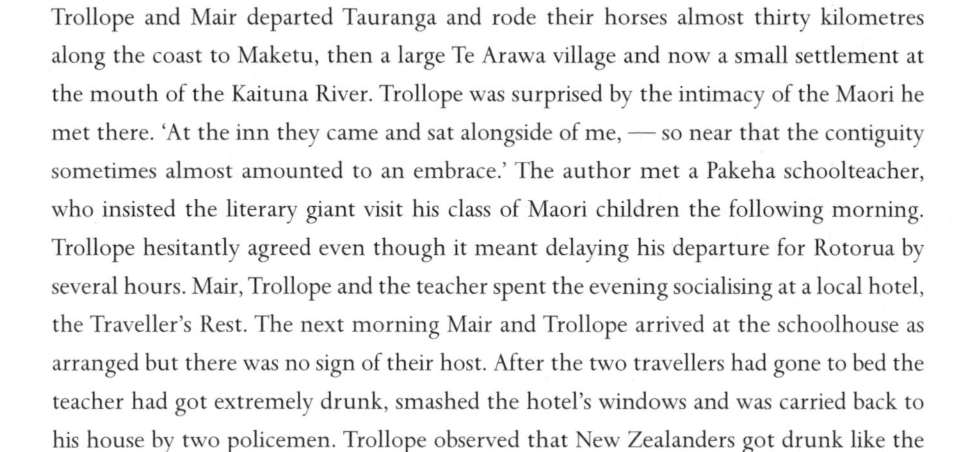

Trollope and Mair departed Tauranga and rode their horses almost thirty kilometres along the coast to Maketu, then a large Te Arawa village and now a small settlement at the mouth of the Kaituna River. Trollope was surprised by the intimacy of the Maori he met there. 'At the inn they came and sat alongside of me, — so near that the contiguity sometimes almost amounted to an embrace.' The author met a Pakeha schoolteacher, who insisted the literary giant visit his class of Maori children the following morning. Trollope hesitantly agreed even though it meant delaying his departure for Rotorua by several hours. Mair, Trollope and the teacher spent the evening socialising at a local hotel, the Traveller's Rest. The next morning Mair and Trollope arrived at the schoolhouse as arranged but there was no sign of their host. After the two travellers had gone to bed the teacher had got extremely drunk, smashed the hotel's windows and was carried back to his house by two policemen. Trollope observed that New Zealanders got drunk like the English and overindulged far more frequently than their Australian neighbours.

Trollope wasn't universally liked in New Zealand. His visit to the Bay of Plenty was fleeting; he stayed a night at Maketu and found time to learn of Gate Pa, the site of a devastating British defeat during the New Zealand Wars; but his time there was sufficient to anger the locals. The *Bay of Plenty Times*, which only began publication in the month of Trollope's visit, reported that 'it appears that we have seen the last of Mr Anthony Trollope, as we learn he purposes proceeding to the Waikato overland. Well, we shan't miss him much. He did not make himself popular here, hardly showed himself in public at all. "Let him gush," as Artemus Ward says.'

Trollope's party turned inland from the Bay of Plenty coast and journeyed south for more than fifty kilometres towards the southern shore of Lake Rotorua. The journey to the small village of Ohinemutu took them over terrain that 'rises and falls in rapid little hills, and is tossed about in a wonderful fashion; — but there is no serious ascent or descent'. They crossed Lake Rotoiti, to the northeast of Lake Rotorua, in a canoe and swam the horses over. Mokoia Island came into view as they continued down the eastern shore of Lake Rotorua and into the village of Te Ngae. The island is the setting for a celebrated Maori story. A beautiful chief's daughter, Hinemoa, lived on the shores of the lake, and defied her family by swimming to her lover Tutanekai on the island. She was guided by the sound of his flute at night. Two intersecting streets in Rotorua city centre are named after the famous lovers and the warm pool Hinemoa bathed in just below Tutanekai's house is a tourist attraction. The romance of the tale seemed lost on Trollope, however. 'As the distance is hardly more than a mile, and as the Maoris are all swimmers, the feat did not seem to me to be very wonderful, — till I heard that the flute was made out of the tibia of a man's leg.'

James Anthony Froude, who visited the 'sunny, dreamy' Mokoia Island, was intrigued not only by Hinemoa and Tutanekai but also the story of a massacre on the island in the early missionary days. The central character was the Nga Puhi leader, Hongi Hika, a famous warrior who visited England in 1820 on the premise that he wanted to know more about the missionary cause. While in England he was given money to 'civilize' and convert his countrymen but he spent the money on arms in Sydney and returned to destroy his enemies. He joined forces with other northern tribes to attack Ngati Whakaue and other Te Arawa on Mokoia Island. They refused to submit so he launched his canoes on the lake and killed everyone he could find on the island.

Froude saw a tree on the island with visitors' names scratched into the bark and a few bones stuck into a cleft, which he was told were the human bones that 'Hangi' [Hongi Hika] had thrown there 'after his dinner'. It's unlikely the bones Froude saw had anything to do with the massacre, but in the nineteenth century there was a tree on the island that was often shown to visitors, containing the skeletal remains of a child. It's not clear how the bones got there.

Trollope found the smell of the sulphur 'putrid' as he reached Ohinemutu, on the southwestern shore of Lake Rotorua. Ohinemutu was the main Maori settlement, around which the government township of Rotorua later grew. It is still distinguishable as a Maori centre of Rotorua today. Trollope described it as 'a poor little Maori village, which seems to have collected itself round the hot springs, close on the borders of the lake, with a view to the boiling of potatoes without the trouble of collecting fuel'. Recalling his trip to the thermal region in 1941, Noël Coward wrote, 'I felt that to be able to boil an egg in a puddle outside your front door, although undoubtedly labour saving, was not really enough compensation for having to live immediately on top of the earth's hidden fires.' Agatha Christie described Rotorua as 'a wonderful place — the air full of sulphur fumes and boiling steam coming up from the ground and great quaking boiling mud pits, and all the Maoris bathing and washing clothes in the hot pools'. Arthur Conan Doyle avoided the place altogether. 'An itinerant lecturer upon an unpopular cause has enough hot water without seeking out a geyser,' he wrote.

It was on a dark evening behind a little Ohinemutu inn that Anthony Trollope entered a natural hot pool for the first time. The Victorian Englishman in his late fifties stripped down to 'very light attire', and as he and Gilbert Mair arrived at the pool they found 'three Maori damsels' already bathing. 'But this was nothing, — nothing, at least, in the way of objection,' wrote Trollope. 'The night was dark; and if they thoroughly understood the old French proverb which has become royally English, why should we be more obstinate or less intelligent? I crept down into the pool, and as I crouched beneath the water, they encouraged me by patting me on the back.' Trollope sat in the pool for half an hour while Mair chatted to the women in Maori. He concluded that his first evening in New Zealand's thermal area had passed 'very pleasantly'. But Mair later revealed in *Reminiscences and Maori Stories* that the famous author had 'discreetly omitted one little episode from his chronicles'. After they had been in the water a while Trollope said to him, 'I wish I had something to lean against,' so Mair 'whispered to a fine young woman of splendid proportions, popularly known as "the Duchess", who immediately set her capacious back against his, whereat he exclaimed, "Well, Mair, this is very delightful,

POSTCARD OF OHINEMUTU, C. 1880–1910. SPECIAL COLLECTIONS, AUCKLAND CITY LIBRARIES (N.Z.), 231-4.

don't you know; but I think I did wise in leaving Mrs Trollope in Auckland."'

Froude felt he could have stayed indefinitely in Ohinemutu. He saw the remains of a grand pa that had been destroyed by an earthquake, and a Maori man swimming in the rain with a pipe in his mouth, holding an umbrella. He and many other visiting writers were fascinated by gruesome stories about the boiling pools. Froude was shown where a Maori man with the 'firewater in him' had fallen in and also the site where an Ohinemutu chief boiled and ate an ambassador representing a neighbouring tribe, before he was boiled in the same pool and eaten in retaliation.

Gilbert Mair liked to regale guests with the tragic story of a man who had tried to enlist in his contingent during the New Zealand Wars. In the 1860s and 70s Mair often recruited several hundred friendly Te Arawa Maori at short notice. When he got news of 600 Maori from Waikato marching to join the hostile Piri-rakau tribe Mair looked for volunteers. The first man to come forward was Wehi-Peihana ('The Frightened Peasant'), a grey-haired, tattooed warrior about seventy years old. He had fought well in the past but Mair told him he was too old and sent him away. Terribly disappointed, Wehi-Peihana came back repeatedly during the day only to be turned away each time. On hearing Mair say he had enough men, Wehi-Peihana leapt in front of the captain, performed war dances and demanded to be picked. Mair still refused and the old warrior cried 'Kahore ahau e mate tara-whare' ('I will not die under the eaves of a house'). Then he stripped down to his shirt and sank into a nearby boiling spring up to his neck. Mair grabbed the man's shirt collar, dragged him out and dipped him into the tepid lake a few metres away. He ran to get a dozen bottles of salad oil but by the time he'd returned the man had got back into the boiling pool and out of Mair's reach. Laying a bundle of manuka poles used for fencing across the pool, Mair walked over to the man and dragged him out again, scalding his foot in the process. But the old warrior was too badly injured to recover and later died, blaming the captain for not letting him fight.

Both Trollope and Scottish traveller James Inglis wrote about the death of Wehi-Peihana. After the accounts were published Mair was teased by his fellow officers for 'pulling the legs' of the visitors, even though the incident was never in doubt. Mair said the only wrong inference was that suicide was common among Maori refused admission to his force.

There was so much boiling water in Ohinemutu in 1885 it was necessary to poke the ground with an umbrella or a stick before crossing it, said George Augustus Sala during an Australasian lecturing tour. Sala was one of the most successful writers of his era. His career flourished after he locked himself out of his home with little money one evening. He wandered the streets observing how the poor people lived and was forced to stay the night in a filthy lodging house. He wrote about his nocturnal adventure for Dickens' journal *Household Words*. Although he talked of releasing a book about his travels in Australasia he never did. Sala contributed a series of articles from 'the verge of the Wonderland of New Zealand' to the *Daily Telegraph* as part of 32 articles titled 'The Land of the Golden Fleece'.

> There is only a very thin crust of earth between you and heaven knows how many vast vats of boiling water down below. Foot it merrily, then, on your way to the 'pa' on the peninsula. Cauldrons are to right of you, cauldrons to left of you, and cauldrons in front. There is an eternal washing day, and the coppers are ever on the boil. And when at last, having baffled the treachery of the tremulous earth, you reach the point of the peninsula, you find yourself in a place of tombs and 'tapu'. Among them is a tiny gravestone, in the midst of a miniature flower-garden, neatly palisaded. This tomb is sacred to the memory of Ellen Hinemoa Wilson, a poor little child who, not long since, was scalded to death by falling into a boiling hole in her father's garden.

Ellen Hinemoa, the first European child born to Ohinemutu settlers, died in early 1877 aged two years and eight months, after falling into a barrel of boiling water being used for washing. Rotorua remains a dangerous and volatile place where visitors are warned to keep to the paths and not jump fences. Scalding pools are sometimes only covered by a thin crust of earth and may only be emitting a few wisps of steam. However, the milder pools in Rotorua were thought to be immensely therapeutic. Father Mahoney, a severely arthritic Catholic priest from Tauranga, was carried to Rotorua to bathe in a spring, after which it was said that he walked back to Tauranga. The pool became known as the 'Priest's Bath'. As the government township of Rotorua developed, a variety of baths were constructed. Rotorua's waters were thought to be especially effective in helping rheumatism, gout, sciatica and lumbago, dyspepsia and skin diseases. Mark Twain didn't have time to travel from Auckland to Rotorua but described the city as the 'Carlsbad of Australasia' and was amused by the claim the waters could cure alcoholism.

> The government's official physician is almost over-cautious in his estimates of the efficacy of the baths, when he is talking about rheumatism, gout, paralysis, and such things; but when he is talking about the effectiveness of the waters in eradicating the whisky-habit, he seems to have no reserves. The baths will cure the drinking-habit no matter how chronic it is — and cure it so effectually that even the desire to drink intoxicants will come no more. There should be a rush

> from Europe and America to that place; and when the victims of alcoholism find out what they can get by going there, the rush will begin.

Rotorua was a 'city of the future' and its health-giving waters were a key attraction. 'Invalid English people, huge and splendidly appointed steamships will carry you direct in less than forty days from Plymouth to New Zealand, where you will find the grandest landscape, the most romantic coast scenery, and the most healing thermal springs in the world,' Sala informed his *Daily Telegraph* readers. He visited the hospital, sanitorium and baths, which included 'Cameron's Bath', also known as the 'Laughing Gas Bath', where a young English aristocrat almost died after inhaling the enticing vapours; the 'Coffee Pot'; the 'Pain-killer' bath; and 'Madame Rachel's Bath', named after a woman who promised women eternal beauty. 'Madame Rachel' is 'clear as crystal, but alkaline to nastiness, and so charged with silica that if you stayed in long enough you would be enamelled,' wrote James Anthony Froude. He noticed that a small twig of tea tree that had been in the water for a week or two was like a 'branch of white coral'.

Twenty Maori chiefs approached Sala after hearing him speak at a ceremonial opening of a bath in Rotorua. The chiefs called him the 'book-a-book-writing pakeha'. Sala was lobbied by local Maori during his stay at Ohinemutu who wanted him to tell the English they were a decaying race and that without their lands they would disappear. The chiefs met him in the billiard room of Ohinemutu's Lake House Hotel and Sala believed it to be one of the strangest spectacles he'd ever witnessed. Chiefs of all ages made speeches in succession, which were translated into English. 'The chiefs, whose attire presented a pleasing variety of "looped and windowed raggedness", but among whom watches and gold chains were not by any means uncommon, spoke with didactic deliberation, but with perfect fluency, never halting for a word, and not without dignity of action,' he wrote. The chiefs swore their loyalty to the Queen but argued they should be allowed to keep the lands they already had and be granted more. In the middle of the meeting a very old chief even arrived from his sick bed to talk with the 'book-a-book-writing pakeha'. 'He tottered in, holding in one tremulous hand a short spear, the symbol of his tribal rank. But I felt the tip of the weapon as he sat down beside me, and it was as blunt as the top of a toothbrush.'

Noël Coward fondly remembered his Maori welcome in Rotorua. 'I was met at the door by a painted warrior who capered round me for some minutes and finally made me pick up two sticks from the floor. After I had achieved this not impossible feat a great uproar broke out and I was presented to the chiefs and the local belles, with whom I rubbed noses; this was damp but convivial.' Maori songs and dances followed, before Coward sang a few numbers, which were met by 'polite bewilderment', and was given gifts.

Zane Grey thought the Maori to be 'extraordinary fishermen' and was also captivated by their speeches and singing after attending a concert in Rotorua. 'I could not recall when I had listened to such sweet singing as that of the Maori girls,' he wrote. During his visit to Rotorua Grey was bestowed with the name of Maui, the figure in Maori mythology who fished up the North Island of New Zealand using a hook of human bone and congealed blood from his own nose as bait. Grey was shown a carving of a fish caught by Maui at a meeting house by Maori guide Rangitiaria Dennan, known as Guide Rangi, who became famous for her work in the village of Whakarewarewa a few kilometres from the centre of Rotorua. Whakarewarewa is now Rotorua's largest and most famous thermal reserve. For more than forty years Rangi showed tourists, heads of state and other dignitaries around Whakarewarewa while explaining Maori history and tradition. After already causing furrowed brows by walking ahead of the royal party, she was officially censored for offering her arm to Queen Elizabeth II in case she slipped, during the 1953–54 royal tour around the thermal area.

After claiming most Maori music had its origins in European works, George Bernard Shaw was challenged by Rangi to attend a private concert in her home in Whakarewarewa. He consented, on the condition he could leave after the first piece. He enjoyed the concert and stayed the whole evening, but remained unconvinced about the origins of the music, as he explained in a letter.

> At the tourist concert at Rotorua, which I was induced to attend only by a promise of at least one turn of genuine Maori music, they gave us some rhythms without melody. Some of them were Spanish. These they gave with great precision and enjoyment, as they did all the German waltz tunes (early XIX century) and landler and barcarolles in which they delight.

Shaw thought Rotorua to be 'an uncommonly pleasant place, although it smells of brimstone like Hades'. He explored the area on foot and according to his guide was the 'fastest walker in the Antipodes'. His wife Charlotte followed in the car because she hated walking. Although in his late seventies, Shaw was fit and strong and his only serious illness had been a bout of smallpox in his twenties. His adventures in New Zealand may have taken their toll, however. He suffered a mild heart attack later that year and a friend told *The Times* that Shaw seemed to have 'aged considerably' since returning from his trip. Tikitere, also known as 'Hell's Gate', where the ground shakes and shudders, where boiling pools heave and hiss and where the air is heavy with sulphur, was the 'most damnable spot' Shaw had ever visited. He said he would willingly have paid £10 not to have seen it. When a photographer suggested Shaw pose at 'Hell's Gate' he replied, 'If you have patience no doubt you will see me in the real setting.'

Sala stopped in Whakarewarewa on his way from Rotorua to the Pink and White Terraces. A French Canadian called 'Mac' drove him in a stagecoach. Mac worked for W.K.

Carter, known as 'King' Carter, who ran a coaching business on the Cambridge to Rotorua route. He would later go into competition with his former boss. Sala wrote, 'to pilot a team of four and sometimes of five horses up and down the zigzags, round the sharp corners, and along narrow ledges overlooking tremendous precipices to mountainous Maoriland; to thread narrow gorges and penetrate dense bush and scrub; to dash with the wheels axle-deep in water, through swollen torrents; to rattle over the boulders of dry watercourses — these are only a few of the episodes of a stage-coachman in New Zealand'.

The geysers at Whakarewarewa were fenced in and run by Maori who caught the tourists on their way to the terraces. The village consisted of a few whare and Maori crouched on their haunches munching a hot potato in one hand and puffing on a short pipe in the other. Invalids wanting to convalesce in the hot springs could hire the whare and one such patient was in residence when Sala visited. The patient had been holidaying in Switzerland when he fell down a precipice in the Alps and injured his spine. Unable to find a cure at home, he travelled to New Zealand and moved into a whare furnished only with a hammock, a chest, a few books and cooking utensils. The old Maori chief who was his landlord doubled as his nurse. When Sala arrived the chief was eager to question the visitor about his patient:

> The ailing gentleman went about leaning on the arm of the tall, dusky savage, with his face all ridged and furrowed with tattooing. After a while he consigned his charge to the care of a younger Maori, and made signs that he would like to converse with me. He spoke English very fluently. After the preliminary grinning and hand-shaking, his face assumed an expression of much gravity, and he asked, Did I know the sick Pakeha? I replied that to the best of my remembrance I had had the honour of meeting him some years before in Paris. Was the mighty Pakeha, the Lord of Rosebery, the sick Pakeha's great-grandfather? With the remembrance still vivid in my mind of a certain beautiful portrait of a child painted by Sir John Everett Millais, R.A. I answered that as far as I knew the Earl of Rosebery was not yet blessed with any great-grandchildren. Did I know the sick Pakeha's grandfather? Growing rather uneasy under this examination, I made answer that I believed that all the sick gentleman's ancestors had been great chiefs and illustrious in their day. Whereupon my Maori questioner gave a grave nod of approval, grunted 'Kapai', and withdrew, apparently perfectly satisfied.

Sala continued through the village of Waikite where he saw the 'monster geyser' shoot up. 'It was angry. It was to me as the breath of the nostrils of "the old dragon underground", "swinging the scaly horrors of his folded tail", fuming and snorting in vain efforts to reach upper earth, and at length fairly boiling over in mad despair.' The geyser at Waikite was one of several spectacular examples to be seen in the Whakarewarewa area in the 1880s. Wairoa sent water up to sixty metres in the air, while Pohutu, today's big geyser, can shoot water no more than thirty metres high. After 'an enchanting drive' of about eleven kilometres Sala arrived at Wairoa. They descended a narrow 'cornice' road and climbed over a mountain into the Tikitapu bush before skirting the shores of the lake of the same name, which was also known as the Blue Lake. Sala described the Tikitapu bush as a 'fern forest of exceeding loveliness', which brought a 'Midsummer Day's Dream' to mind.

> Yonder must be the bank on which the wild thyme grows. There must be sitting, amidst dancing and delight, the Fairy Queen. Yes; Oberon and Titania must be somewhere about. Nestling among those tiny, trailing little ground ferns, quivering and blushing as though with joy in the chequered sunlight of red gold, must be Peaseblossom and Mustardseed, and a host of kindred elves; while, high up aloft, perched on the summit of a tall, canopied, palm-like fern tree, must be Puck, shaking his airy sides to think what fools we mortals be; but anon, in more placable mood, chanting that 'the man shall have his mare again, and all shall be well'. It must be fairyland.

Sala met a 'fairy' in the bush, a 'rosy-cheeked girl of eighteen on horseback, very neat short riding habit, coquettish-looking hat and feather, handkerchief in the pocket of her side-saddle, buckskin gauntlets, and a dainty whip'. Arthur Conan Doyle believed New Zealand to be something of a 'fairy centre'. He was embroiled in the controversial 'Cottingley Fairies' case, in which English schoolgirls Frances Griffiths and Elsie Wright claimed to have photographed fairies in the Yorkshire village of Cottingley. The pictures were taken in 1917 but become infamous when Conan Doyle publicised them in the *Strand Magazine* in 1920. Along with British theosophist Edward Gardner, he thought they were genuine and argued his case in *The Coming of the Fairies.* Critics ridiculed him, saying the fairies were obviously cardboard cut-outs. Frances Griffiths maintained the fairies were real but in the 1980s Elsie Wright admitted they were fake. In a letter to a Christchurch newspaper 'H.B.' noted that Conan Doyle claimed the fairies in the photographs were reminiscent of ones in picture books. If they looked like picture book fairies, he asked Doyle, why didn't they act like picture book fairies? After all, weren't they supposed to have the power to turn humans into animals and vice versa?

Conan Doyle wrote of New Zealand's fairies in *The Coming of the Fairies*. One woman claimed to have seen the creatures 'in all parts of New Zealand, but especially in the fern-clad gullies of the North Island'. Mrs Hardy, the wife of a settler in 'the Maori districts' of New Zealand, apparently saw fairy horses:

> One evening when it was getting dusk I went into the yard to hang the tea-towels on the clothes-line. As I stepped off the verandah, I heard a sound of soft galloping coming from the direction of the orchard. I thought I must be mistaken, and that the sound came from the road, where the Maoris often gallop their horses. I crossed the yard to get the pegs, and heard the galloping coming nearer. I walked to the clothes-line, and stood under it with my arms uplifted to peg the towel on the line, when I was aware of the galloping close behind me, and suddenly a little figure, riding a tiny pony, rode right under my uplifted arms. I looked round, to see that I was surrounded by eight or ten tiny figures on tiny ponies like dwarf Shetlands.

Even Conan Doyle thought fairy horses a little far-fetched. Several people claimed to have seen them but 'their presence makes the whole situation far more complicated and difficult to understand. If horses, why not dogs?'

Trollope rode past Lake Tikitapu, or the Blue Lake, the smallest of four lakes between Lake Rotorua and Lake Tarawera. He and Mair were on their way to the Pink and White Terraces but took a slight detour to Kaiteriria, on the southwest tip of Lake Rotokakahi, or the Green Lake. In the final campaigns against Te Kooti from 1870 to 1872 Mair trained and commanded around a hundred young Te Arawa men at Kaiteriria. Te Kooti was an enemy of both Te Arawa and the Crown, which offered a £5000 reward for his capture. The Te Arawa men lived in their own huts surrounded by a palisade with gates and sentinels. Trollope called it a 'Europeanised' pa. 'There seemed to be no danger of any disturbance among the men. As long as they are paid, and fed well, and not overworked, these Arewa Maoris are too well alive to the advantages of their military service to risk them by mutiny or disobedience.'

Trollope wrote at length about the New Zealand Wars and he thought Maori a brave, dignified people, initially warm and hospitable towards the British. In *Australia and New Zealand* he wrote of how the colonists had behaved well towards Maori but that contact with Christianity and Europeans was detrimental and that it had become inevitable Maori would die out. 'It is acknowledged on all sides that the Maoris are melting.'

At the head of Lake Tarawera, Trollope chanced upon a Maori community in an abandoned mission station. There was a deserted church and parsonage surrounded by blooming English primrose, a decaying corn-mill and a large amount of cleared but uncultivated land. The Pakeha occupants had been driven out during the wars. From there, Trollope was rowed for four hours in a canoe across the lake to the mouth of the stream emanating from Lake Rotomahana. Mair and Trollope got into the tepid water to start the walk to Lake Rotomahana. It was almost dark by the time they got to camp for the night, a whare on the shores of the lake, and Mair warned Trollope to watch his footing. 'In one place the Governor's aide-de-camp's dog had been boiled alive in a mud-jet, and in another a native girl had dropped a baby, and had herself plunged in after the poor infant, — hopelessly, tragically gone for ever amidst horrible torments. I heard more, however, of the Governor's aide-de-camp's dog than I did of the girl and the baby.' They cooked bacon and potatoes in the boiling springs and Trollope bathed in a hot pool, where, referring to his enjoyable experience behind the Ohinemutu inn, he was joined by a naked Maori minder of the 'less interesting sex'.

Before that terrible night in June 1886 when Mt Tarawera erupted, the Pink and White Terraces on the shores of Lake Rotomahana were New Zealand's most famous tourist attraction. These giant glistening staircases were formed by geysers spouting hot, silica-rich waters over the hillsides, which cooled and crystallised into magnificent, marble-like pink and white pools of different temperatures. They were edged with intricate stalactites and were brimming with turquoise water. The lower pools were cool enough to bathe in but the closer you climbed to the top, the hotter the pools got. The white terraces were 60 metres high and spread to 90 metres at their widest point; the pink terraces, which were wider at the top and narrowed as they fell, lay about one and a half kilometres away on the opposite shore of Lake Rotomahana.

The terraces formed a sublime landscape: they were more than simply beautiful. Such landscapes dwarf human achievement and have the power to astound and transfix. They are often given otherworldly or spiritual qualities and writers who visited the terraces attempted to convey the magnificence of the structures by using imagery of the earth's finest gems, the heavens and the supernatural. Trollope camped on the side of the lake near the white terraces, which he climbed once it was light. He found,

> ... a raised fretwork of stone, as fine as chased silver ... on one terrace after another there are large shell-like alabaster baths ... And on the outside rims, where the water has run, dripping over, century after century, nature has carved for herself wonderful hanging ornaments and exquisite cornices, with that prolific hand which never stints itself in space because of expense, and devotes its endless labour to front and rear with equal persistency.

The white terraces looked like 'a crystal staircase, glittering and stainless as if it were ice, spreading out like an open fan from a point above us on the hillside and projecting at the bottom into a lake, where it was perhaps 200 yards wide,' wrote James Anthony Froude in *Oceana; or, England and Her Colonies.* The landscape reminded George Augustus Sala of the Acropolis, with 'volutes and cornices, grooves and mouldings, scrolls and indentations,

'WHITE TERRACES' (1888) BY CHARLES BLOMFIELD. Alexander Turnbull Library, Wellington, New Zealand. G-472.

flutings and embossings, wrought by no human sculptor's hand, but by the hand of Nature'. He also told his readers that if they had seen the Cathedral of Milan and 'the delicate white marble drying in the spring sunshine after a heavy rain-storm which has brought out the hues deep latent in the stone,' they 'may be able to form some idea of the phantoms of rainbow which seem to linger on the surface of the white terrace, the tint of which, again, is not a cold or glaring white but a warm or creamy white — the Wedgwood-Flaxman white'.

Sala met a well-known Auckland photographer, Josiah Martin, camping opposite the white terraces. He was struck by the glamour and prestige of Martin's temporary home address. 'At Rome how often have I envied the occupants — whosoever they might be — of "Number Five, Appian Way", and "Number Nineteen, Forum of Trojan". But now that I have seen the marvels of Hotwaterland I really think that the most picturesque address that one could give would be "The Tent, opposite the White Terrace, Lake Rotomohana, N.Z".'

Alfred Domett, poet, journalist, New Zealand premier and a friend of Robert Browning, described the terraces in his work *Ranolf and Amohia: A South Sea Day Dream*. The epic poem about a white sailor and a Maori princess, which was inspired by the Mokoia Island legend of Hinemoa and Tutanekai, was published in 1872 just after Domett returned to England after almost thirty years in New Zealand. Although he said he found it difficult to read, Tennyson praised the poem for its 'power of delineating delicious scenery'.

> Slowly climb
> The Twain, and turn from time to time
> To mark the hundred baths in view —
> Crystalline azure, snowy rimmed —
> The marge of every beauteous pond
> Curve after curve — each lower beyond
> The higher — outsweeping white and wide,
> Like snowy lines of foam that glide
> O'er level sea-sands lightly skimmed
> By thin sheets of the glistening tide.

The pink terraces weren't considered as beautiful as the white but the pools were better for bathing. 'In the bath, when you strike your chest against it, it is soft to the touch, — you press yourself against it and it is smooth, — you lie about upon it and, though it is firm, it gives to you,' wrote Trollope. 'You plunge against the sides, driving the water over with your body, but you do not bruise yourself. You go from one bath to another, trying the warmth of each ... I have never heard of other bathing like this in the world.' Froude wrote as evocatively about the appearance of the pink terraces as he had the white. 'The crystals were even more beautiful than the others which we had seen, falling like clusters of rosy icicles or hanging in festoons like creepers trailing from a rail. At the foot of each cascade the water lay in pools of ultramarine, their exquisite colour being due in part, I suppose, to the sky refracted upwards from the bottom.'

A great boiling pool of 'exquisite blue' at the top of the pink terraces transfixed James Inglis, who wrote in *Our New Zealand Cousins,*

> At times the soft cloud of swirling steam enwraps all this from your gaze; and then coyly, as it were, the Angel of the Pool draws aside the veil, and affords a still more ravishing glimpse of the bewitching beauty that haunts you, takes

> possession of your entire being, and almost tempts you to sink into the embrace of the seductive lava. This is really no over description. I had that feeling strongly myself, and it was shared by other members of the party. The witchery of this exquisite bath, albeit it would boil one to rags in an instant, is such that one feels a strange semi-hysterical impulse to sink softly in and be at rest … The remembrance of these marvels will haunt me to my dying hour.

As Trollope lay in the warm water of the pink terraces admiring the scenery, he imagined what the future held for the area: a bustling hotel at Rotomahana, and regular boat and bathing trips for tourists. But the man who had happily shared a pool with three 'Maori Damsels' remained troubled about how men and women could respectably bathe together. Enclosing parts of the terraces would spoil their beauty while insisting on demure bathing costumes would spoil the sensuous experience of the pools. Restricting men and women to use the pools at different times of the day wasn't practical. The women could have the pink terraces and the men the white — but with a lake between them the two groups wouldn't be able to communicate — and it would be difficult to stop 'interlopers and intruders' joining the opposite sex.

Just as Trollope predicted, the terraces became increasingly popular with tourists. The village of Te Wairoa accommodated growing numbers of visitors, who paid Maori handsomely for the privilege of seeing the terraces. By the time of Sala's visit in late 1885, tourists eager to record their pilgrimage to the eighth wonder of the world had defaced the pristine surfaces of the terraces. Names, addresses and dates had been scribbled on the silica. His group was one of the last to experience the magnificent terraces and now visitors have to satisfy themselves with excavated buildings and artefacts while the glories of the terraces are but a figment of the imagination. Trollope left the terraces and returned to Kaiteriria and his next port of call was Lake Taupo; a long day's ride away. He stopped occasionally to bathe in warm waters and around the halfway point he crossed the Waikato River for the first time. He followed the river towards the settlement that's now called Taupo, on the northeastern corner of the country's largest lake, with which it shares its name.

Trollope passed through the thermal area of Wairakei, less than ten kilometres from Taupo. It hadn't been developed for tourists then but in the late 1870s Robert Graham, who established the first hot springs resort northwest of Auckland at Waiwera in 1845, built the 'Geyser House Hotel' as it became known, on more than 1600 hectares of land at Wairakei. Graham died in 1885 but his wife Jane and their sons continued to run the complex, which served as a post and telegraph office and consisted of natural baths and several wooden, straw and reed huts designed to withstand earthquakes. The buildings were acquired by the Tourist Department in the late 1940s and the refurbished hotel opened as Hotel Wairakei. Now a privately run hotel, the Wairakei Resort stands on the original Graham property.

Rudyard Kipling stayed in 'Mr Robert Graham's Establishment' in Wairakei in 1891. Inspired by the boiling mud pools and thermal steam, the young author wrote a short story called *One Lady at Wairakei*. The story first appeared in the *Saturday Supplement* of the *New Zealand Herald* on 30 January 1892, after the newspaper 'made arrangements' with Kipling 'to apply his art within the New Zealand setting'. The story languished in obscurity until Victoria University literary scholar and poet Harry Ricketts reproduced it in book form in 1983. *One Lady at Wairakei* is based on the narrator's conversation with 'Truth', who appears in the form of a woman from the depths of a mud pool. 'Truth' predicts a New Zealand literature will flourish once the country becomes economically independent.

> 'Tell me the truth, the whole truth and nothing but the truth, about New Zealand,' I said promptly.
>
> 'Banks — railways — exports — harbour boards, and so forth — eh?' She smiled wickedly. 'You will find all that in books.'
>
> 'No. I want to know how the people live, and what they think, and how they die; and what makes them love and fight and trade in the particular manner in which they fight and love and trade. That isn't in the books.'
>
> 'No — not yet,' said Truth thoughtfully, drawing her pink fingers to and fro in the water. 'It will come some day.'
>
> 'That's what I want to know. When is it coming?'
>
> 'What?'
>
> 'The story of the lives of the people here. I want to read it.'
>
> 'Perhaps they haven't any lives. You said they were all in the hands of the banks. How can you expect an encumbered estate, mortgaged to the hilt, to have a life of its own?'
>
> 'Truth, you're prevaricating. You know I didn't mean that. Banks have nothing to do with the inside lives of peoples. I have not the key to the stories myself but they are here in the country somewhere — thousands of them. When are they going to be written, Truth, and how are they going to be written, and who are going to write them?'
>
> 'My young men and my young women. All in good time. You can't fell timber with one hand and write a tale with the other. But they'll come, and when they come —'
>
> 'Yes.'
>
> 'The world will listen to them …'

Rupert Brooke found Wairakei disturbing. He stayed in the area while he waited for his ship to depart from Wellington for Tahiti and in a letter from the incorrectly named 'Warapei of the hot springs' on Christmas Day 1913 he wrote,

> New Zealand is a queer place. If you go [for] a walk along the road, and happen to look down at the puddles, you will notice they keep bubbling. Stoop down and put your finger in them and you know why. They're boiling. You turn to examine what looks like a rabbit hole in the wayside. Suddenly a strange rumbling proceeds from it. You stand back frightened. An enormous geyser of steam and boiling water bursts from it ... A terrifying place.

George Bernard Shaw visited Wairakei in 1934 and predicted that New Zealand would harness its geysers for power. He was right. The world's second commercial geothermal power station was commissioned at Wairakei in 1958. The station and more recent geothermal projects now supply about seven percent of the country's electricity.

'Planet Earth, it seems in these wonderlands, is signalling from below its disapproval of us,' wrote J.B. Priestley. 'To go from them to a region of pure white steam is like going from the poetry of Edgar Allan Poe to the poetry of Wordsworth.' Priestley painted a picture of the steam released by the geothermal station at Wairakei and he felt an almost feminine presence, rising out of the ground 'whiter than anything in the world' before gradually thinning out, floating away and disappearing. He imagined that the sporadic puffs of steam in the distance were giants hiding in the bush smoking. He thought although the scene owed much to technology, with a little imagination it could be as Wordsworth wrote at the end of 'To the Cuckoo',

> ... the earth we pace
> Again appears to be
> An unsubstantial faery place

Trollope arrived at the point where the Waikato River meets Lake Taupo, and found a small settlement called Tapuaeharu (now Taupo), consisting of 'a large redoubt held by European armed constabulary, and of an inn'. He and Mair were rowed south across the lake by six constables and spent the night at the Maori village of Tokaanu, where 'old tattooed natives came and grinned at me. Young women, tattooed, as are all the women, on the under-lip, sat close to me and chattered to me; and young men kindly shook me by the hand. I encountered nothing but Maori friendship; — but at the same time I encountered no Maori progress.'

Kipling wrote about coming out on 'great plains where wild horses stared at us, and caught their feet in long blown manes as they stamped and snorted'. A number of wild horses still exist in the Kaimanawa Mountains region to the south of Lake Taupo, a region where wild horses were first reported as early as the mid-1870s. Kipling believed he ate a kiwi, 'a roast bird with a skin like pork crackling, but it had no wings nor trace of any'. Nobody really knows whether it was true or just his travelling companions playing a joke. Little evidence exists of Rudyard Kipling's visit to the Taupo area, but he seemed to both infuriate and fascinate his driver on the journey, as he wrote in *Something of Myself*:

> We passed a horse's skull beside the track, at which he began to swear horribly but without passion. He had, he said, driven and ridden past that skull for a very long time. To him it meant the lock on the chain of his bondage to circumstance, and why the hell did I come along talking about all those foreign, far places I had seen? Yet he made me go on telling him.

It was during a stormy Easter in 1926 that Zane Grey arrived in Taupo. The hotels were packed and the town was brimming with fishermen. He couldn't find a suitable campsite near Taupo so the party crossed the lake westwards to the mouth of the Waihora Stream in Western Bay, an area surrounded by vertical rock cliffs. Mr Wiffin, a government official, and a guide named Ricket, were not enthusiastic about the plan. The party encountered a huge swell and lost sight of a second boat carrying provisions. Grey wanted the boats, like two hunters, to stick together for safety. But the boatman in the second craft returned alone, with near-fatal consequences. He closed the engine room to keep water out and a gas explosion blew up part of the boat. Fire engulfed the vessel and the boatman jumped into the icy lake in the darkness. He swam ashore, bound his feet with strips of his waistcoat and walked to a farmhouse where he collapsed suffering from exposure and exhaustion.

Grey's party continued on. They explored Western Bay, with its wild boars, kingfishers, tui, bellbirds, fantails, grey fuzzy moss and lichens, daisies and dainty forget-me-nots. They moved to the south of Lake Taupo to the mouth of the Tongariro River and established a camp above the river in a grove of manuka and kowhai trees. Grey likened the Tongariro River to the 'green-white rushing Athabasca' in the Canadian Rocky Mountains that he had written about in *The Great Slave*. On the horizon 'rose the magnificent mountain range, wreathed at dawn by sun-flushed clouds, clear and sharp and dark at noonday, and at sunset half obscured in lilac haze'. The Tongariro River, and in particular an area called the Dreadnought Pool, became one of Grey's favourite places. 'Tongariro! What a strange beautiful high-sounding name! It suited the noble river and the mountain from which it sprang. Tongariro! It was calling me. It would call to me across the vast lanes and leagues of the Pacific. It would draw me back again. Beautiful green-white thundering Tongariro!'

Grey liked the Tongariro River so much he wanted it all to himself. He certainly didn't want the tourists around. According to Bryn Hammond in *The New Zealand Encyclopaedia of Fly Fishing*, Grey negotiated with Maori landowners to buy a 'large central stretch' of the river, on which he wanted to erect a fishing lodge he and his friends could use. Originally he wanted to purchase the whole river; but locals were outraged. He annoyed the anglers at Tongariro as he had those in the Bay of Islands, not only by criticising their fishing techniques but also by stationing minders at pools until he wanted them. Grey advocated that treble hooks be banned and that Tongariro become a fly only river. Both ideas were eventually adopted, but it was the manner in which he argued his case as he journeyed around the North Island that created the friction.

The government, which had enticed Grey to New Zealand to market the country as a tourist destination, was concerned at his proposal to deny public access to part of the river. Rich foreigners and other New Zealanders were trying to do the same thing in order to frustrate Grey's plans. But under the 1926 Maori Land Claims Amendment and Adjustment Act, Maori conceded the rights to the bed of Lake Taupo and the streams flowing into it. Anglers were provided with access on all the major tributaries and the rights of all New Zealanders to fish their country's waters were secured. 'That close to completion was Grey's outright purchase of the Tongariro River, as far as he was concerned it was already his, and well might have been,' wrote Hammond.

✶

George Bernard Shaw, his wife and the manager of the Chateau Tongariro, Richard Cobbe, walked down the wide staircase into the spacious lounge of the Chateau at 8.30 p.m. on Sunday 1 April 1934. Some 240 people rose to greet them. They had gathered in the luxurious hotel, 'large and pretentious' according to Priestley, built in the late 1920s at the foot of Mt Ruapehu in the Tongariro National Park, to hear the esteemed Irish playwright. The Tourist Department, the same department that had arranged Shaw's tour around the country, took over the running of the hotel in late 1931 after the business failed. But instead of promoting the hotel, Shaw continued to espouse his political views. He told the crowd he wouldn't be giving a speech because 'for a long time he had been trying to induce the world to make public speaking a criminal offence'. He claimed too many men had been elected to government because they did nothing but deliver good speeches. He did, however, submit to an hour's questioning.

Everywhere he went the 'political medicine man' was asked what he thought of New Zealand; whether the British cared about the country; and his views on world affairs. He didn't think New Zealand was self-sufficient enough, its immigration policy was too restrictive, and he thought many of the country's institutions, like the railways and mental hospitals, were socialist even if New Zealanders didn't consider them to be. He recommended the creation of a film industry 'or you will lose your souls without even getting American ones'. He claimed never to have seen a Maori unhappy 'in spite of our endeavours to make them religiously miserable' and thought they were probably better off before European settlement. New Zealanders resembled nineteenth century Englishmen in his view, and being an 'old Victorian' he felt more at home in New Zealand than London.

On this particular night, Shaw advocated the preservation of New Zealand's sights for locals not tourists and warned that to prosper, farming would have to be more scientific. He revealed that he wanted to continue writing as long as he lived. 'I do it naturally just as I breathe or digest my food, and I do not think anything will stop me.' Shaw closed the event by saying, 'May I be allowed to move a hearty vote of thanks to myself,' and the audience responded by singing 'For He's a Jolly Good Fellow'.

'OUR ADVISOR GENERAL' BY STUART PETERSON

FROM NZ FREE LANCE, 11 APRIL 1934. ALEXANDER TURNBULL LIBRARY, WELLINGTON, NEW ZEALAND. N-P 1076-3.

Rupert Brooke stayed at a sheep farm 'near the foot of the big mountains in the centre of the North Island'. The farm was owned by the Studholmes, a couple Brooke had met on the boat from Fiji. Brooke called the farm 'Ruanni'. But New Zealand author E.H. McCormick believed Brooke was talking about 'Ruanui', a little over twenty kilometres from the small town of Taihape, on the southern edge of the central volcanic plateau, past the three peaks of Tongariro, Ngauruhoe and Ruapehu. In a letter to his mother Brooke described the Studholmes' house as large and 'like a small English country house, with a lovely garden'. He planned to stay two days but as his ship to Tahiti was delayed he stayed a week 'mostly lying out on the lawn and dozing' as he was recovering from a cold. This wasn't his only ailment. While in Fiji his foot had become infected after he cut it and he developed coral poisoning. He was still limping a few months later. Brooke thought Studholme a 'typical rich English "gentleman"' and that some of his opinions were 'simply *filthy*'. But the family had been very kind to Brooke, so he didn't argue with the farmer. McCormick, who knew Studholme, thought Brooke and his host would have been discussing the great waterfront strike of 1913, described in one newspaper as 'the longest and fiercest strike we have known'.

When J.B. Priestley arrived in Waitomo in 1973 he did something unusual. Despite spending five nights in the village he *didn't* visit its world famous glow-worm caverns. 'The truth is, I don't want caves,' he wrote in his travelogue *A Visit to New Zealand*.

Even though Priestley was 78, he wasn't afraid of adventure and he travelled to New Zealand because he 'needed a challenge'. Recovering from an operation for piles he had become sick of well-meaning people fussing over him. 'I saw myself declining into a fat-lazy-fireside old codger, demanding and unproductive, a 200-lb parasite.' As a distinguished guest of the New Zealand government, Priestley was treated to plenty of sightseeing and his itinerary included five nights in Waitomo, a tiny village with a population of a few hundred people and hundreds of thousands visitors each year. Waitomo lies nearly sixty kilometres south of Hamilton, off the main road north that skirts around the western side of the volcanic plateau, in a landscape of native bush, green fields, underground streams and glow-worm adorned limestone caves that came to international prominence in the late nineteenth century. The caves were 'discovered' by English surveyor Fred Mace and a local Maori chief, Tane Tinorau, in 1887, but Maori had already known for some time that a stream disappearing into the side of a bush-covered hill led to a strange and mysterious place. They avoided the caverns for fear of disturbing the spirits they believed to be inside.

Mace, a surveyor working throughout the King Country from his base at Otorohanga, heard rumours about the caves and persuaded Tinorau to accompany him into the hillside. The two men began their journey where the stream goes underground, the exit point for today's tours. Taking candles, they explored by raft and on foot and found a series of lofty limestone caverns formed over millions of years, encrusted with an array of stalactites and stalagmites and bejewelled with thousands of glow-worms. The authorities were alerted and by the turn of the twentieth century tourists were regularly visiting Waitomo to see the limestone caves and to enjoy the highlight of the trip, a boat ride through the 'glow-worm grotto'.

In the autumn of 1973, J.B. Priestley's wife Jacquetta joined the tourists filing through this magical underground world, but the writer refused to accompany her. He agreed to go on other excursions in the area, including one trip to see a live kiwi and another to meet a woman who made the feathered cloaks that were traditionally worn by Maori chiefs. But nothing would entice him underground. He didn't want to relive the sensation of being buried alive.

On a hot, chalk-dusty June day in 1916 a young Priestley was dividing up rations of bread, meat, tinned milk and tea in a small dugout in a trench below Vimy Ridge in France. It was a thankless assignment as no one ever seemed to be satisfied with their share. While Priestley was sorting through the rations he heard a 'rushing sound'. It was a familiar, frightening noise and he recalled his mind going into 'slow time'. He knew he had to run away but he also knew he didn't have time. A big shell called a 'Minenwerfer' landed just a couple of yards away from him and 'the world blew up'. Entombed in earth, Priestley was lucky to be rescued. His comrades didn't know that he was buried but 'several fellows knew the platoon rations were in there somewhere: that stuff would have to be dug out'. Amazingly Priestley escaped with minor injuries and some temporary deafness and after a few months' convalescence back in Britain he returned to the front.

Although he said he hadn't become a 'victim of claustrophobia' he avoided travelling on the London underground. During the Second World War he ventured below ground again — he 'crawled along, like a giant worm, to the very coal face' in order to write a piece about miners. But he didn't enjoy the experience. It was a matter of principle. If the miners had to endure a confined space every day he could surely face going underground with them once. Halfway around the world and 57 years later Priestley was happy relaxing at the Waitomo Hotel and wrote that he saw 'no point in going underground again just to say I had seen some caves that I didn't want to see'.

Several other writers, however, have eulogised over the caves with their magnificent limestone sculptures and their sparkling glow-worms. They have described 'glistening halls', 'alabaster and Parian marble-like scenes of unsurpassed loveliness' and 'the most delicate tracery, some pure white, some cream … all glistening like icicles upon the background of more heavily moulded patterns'. Noël Coward wrote about 'millions of glow-worms glittering on the rocks overhead like stars'. George Bernard Shaw told journalists the caves were 'incomparable' and 'sufficient to blot out all memories of ordinary scenery'. Zane Grey wrote that although he didn't expect much after seeing the Caves of Bellamar in Cuba and the Mammoth Cave of Kentucky, he found 'something vastly different, most unique, and strangely beautiful in the extreme'. He was led into the caves to the subterranean river and into a dark 'Stygian cave forlorn', quoting Milton's 'L'Allegro', 'the roof of which was studded with myriad of tiny blue-white lights, like wan stars in a velvet-black heaven. From the obscure silent river shone a perfect reflection of these glow-worm lights.'

Shaw admired the fact that, as a natural tourist attraction, the caves had an intrinsic value; their greatness had nothing to do with mankind. 'New Zealand is fortunate in that it has sights which are worth seeing for themselves. In some other countries, for instance, a tourist is shown a cottage and told somebody of greatness lived there. All you see is the cottage. It is true, perhaps, that it has been the abode of somebody, but to the tourist it is nothing more than a cottage and an ordinary one at that. But in your country you have those geysers and wonderful caves. They are sights anybody would be pleased to see.'

The Waitomo Caves, like the Pink and White Terraces, are a sublime landscape; at once awe-inspiring and threatening. The caves and their adornments have been created over millions of years and Waitomo's imposing limestone stalactites and stalagmites grow by less than one cubic centimetre in the average human lifetime. The sculptures have been formed by water dripping from the roof of the cave and flowing over its limestone walls, creating crystalline deposits along the way — and the constant echo of dripping water that can be heard in the caves is a reminder of their agonizingly slow construction. Like the terraces, the caves are given otherworldly qualities. Some of the structures have church-like names including the 'Catacombs' and the 'Pipe Organ', which one writer described as a 'stalagmatic mass rising tier upon tier, like the front of an organ with marble pipes'.

In her essay 'Stars Under the Earth', English-born poet Blanche Baughan, who came to New Zealand at the turn of the nineteenth century and greatly admired the country's scenery, wrote that 'a visitor once, a woman, was lifted out of the boat at the end of the trip in a fainting condition, overwhelmed, it can scarcely be by terror, for there is nothing in this sweet still sanctuary to terrify, but probably by the deep appeal made here to some of the deepest human sensibilities'. The sublime impact of the glow-worm grotto can be put into perspective against the effect that a solitary luminescent insect had on the Romantic poet William Wordsworth:

> At night the glow-worm shone beneath the tree;
> I led my Lucy to the spot, "Look here,"
> Oh! joy it was for her, and joy for me!

The Waitomo glow-worms seem both powerful and endearingly vulnerable. Unless tourists maintain a respectful silence in the caves the creatures won't put on their magnificent display. Shaw's biographer Michael Holroyd wrote the Waitomo glow-worms were 'a firmament of blue shimmering lights that, since noise would extinguish them, completely silenced GBS'. Up to that point on his New Zealand tour, Shaw had been very talkative. In fact he talked so much during his month-long trip that newspaper articles about him were compiled into a book entitled *What I Said in New Zealand.*

Shaw's silence in the glow-worm grotto didn't last for long. After praising the beauty of the caves he used his experience at Waitomo to make a political point. He said he was surprised to hear that many New Zealanders, even those living close to the caves, had never seen them; supporting an argument he had already made in Auckland about New Zealanders having a 'greater interest in what they call "Home" than in their own country. It was time New Zealanders made themselves familiar with their own country. From what he had seen of it, they would find it worthwhile.' Shaw was critical of New Zealanders' sentimentality towards Britain and their dependence on the British market. He travelled to the country towards the end of his career and his last plays draw on his experiences in New Zealand and other British colonies. They explore how people might best govern themselves and realise their full potential. A play Shaw completed during his New Zealand trip, *The Simpleton of the Unexpected Isles,* is a farcical tale set in a distant outpost of empire with a 'Day of Judgement' theme, in which angels eliminate all those who are worthless.

'What a lot of green chumps they must be up at Cambridge!' reported the *Auckland Star.* It was shortly after Sala's Rotorua visit and the article pilloried the author for insisting on high fees wherever he went.

> They telegraphed to the great Prince asking if he would give a lecture as he passed through for the benefit of the Free Library ... The great Prince ... wired back the query — 'What fee will you give?' and the simple bucolics were so flabbergasted by the sordid turn which this gave to the negotiations that they have not yet recovered their breath. What a rude awakening they must have had from their fond fancyings of princely bounty freely extended to help the cause of literature and popular education!

Anthony Trollope's main reason for visiting the 'interior' was to see the terraces, so he didn't travel as far west as Tongariro or Waitomo. After reaching the southern shores of Lake Taupo he crossed back and rode north to Cambridge. It took three days during which 'the desolation of the country was its chief characteristic'.

Trollope and Mair spent a night in Cambridge. In the morning the pair sat down to a hotel breakfast of bacon and eggs, the same meal ordered by 11 other guests. Mair recalled the scene around a 40 foot table while the other guests vied with each other as to who would offer the esteemed visitor the table's only mustard pot.

> Mr Trollope gruffly thanked the first to offer it, gave a deep grunt at the second, a suppressed roar at the third. At last one boarder rose from the far-away end, and bowing courteously inquired, 'May I offer you the mustard, sir?'
>
> The literary giant sprang to his feet and bellowed, 'Damn your eyes, sir! Look at me! Do I look physically incapable of getting what mustard I require?' The too polite boarder fell back in his chair and there was a terrific silence, only to be broken when Mr Trollope grunted to me, 'Mair, I was a damn fool to sit down with thirteen at a table.'

Mair broke the strained silence by laughing, Trollope followed and then the whole crowd erupted, before the travellers said their goodbyes. Trollope was met by a party of men including John Logan Campbell who had arrived to take the author back to Auckland by coach. They were driven by Mr Quick, 'that gallant American coach proprietor', through Ohaupo, just south of Hamilton, to Pirongia (then called Alexandra) a little further to the left where a fort was being built 'as a place of refuge for the inhabitants, should the king's people ever attempt to make a raid upon the town' and north again through Hamilton.

Hamilton was 'a cleaned-up, nicely painted shanty town, doing very well at present but ready if necessary to be pulled down and carted off elsewhere,' wrote J.B. Priestley. As his party was about to leave the city, the director of the local museum came running up insisting that Priestley's wife, the eminent archaeologist and writer Jacquetta Hawkes, couldn't depart without seeing the museum. It was 'an odd sketchy sort of place, with narrow wooden stairs going up to a fair-sized room that looked as if it had only just stopped — reluctantly too — being a warehouse,' Priestley wrote. He was shown some old Maori combs and wondered whether, as Jung had suggested, the soul of a conquered people enters their conquerors, and whether young New Zealanders would consider Maori history, customs and traditions to be increasingly important.

Trollope wrote that the lands from Cambridge to Ngaruawahia (then called Newcastle) 'were for the most part among fields green with English grasses', and the land became poor again in the last stretch almost as far north as Drury, around 30 kilometres from Auckland. On his return to the city it was reported in the *Daily Southern Cross* that he approved of the advances made by settlers in the Waikato and he thought New Zealand was making more progress than Australia. He declared the Lake region around Rotorua was 'without a parallel in the world, and the more that one meditates upon the scenes around him there the more enraptured he becomes with the unrivalled beauties of the place'.

Ngaruawahia is the place where Jules Verne's fictional party of travellers in *Les Enfants du Capitaine Grant: Voyage autour du monde* (variously published in English as *A Voyage Round the World, Captain Grant's Children, Among the Cannibals*, and *The Castaways; or, A Voyage Round the World*) were captured by Chief Kai-Koumou. The work, published in 1867–68, is a three-part story about a missing sea captain, in which his two children and a group led by Lord Glenarvan search for him in different countries. With only the latitude of their father's shipwreck to work from, they search for him in a round-the-world, straight-line journey through South America, Australia and New Zealand. After being shipwrecked at Kawhia to the southwest of Hamilton, the party is captured by Maori at the point where the Waipa River meets the Waikato. They had unwittingly camped among Maori who were part of a tribe that had been decimated by Pakeha soldiers and were in retreat. Verne described the emergence from the morning fog of a canoe on the Waikato, carrying Chief Kai-Koumou ('He who eats the limbs of his enemy') and 10 European prisoners with bound feet. The chief was well known to Paheka soldiers as a formidable warrior.

> From the moment of embarking, the natives, who were very taciturn, like all savages, had scarcely exchanged a word, but from the few sentences they did utter, Glenarvan felt certain that the English language was familiar to them. He therefore made up his mind to question the chief on the fate that awaited them. Addressing himself to Kai-Koumou, he said in a perfectly unconcerned voice: 'Where are we going, chief?'
>
> Kai-Koumou looked coolly at him and made no answer.
>
> 'What are you going to do with us?' pursued Glenarvan.
>
> A sudden gleam flashed into the eyes of Kai-Koumou, and he said in a deep voice:
>
> 'Exchange you, if your own people care to have you; eat you if they don't.'

The party was taken to Lake Taupo and imprisoned. Glenarvan shot another Waikato chief Kara-Tete and at the funeral the dead man's wife and six slaves were killed in line with tradition. They could now accompany the chief into the other world. As soon as the slaves were killed,

> … the whole crowd, chiefs, warriors, old men, women, children, without distinction of age, or sex, fell upon the senseless remains with brutal appetite. Faster than a rapid pen could describe it, the bodies, still reeking, were dismembered, divided, cut up, not into morsels, but into crumbs. Of the two hundred Maories present everyone obtained a share. They fought, they struggled, they quarrelled over the smallest fragment. The drops of hot blood

> splashed over these festive monsters, and the whole of this detestable crew grovelled under a rain of blood. It was like the delirious fury of tigers fighting over their prey, or like a circus where the wild beasts devour the deer. This scene ended, a score of fires were lit at various points of the 'pah'; the smell of charred flesh polluted the air; and but for the fearful tumult of the festival, but for the cries that emanated from these flesh-sated throats, the captives might have heard the bones crunching under the teeth of the cannibals.

Determined to escape a similar fate, Verne's travellers staged a dramatic escape from their Maori captors and fled New Zealand, causing a volcano to erupt in the process. Verne's gruesome description of the funeral is thought to have influenced Anton Chekhov. In *A Hunting Drama*, a short story Chekhov published in a St Petersburg newspaper in 1884 and 1885, the famous Russian short story writer and playwright wrote 'It's barbarity! It's New Zealand!' John Goodliffe, the author of *These Fortunate Isles: Some Russian perceptions of New Zealand in the nineteenth and early twentieth centuries* believes there is 'little doubt' that Chekhov's image of New Zealand was connected with Verne's description of the Maori chief's funeral. *Les Enfants du Capitaine Grant* was extremely popular in Russia.

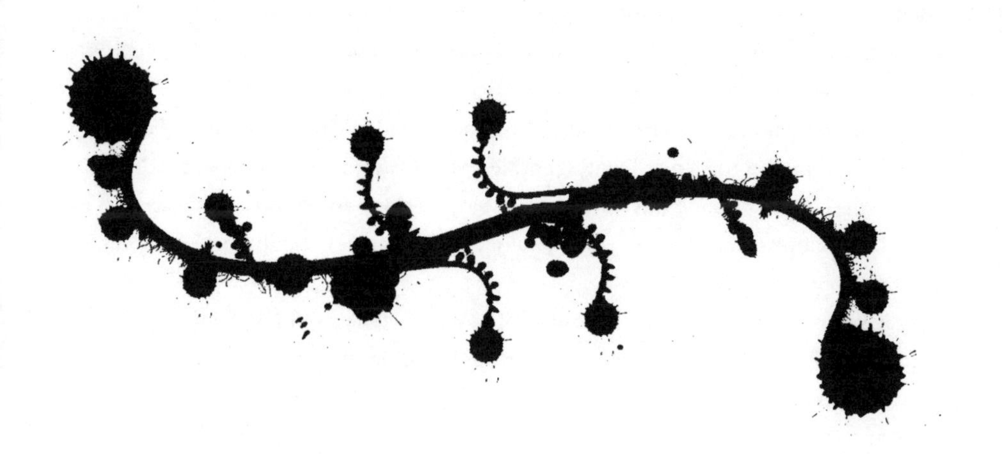

SEE NAPIER AND SPIT

THE COLLAPSE OF A NEW YORK publishing firm began a chain of events that took Mark Twain to New Zealand. Charles L. Webster & Co. was formed in 1884 by Webster and his wife's uncle, Samuel Langhorne Clemens, better known as Mark Twain. The company was established to publish Twain's works and its first book, *The Adventures of Huckleberry Finn*, was a phenomenal success. The company took on other authors, and it published Ulysses S. Grant's memoirs, again with great success. Webster left the firm in 1888 and died three years later. In 1891 the company began publishing the *Library of American Literature*, investing $100,000 into the venture. It was an ambitious project. Twain believed the company needed a Paige typesetter, a machine he thought would prove to be both lucrative and labour-saving. He poured $190,000 into the undertaking even though a working model of the typesetter had yet to be produced and a rival machine was now dominating the market. The company sold the subscription-book department, which included the *Library of American Literature* to William Evarts Benjamin. It was rumoured to be worth more than twice what Benjamin paid. Twain tried to borrow money to keep the business afloat and he wrote to alleviate the stress. In one letter he wished his partner a Merry Christmas and added, 'I wish to God I could have one myself before I die.'

Twain turned to Henry H. Rogers, a particularly ruthless businessman, for help. Rogers had the typesetter tested and stopped Twain investing any more money in it. But it was too late to save the company and Rogers helped the author through bankruptcy proceedings. Twain was left with debts of around $100,000, not including the $60,000 the publishing firm owed to his wife. The creditors accepted a settlement of 50 percent of the liabilities, but with his wife's urging Twain resolved to pay the debt in full. He planned to raise the money on a global lecture tour and by writing a book of his travels. According to the *New York Times* he was 'inspired by a lofty motive, to which the history of literature cannot show a parallel'. Twain travelled to around a hundred cities and the publication of *Following the Equator* in the United States (entitled *More Tramps Abroad* in England) put Twain back in the black. The book was considered to be a 'scathing and caustic' work, written by a tired and grieving man. Not only had Twain just finished his frenetic world tour, but his daughter, Suzy, had recently died.

If Twain hadn't needed to make a lot of money fast, he would probably never have visited New Zealand. He had rejected other opportunities to tour the antipodes 'partly because of the great length of the journey and partly because my wife could not well manage to go with me'. But in November 1895 Twain arrived in New Zealand with his wife Livy and one of his daughters, Clara. He engaged the services of R.S. Smythe, a veteran impressario that one Auckland newspaper suggested should be called 'Lucifer, the light-bringer, for he always brings a star with him'.

Auckland harbour appeared 'vast and beautiful' and there was 'land all about for hours', as Twain and his family sailed through the Hauraki Gulf on the afternoon of Tuesday 26 November 1895. They were on board the Union Company's SS *Rotomahana* ('roomy, comfortable, well-ordered, and satisfactory'), bound for Gisborne. It was a perfect summer's day and whales played in the distance. 'Nothing could be daintier than the puffs of vapour they spout up, when seen against the pink glory of the sinking sun, or against the dark mass of an island reposing in the deep blue shadow of a storm cloud,' Twain wrote.

The *Rotomahana* sailed through the Hauraki Gulf into the Colville Channel where Great Barrier Island appeared on her port side and the Coromandel Peninsula on her starboard. The sight of Great Barrier prompted Twain to write about a terrible shipwreck, presumably that of the *Wairarapa* which hit a cliff in dense fog the previous year, killing 121 people. A court of inquiry blamed the captain for taking the wrong course at Three Kings Islands, a small group of islands about fifty-five kilometres northwest of the coast, and for not making allowance for the sea currents. Twain wrote that the captain had committed suicide as soon as he realized he'd wrecked the ship, knowing that 'whether he was to blame or not the company owning the vessel would discharge him and make a devotion-to-passengers'-safety advertisement out of it, and his chance to make a livelihood would be permanently gone'.

Twain was sailing towards Poverty Bay. It was named by Captain Cook and was the site of the explorer's first landing in New Zealand in October 1769. The small half-moon shaped bay is guarded by the Gable End Foreland, described by James Inglis in his 1887 book *Our New Zealand Cousins* as a 'sheer, abrupt, rocky face like the gable of a mighty house, a formation, as one can see by the detached fragments and hummocks in the sea at its base, evidently the result of some tremendous landslip'. It was a treacherous place for sailors. Inglis had trouble getting ashore as the launch 'bobbed around like a cork' while 'the gangway was slung from the ship, and was now high in mid-air, now banging on the funnel, or deck, or cabin hatch of the launch'.

Inglis landed in the 'neat and thriving' town of Gisborne, situated at the convergence of the Waimata and Taruheru rivers. He tasted 'exquisite cheese' from a new factory and admired the condition of the bridges, footpaths, shops and the picturesque way the winding river skirted the town. The 'rapacity' of Gisborne's 'trim and pretty streets' shocked novelist Eric Linklater when he visited in 1951. From a hill above the harbour he described the scene looking inland, 'across the town, to a flat alluvial plain of immense fertility and brilliant colour'. He liked the design of Gisborne's centre where 'the river has gardened banks' and 'the business streets are broad and clean'. But Linklater thought the rapidly spreading residential area was 'consuming the far fields, gnawing at pasture, devouring national wealth'. The 'farmer's paradise' at Gisborne, where huge numbers of sheep and cattle could graze on fast-growing rich pasture, was being swamped by 'bungalows and rose-beds'.

The turbulent waters of its river mouth prevented Mark Twain visiting Gisborne. The author reached Poverty Bay three hours ahead of schedule after a fine, 23-hour journey from Auckland, but gales and heavy seas forced the *Rotomahana* to anchor more than a kilometre from land. A crowd watched as a steam-tug, the *Snark*, left shore to pluck 25 people off the ship and deposit a group of departing passengers, including the Greenwood Travelling Dramatic Group, in their place.

Mr W. Good from the *Poverty Bay Herald* interviewed Twain on board the steamer and reported the author wouldn't come ashore for his scheduled performance in Gisborne. The steamer couldn't wait and Twain wasn't prepared to step on the *Snark*. The author said he had had 'many rough experiences in his time' but that he'd 'seen nothing to equal the bobbing about of the *Snark* alongside the *Rotomahana*'. Among the passengers picked up by the tug were four prisoners being transported to Napier. Twain asked how long one convict's sentence was. On being told 12 months he was reputed to have joked, 'Waal, I guess it ought to be shortened to six months after that trip in the tender'. One of the prisoners was heard complaining bitterly about having to go to jail in such terrible weather. Twain told the reporter that his brief visit to Poverty Bay would probably find its way into his book — it did:

> We were a mile from shore; a little steam-tug put out from the land; she was an object of thrilling interest; she would climb to the summit of a billow, reel drunkenly there a moment, dim and gray in the driving storm of spindrift, then make a plunge like a diver and remain out of sight until one had given her up,

> then up she would dart again, on a steep slant toward the sky, shedding Niagaras of water from her forecastle — and this she kept up, all the way out to us ... In sight on deck were the crew, in sou'westers, yellow water-proof canvas suits, and boots to the thigh. The deck was never quiet for a moment, and seldom nearer level than a ladder, and noble were the seas which leapt aboard and went flooding aft. We rove a long line to the yard-arm, hung a most primitive basket-chair to it and swung it out into the spacious air of heaven, and there it swayed, pendulum-fashion, waiting for its chance — then down it shot, skilfully aimed, and was grabbed by the two men on the forecastle.

At the time Twain should have been giving a well-publicised lecture in Gisborne he was sailing south along the east coast towards Hawke's Bay. Livy Clemens celebrated her fiftieth birthday on board ship 'under world time', Twain wrote to a friend. The cancelled lecture was just one of a series of mishaps and misadventures that had plagued Twain's tour. The boat on which he left Vancouver ran aground causing a week's delay; a cholera outbreak prevented him landing at Honolulu, disappointing more than six hundred ticket holders; and in Australia there was more trouble. Twain developed painful carbuncles and was incapacitated for a week. Then he lost his agent when R.S. Smythe, who travelled from Melbourne to Sydney in the *Cuzco,* was quarantined with the other passengers, so his son Carlyle had to take Twain through New Zealand.

Frank Bullen toured Australasia, lecturing and writing a series of articles for the London *Standard.* His work was published in 1907 in the book *Advance Australasia.* He visited the freezing works in Gisborne, owned by the Nelson brothers William and Frederick. The new industry attracted tourists and helped the region become prosperous. Part of a large chimney from the works, which were built from timber with corrugated iron roofing, can still be seen at the end of Loisel Street. Bullen was curious to see the place after reading Upton Sinclair's *The Jungle*, a novel that exposed the dirty conditions in the Chicago meatpacking industry.

Bullen claimed his visit to the works with a government stock inspector wasn't announced, so nothing could have been cleaned up beforehand. He was impressed with the conditions.

> Apart from the grim side of the business, the immense and continuous blood-shedding and the suggestive crimson rivulet flowing steadily into the river beside the works, there was an air of great calm and peace over everything. There is nothing squalid or dirty about the place, from the rows of pretty workmen's

dwellings to the immense cooling chambers crowded with freshly skinned and disembowelled carcases, depending from rails overhead and chilling off before commencing their journey towards the freezing chambers (Linde's Ammonia process), where the temperature rapidly converts those fresh, soft, pink and white bodies into no bad resemblance of a block of stone.

He was impressed by the quality of the meat coming out of the works. 'Better-looking meat than that mutton and beef I have never seen, even at Christmas-time at home.'

A little under one hundred and forty kilometres southwest of Gisborne stands the city of Napier. It lies at the southern end of Hawke Bay, the arc that bites into the east coast of the North Island from the Mahia Peninsula down to Cape Kidnappers. James Inglis observed the seashore here was 'fringed with shifting banks of shingle, which has been carried down from the main range by the swift rivers that tear through the gorges and denude the hill country, on a scale which is, perhaps, paralleled nowhere else on the face of the globe'. He wrote that the spit, behind which lay the town, used to be an island and it was thought Captain Cook sailed between the spit and the mainland over the site on which the town was later developed.

'Napierites' must have strong legs, Inglis commented, as although the 'trim, bustling town' was situated on the flat, the houses of the shopkeepers and merchants were high on the sides of the bluff. 'They are perched aloft at every conceivable altitude, and look down at you from towering elevations. They crown rugged heights. They line precipitous gullies. They stick like limpets to sheer walls of rock. Embowered amid artificially made gardens they peep at you from shady foliage in places where you would think it hard for the trees themselves to keep a foothold.'

Rudyard Kipling was 'highly delighted' with the country he saw from the train on the way up from Wellington. He stayed overnight in Napier's Criterion Hotel a short distance from the waterfront on Thursday, 22 October 1891. Kipling said he was surprised to find 'such a large and well-conducted establishment in a town the size of Napier'. The man who would later be his protégé, Frank Bullen, thought Napier was different to any other town he'd seen in Australasia and that its glory was the bay. It was developed with an English feel; English architect Robert Lamb modelled the town's Marine Parade frontage on Brighton; Victorian and Edwardian baroque public buildings gave the town grandeur; and streets were named after many eminent British writers like Dickens, Carlyle, Thackeray and Browning.

Like Gisborne, the pace of life was slow in Napier, no one seemed in a hurry and a 'Sabbath calm' seemed to pervade the streets, even in the middle of the day. Bullen encountered many people who tried, unsuccessfully, to convince him that their town was growing fast. Compared to provincial towns in Britain, he thought New Zealand towns seemed to be almost at a standstill. He imagined the local misapprehension was based on the fact that people 'have lived here so long, or have only travelled to similar or even smaller places that they know every brick and plank in the place, and watch the erection of each new edifice, however tiny, with an almost parental solicitude'.

Twain was finally able to go ashore in Napier, with its new pier and 'beautiful green bluffs'. But his troubles persisted. Carbuncles had plagued him throughout his Australasian journey and he suffered again in Napier, the fourth such flare-up. His doctors advised him to postpone his first lecture at the now demolished Theatre Royal on Tennyson Street, a few blocks back from the waterfront. But there wasn't time to notify the public. 'After seeing Mr Clemens we are of the opinion that his condition needs rest and quiet for a few days, and we recommend that the lecture appointed to take place on Friday, the 29th instant, be postponed,' advised the doctors. 'We should have preferred that tonight's lecture had also been postponed, had it been possible to give timely notice to the public.' Because the first lecture had to go ahead, Twain was told to 'spare his audience — by sparing himself'. The author opened with a yarn about his boyhood that the *Hawke's Bay Herald* reported was a bit 'long-winded', but then his stories picked up pace. The 'heaven-born genius' showed he 'could so twist words and contort phrases as to keep an audience in an agony of amusement', the newspaper reported. He performed 'The Passing Stranger', spoke of Huck Finn's conscience and the lost dime, and told a joke about missionaries. A sign at the theatre notified patrons that dogs were 'positively forbidden in the Dress Circle'. Twain wrote in his notebook this implied 'tacit permission to fill up the rest of the house'. The *Herald* sympathised with Twain's illness and thanked him for 'sacrificing himself on the altar of our curiosity'.

MARK TWAIN,
REAL NAME SAMUEL LANGHORNE CLEMENS
(Photographer unknown).
Alexander Turnbull Library, Wellington, New Zealand.
F-37422-1/2.

Napier was an ideal place to convalesce, Twain wrote to his close friend and confidant the Rev. Joseph Twichell the next day. On the day before his sixtieth birthday he followed the doctors' advice and relaxed by writing letters, reading newspapers, checking rail timetables and studying Indian history in preparation for his trip to the subcontinent. He wrote to Twichell that although he lectured the previous evening without 'inconvenience' the carbuncle now confined him to bed. Twain reported that his wife and daughter were coping with the travel better than he thought they would and were enjoying the trip. He was glad he had become unwell in a hotel by the sea instead of in a noisy city.

> Here we have the smooth and placidly-complaining sea at our door, with nothing between us and it but 20 yards of shingle — and hardly a suggestion of life in that space to mar it or make a noise. Away down here fifty-five degrees south of the Equator this sea seems to murmur in an unfamiliar tongue — a foreign tongue — tongue bred among the ice-fields of the Antarctic — a murmur with a note of melancholy in it proper to the vast unvisited solitudes it has come from. It was very delicious and solacing to wake in the night and find it still pulsing there.

Twain liked Frank Moeller's Masonic Hotel but didn't care for the caged canaries on the long porch because they sounded like 'the equivalent of scratching a nail on a window-pane'. He jotted in his notebook, 'I wonder what sort of disease it is that enables a person to enjoy the canary.' He claimed to have been told that in New Zealand teeth weren't filled but pulled out and replaced with false ones. The ailing Twain wrote, 'I wish I had been born with false teeth and a false liver and false carbuncles. I should get along better.' On Saturday the *Hawke's Bay Herald* reported that Twain's condition had improved. 'If he remained in Napier for a couple of months and took it easy he would be a renovated man.'

At the time of Twain's visit there were two shingle spits in Napier. Playing on the well known saying 'See Naples and die', Twain invented 'See Napier and spit'.

In February 1931 much of the town, along with neighbouring Hastings, was destroyed in a devastating earthquake. The water alongside the spits receded as huge areas of the seabed rose and the lagoon was reclaimed. The disaster left 256 people dead and large numbers homeless. After the earthquake Napier was reinvented as an Art Deco town and the Masonic Hotel where Twain stayed was rebuilt as the town's largest hotel. The Criterion, where Kipling stayed, was also rebuilt on the same site as the old hotel.

Twain departed for Palmerston North on a perfect summer day. A cool breeze blew as the author left on the 175 kilometre journey by express train. Twain travelled extensively on the railways. Although the country used to have an intricate passenger network, only a few main passenger lines are left and much of Twain's route is now plied only by freight trains. Of the New Zealand trains he wrote 'nothing that goes on wheels can be more comfortable, more satisfactory', especially given the 'constant presence of charming scenery and the nearly constant absence of dust'. The speed wasn't so impressive. He joked that the New Zealand express train was called the 'Ballarat Fly', after describing 'one of those whizzing green Ballarat flies' in his room in Napier. He thought the fly was 'the swiftest creature in the world except the lightening flash,' and wrote that if a ship had the same proportion of energy that the insect had in its body 'we could spin from Liverpool to New York in the space of an hour — the time it takes to eat luncheon'.

It took close to an hour for Twain and his family to reach Hastings, just 20 kilometres south of Napier. A couple of hours later they stopped for a 20-minute lunch break at the central Hawke's Bay settlement of Waipukurau. It was brief but memorable and Twain experienced what he believed to be 'mental telegraphy' during lunch. He'd recently written about the phenomenon in 'Mental Telegraphy Again', published in *Harper's Magazine* and reprinted by Australasian newspapers. It was partly the story of how he secured his agent for the Australasian tour. When he decided to tour the antipodes he wrote from Paris, where he was living, to his friend in London, Henry Morton Stanley, who had undertaken his own lecturing tour to Australia and New Zealand in 1891–92. Stanley advised Twain to contact R.S. Smythe, who'd organised his tour. Three days after Twain sent a letter to Smythe, he received a letter from the impressario posted two months earlier offering the exact terms he'd been hoping for. 'Mr Smythe's letter probably passed under my nose on its way to lose three weeks travelling to America and back, and gave me a whiff of its contents as it went along. Letters often act like that. Instead of the thought coming to you in an instant from Australia, the (apparently) unsentient letter imparts it to you as it glides invisibly past your elbow in the mail-bag,' he wrote.

During the lunch at Waipukurau, Twain was the only one who could see a couple of paintings hung on the wall he was facing. They were some distance away but the writer thought he could make out a scene in South Africa when the Zulus killed Napoleon III's son.

> I broke into the conversation, which was about poetry and cabbage and art, and said to my wife —
>
> 'Do you remember when the news came to Paris — '
>
> 'Of the killing of the Prince?'
>
> [Those were the very words I had in my mind.] 'Yes, but *what* Prince?'
>
> 'Napoleon. Lulu.'
>
> 'What made you think of that?'
>
> 'I don't know.'

His wife hadn't seen the pictures and Twain hadn't mentioned them. The writer expected her to reply to his question with a recent item of news from Paris. The couple lived in the French capital for a few years and had only recently left it. But what she actually recalled was an event that happened when they were in Paris 16 years previously. Twain believed it a clear case of mental telegraphy. He had transferred the image in his mind to hers. The pictures on the wall were not of Napoleon's son Lulu and Twain had 'telegraphed an error'. This to him was proof.

Twain and his party moved on. They travelled inland from Waipukurau, through a huge native forest running from Takapau to Woodville, east of Palmerston North. The forest, which contained a variety ferns, shrubs and trees including rimu, totara and the northern rata, continued as far south as the Opaki Plains just north of Masterton, roughly halfway between Palmerston North and Wellington. Settlers called it 'Seventy Mile Bush' and Maori called it Te Tapere Nui o Whatonga ('the great domain of Whatonga'). Only remnants exist of the dense bush that was home to the huia, the kokako and the kiwi. In *More Tramps Abroad* Twain described seeing 'wonderfully dense and beautiful forests, tumultuously piled skyward on the broken highlands' several times on the way to Palmerston North. The 'noblest' of these trees, the kauri, was 'furnishing the wood-paving for Europe'.

> Sometimes these towering upheavals of forestry were festooned and garlanded with vine-cables, and sometimes the masses of undergrowth were cocooned in another sort of vine of a delicate cobwebby texture — they call it the 'supplejack,' I think. Tree ferns everywhere — a stem fifteen feet high, with a graceful chalice of fern-fronds sprouting from its top — a lovely forest ornament. And there was a ten-foot reed with a flowing suit of what looked like yellow hair hanging from its upper end. I do not know its name, but if there is such a thing as a scalp-plant, this is it.

From the junction town of Woodville there are two roads running south to Wellington that pass either side of the Tararua Range. One runs towards the west coast through Palmerston North and the other continues down the middle of the lower North Island. Pahiatua is a small town on the inland route. Australian poet and writer Henry Lawson described the peaceful looking Pahiatua as being 'peculiar for the number of old men at graft, also murders, fines and mysterious disappearances'. Lawson arrived when the bush was being burned off and all he could see was a public house and a street shrouded in smoke. Main Street, which was originally built to accommodate the railway, was the widest in the country. Pahiatua would be an important town one day, he wrote, 'because we never yet came across a township that wasn't going to be an important town some day, except one, and that was going to be an important city'.

Twain took the coastal route south. 'A romantic gorge, with a brook flowing in its bottom', greeted the author as he approached Palmerston North. The Manawatu River begins on the eastern side of the Ruahine Range, the North Island's backbone, but instead of flowing east to exit at Hawke Bay, it turns back through the range to exit on the west coast, at Foxton. There's a theory that the river's bizarre course was caused by a sag in the ranges through which the river flowed, forming the gorge as the mountains rose. In Maori legend the gorge was cut by a huge totara tree that smashed through the mountains on its way to the sea. David Kennedy, a Scottish singer, published *Kennedy's Colonial Travel* in 1876 after touring the colonies for several years. He wrote that the steep gorge was 'peculiar in its grandeur' and had 'luxuriant bush'.

> Heavy rain-clouds, brooding over the gorge, trailed deeply into the tree-tops, and through these smote piercing gleams of sunshine, that, striking the opposite heights, lit up the bright verdure with flakes of still more vivid green. The gorge shot out headlands and bluffs — the splendid vista stretching along till it had ended in abrupt high portals, through which we saw an open window of white sky, and the distant low-lying country framed in like a picture by the natural gateway.

A 'straggling' city that nevertheless offered a delightful 'spaciousness' was Frank Bullen's impression of Palmerston North. Bullen liked his hotel and what locals called the finest opera house in the southern hemisphere, even though he thought this a slight exaggeration. The buildings were stately and the town was a 'bright, breezy, ambitious place, whose citizens manifest the most robust faith in its future'. However grand, the opera house didn't survive. It was sold and then demolished in the 1990s.

Palmerston North is situated on the banks of the Manawatu River and developed in the heart of rich sheep and dairy-farming lands, after settlers cleared much of the surrounding bush. The city is now home to one of the country's largest universities, Massey. J.B. Priestley was driven through 'spic-and-span but monotonous streets of detached villas' to the Palmerston North home of Professor Batt, the university's head of biochemistry and 'a youngish lively man with an attractive wife'. Priestley endured a 'longish tedious journey' from Wellington to attend a lunch in Batt's house. He didn't really want to go but to his surprise he enjoyed the soirée, at which his wife proved to be the big attraction. She was the daughter of Gowland Hopkins, a biochemist who had won a Nobel Prize for his study of vitamins. Priestley thought the lunch guests were interesting and that he was 'probably the only droning old bore' present. He was intrigued to hear that American academics often applied for posts in New Zealand. When he was planning to write his book of the country he had been warned that Americans had no interest in New Zealand. But Priestley noticed American tourists wherever he went and that a number of Americans worried about nuclear war had immigrated to New Zealand.

Mark Twain didn't enjoy Palmerston North. He barely mentioned the city in *More Tramps Abroad*, but reserved a few scathing comments for his notebook. There was a memorable 'Queen of Sheba style of barmaid' at the Club Hotel on the southeast corner of The Square on Church Street. She condescended to answer the bell but refused any domestic chores, believing them to be chambermaid's work. He also wrote of the drunks in the hotel and a 'fat, red, ignorant' landlord who couldn't get a key for his room until midnight. An 'elderly & not very handsome woman' had little sympathy for Twain's plight and she told the author that *she* wasn't scared to sleep in an unlocked room.

The hotel's rooms were small, had thin partitions and disappointingly, to Twain's disgust, smoking was banned. A baby started crying early in the morning, then someone ('either the cat or a partially untrained artist') started playing the piano. It was 'the most extraordinary music — straight average of 3 right notes to 4 wrong ones, but played with eager zeal and gladness — old, old tunes of 40 years ago, such as I heard at Timaru — & considering it was the cat — for it *must* have been the cat — it was really a marvellous performance. It convinces me that a cat is more intelligent than people believe, & can be taught any crime,' he wrote. The original Club Hotel that so annoyed Twain burned down and its replacement has been absorbed into a shopping complex.

THE CLUB HOTEL. Palmerston North City Archives

A reporter from the *Dominion* quizzed George Bernard Shaw for over half an hour in Palmerston North. The playwright was in the city for one night on his way from Wanganui to Wellington. The reporter asked Shaw why not a 'single notable author, poet, or dramatist' had become successful staying in New Zealand. 'Any man who follows a profession is more or less bound to follow his market,' Shaw replied. 'New Zealand is not a literary centre, but England and London and Paris are literary centres, and you really have to follow your market to a certain extent. That is the only thing to do if New Zealand is to develop this. I did not know that New Zealand has not produced a single notable author, poet, or dramatist. Perhaps it may congratulate itself upon that — it is a very questionable occupation.'

Twain found the four-hour train journey from Palmerston North to the coastal town of Wanganui on the banks of the Whanganui River so comfortable he wouldn't have minded if the trip had taken twice as long. 'Nothing that goes on wheels can be more comfortable, more satisfactory, than the New Zealand trains. Outside of America there are no cars that are so rationally devised. When you add the constant presence of charming scenery and the nearly constant absence of dust — well, if one is not content then, he ought to get out and walk.'

The road from Palmerston North to Wanganui passes through Bulls. It was here that J.B. Priestley was taken to a teashop by his driver Mr Mills, to regale his famous passenger with a joke from his childhood: 'Wellington gets its milk from Bulls.' Priestley noticed the curious and misleading description of all roadside eating and drinking establishments in New Zealand as 'teashops' or 'tearooms', which suggested to the English 'lady-like establishments delicately run by the daughters of late Indian army colonels'.

Frank Bullen left the flat terrain of Palmerston North and headed towards Wanganui 'though a most beautifully diversified country, the level plain gradually narrowing as we went north, although there were occasional stretches of rich-looking valley land'. He changed trains at Aramoho, only a few kilometres from Wanganui. The Palmerston train continued to New Plymouth to connect with the Auckland-bound steamer. Bullen found it hard to believe so 'beautiful and imposing a town' as Wanganui, with such fine buildings, could be run by fewer than ten thousand residents. Horseback riding, the Salvation Army, 'comely girls in cool and pretty summer gowns' and many Maori, some of whom were 'very tastefully frescoed'. This was Twain's impression of Wanganui. He hated one of the town's war monuments, which he found disturbing. It's been said that the monument, which Twain mistakenly remembered as two separate structures, is the country's 'first genuine war memorial'. It can still be found in Moutoa Gardens, at a bend in the river near its mouth, and features the statue of a weeping woman and the words: 'To the memory of those brave men who fell at Moutoa 14 May 1864 in defence of law and order against fanaticism and barbarism. This monument is erected by the province of Wellington.'

The Battle of Moutoa was caused by a land purchase by settlers in 1840, and subsequent tensions between lower river Maori, who developed links with the European settlement, and the upper river Maori, who wanted to claim back the land from the Pakeha invader. The lower river Maori prevailed, and the settlers were so relieved they organised the memorial, which lists the names of the fifteen Maori defenders and a Catholic lay brother who was reportedly shot while pleading with both sides to stop fighting.

Twain remembered two monuments: one honouring white men 'who fell in defence of law and order against fanaticism and barbarism' and one erected by white men honouring Maori who fought against their own people. Writing about the 'first' monument he believed 'fanaticism' was the wrong word to use. 'Patriotism is patriotism. Calling it fanaticism cannot degrade it; nothing can degrade it.' The monument to Maori fighting against their own people, which Twain mistakenly recalled as a separate structure, he thought could only be rectified with dynamite. 'It invites to treachery, disloyalty, unpatriotism. Its lesson, in frank terms is, "Desert your flag, slay your people, burn their homes, shame your nationality — we honour such."'

Twain saw the 'Maori Council House over the river — large, strong, carpeted from end to end with matting, and decorated with elaborate wood carvings, artistically executed', which was probably at Putiki Pa on the south bank of the Whanganui River. He met a politician who told him that the Maori population was increasing slightly.

> It is another evidence that they are a superior breed of savages. I do not call to mind any savage race that built such good houses, or such strong and ingenious and scientific fortresses, or gave so much attention to agriculture, or had military arts and devices which so nearly approached the white man's. These, taken together with their high abilities in boat-building, and their tastes and capacities in the ornamental arts modify their savagery to a semi-civilization — or at least to a quarter-civilization.

Twain congratulated the British on subduing rather than exterminating the Maori as they had the 'Australians and the Tasmanians'. They left the Maori good land, and gave them protection from land sharks and political representation, he wrote. In the early 1950s James Michener wrote in *Holiday* that the relationship between 'brown and white in New Zealand is far superior to that between black and white in America'. Maori were able to elect their own members of parliament, intermarry, live and work where they wanted and had fought bravely during two world wars. But he noticed that race relations were 'not all sweetness'. Many Maori villages were 'slums', he wrote, adding that some Maori felt uncomfortable with Paheka who 'shout public acceptance but practice private ostracism'.

Bad weather and illness had disrupted Twain's performance schedule, but he encountered a much more bizarre threat to his tour in Wanganui. On his second afternoon in the town, an agitated visitor accosted him.

> A lunatic burst into my quarters and warned me that the Jesuits were going to 'cook' (poison) me in my food, or kill me on the stage at night. He said a mysterious sign was visible upon my posters and meant my death. He said he saved Rev. Mr Haweis's life by warning him that there were three men on his platform who would kill him if he took his eyes off them for a moment during his lecture. The same men were in my audience last night, but they saw that he was there. 'Will they be there again to-night?' He hesitated; then said no, he thought they would rather take a rest and chance the poison. This lunatic has no delicacy. But he was not uninteresting. He told me a lot of things. He said he had 'saved so many lecturers in twenty years, that they put him in the asylum.' I think he has less refinement than any lunatic I have met.

Despite the warnings Twain performed without incident at the now demolished Oddfellows' Hall, a couple of doors down from its replacement that opened just days after the author's visit and still exists in Ridgway Street. The venue was full on the first night and many people had to stand in the dress circle. The humourist gave his appreciative audience a night of 'magnificent entertainment', according to the *Wanganui Chronicle*. 'A man known by name and fame to every English-speaking country, who has charmed countless thousands by the keen humour of his writings, but whom we in little Wanganui never expected to personally meet, has not overlooked us in his tour round the world, and in turn the courtesy of his visit was rewarded by the partronage of a crowd as large as could be packed into the house.'

On the second night the same paper reported Twain 'gave every man, woman and child a "Yankee start"'. 'He was finishing off with a ghost story — the story of the golden arm — and as it progressed he gradually worked up the feelings of his hearers to such a pitch that one and all appeared to be breathlessly awaiting the terrible conclusion. It came, and in a manner that was totally unexpected, for with a sharp, sudden and loud exclamation he broke abruptly off, the ladies especially nearly jumping out of their seats at the resultant shock.'

'Did you see the Wanganui River?' George Bernard Shaw was asked by a reporter after he had travelled down the Parapara Road on his way from Tongariro in the central North Island to Wanganui. The Parapara Road gradually draws towards the impressive

Whanganui River and joins its course just north of Wanganui. 'I saw a river this morning,' the author replied. 'It was larger than others I have seen, I suppose that was the Wanganui, but I have not been on it.' Shaw said he'd endured an 'arduous' journey through hills that it 'was a pity the Almighty had not used a plane on'. Shaw had a problem with New Zealand's scenery. He understood the need to burn the bush for pasture but for him cut and burnt trees spoiled the landscape. He seemed to think there were still plenty of trees around though. People kept telling him which piece of bush they thought was the 'best left standing', but he claimed to have hardly been out of bush since his arrival.

In New Plymouth, about one hundred and thirty kilometres northwest of Wanganui, a packed audience in the Alexandra Hall greeted Twain as though he was an old friend. The hall stood on what is now the TSB Showplace (formerly the New Plymouth Opera House) site on Devon Street West in the central city. He began his performance with anecdotes from his childhood in Mississippi and moved on to Huck Finn and Jim the slave and concluded with a 'highly humorous dissertation on the study of the German language'. Twain 'kept the audience in a perpetual state of half-subdued laughter, disturbed now and then by a spontaneous and uncontrollable outburst, as a particularly fetching point found its way home'.

New Plymouth lies about halfway between Auckland and Wellington on the North Island's west coast. It was known as the 'garden region' but the grass was the only 'beauty' to be seen according to Twain. New houses were being built on recently cleared land so Twain scribbled in his notebook that the area looked like one huge clearing with miles of charred trees, with a sprinkling of old cottages standing alongside newly painted ones. Before arriving in New Plymouth by train Twain performed in the packed Drill Hall in Hawera, then a town of a couple of thousand people. During the journey from Hawera to New Plymouth Twain passed to the right of the imposing dormant volcano Mt Egmont/Taranaki which dominates New Plymouth. He didn't get a good view of the peak because it was shrouded by cloud.

'On the summit of the mountain I found the skeleton of a rat, carried there, no doubt, by a hawk. After staying for some time on the summit, in the vain hope that the clouds which enveloped it would disperse, we retraced out steps, and accomplished the descent with comparative ease,' wrote Ernest Dieffenbach, who travelled to New Zealand in the late 1830s as surgeon and naturalist on the *Tory*. Dieffenbach was born in Germany but fled to Switzerland to complete his medical training after getting involved in student demonstrations. He was forced out of Switzerland after qualifying as a doctor and spent a few years working in London before voyaging to New Zealand, the Chatham Islands and New South Wales. In *Travels in New Zealand* he claimed that he was 'the first to visit or describe Mount Egmont'. He recorded that the exterior cone was made up of 'a hard lava of a bluish-grey colour, which resounds to the hammer like phonolite or clinkstone, and breaks into large tabular fragments'.

'The little town is beautifully situated under Mount Egmont,' Trollope wrote of New Plymouth with its 'lovely summit of snow, sharp almost as a church steeple'. He couldn't view the 'grandly timbered' land around the mountain thirty miles beyond the town as Maori held it. Taranaki became the flashpoint for the New Zealand Wars, which began in 1860. The Taranaki chiefs had not signed the Treaty of Waitangi that recognised the sovereignty of the British Queen and during a decade of guerrilla warfare that followed, settlers moved into Waitara, just north of New Plymouth, but they had little control elsewhere in the area.

The 'Fly' took Twain back down the west coast of the lower North Island to Wellington. He told a reporter that the route was made up of 'continual stoppages at little stations, where apparently nothing was done, and which appeared to him to be simply arranged to fill in time, and the gentle, albeit sometimes jolty, ride from station to station, as though the train were out for an easy constitutional'. Between New Plymouth and Stratford he noted in his diary that the road was so rough it was difficult to stay in his seat, and if milk were put on the train it would be churned. Twain was late heading towards the country's capital because of a mix-up over train timetables, and faced the prospect of cancelling his first performance.

Paikakariki is a coastal town 40 kilometres north of Wellington. The *New Zealand Mail* columnist 'Scrutator' suggested Twain should try some Maori rhymes. 'For instance, can he find a rhyme to Paikakariki, a word whose quaintness of sound so tickled the fancy of Rudyard Kipling that he had told a friend of "Scrutator's" he had jotted it down for "use somehow, somewhere, someday". I read my Kipling pretty diligently but I haven't come across Paikakariki yet in any of his new work.'

Although the name Paikakariki didn't inspire Twain, he did feature several other New Zealand place names in a poem. In *More Tramps Abroad* he listed a 'curious collection' of names he compiled in order to make a poem out of them, including Kaiwaka, Tauranga, Tongariro, Kaikoura, Wakatipu, Hauraki, Rangiriri, Taranaki, Whangaroa, Whangarei and Kawakawa. His favourite name was the Australian Woolloomoolloo, because it had eight Os and was the 'most musical and gurgly', but a variety of names from both countries were incorporated into 'A Sweltering Day in Australia', which was to be 'read soft and low, with the lights turned down' and included the verses:

Sweet Nangwarry's desolate, Coonamble wails,
And Tungkillo Kuito in sables is drest,
For the Whangarei winds fall asleep in the sails
And the Booleroo life-breeze is dead in the west.

Mypongo, Kapunda, O slumber no more
Yankalilla, Parawirra, be warned
There's death in the air!
Killanoola, wherefore
Shall the prayer of Penola be scorned?

Cootamundra, and Takee, and Wakatipu,
Toowoomba, Kaikoura are lost
From Onkaparinga to far Oamaru
All burn in this hell's holocaust!

Paramatta and Binnum are gone to their rest
In the vale of Tapanni Taroom,
Kawakawa, Deniliquin — all that was best
In the earth are but graves and a tomb!

Narrandera mourns, Cameron answers not
When the roll of the scathless we cry
Tongariro, Goondiwindi, Woolundunga, the spot
Is mute and forlorn where ye lie.

Twain suggested a poet laureate might have done a better job, 'but a poet laureate gets wages, and that is different. When I write poetry I do not get any wages; often I lose money by it.'

FOLLOWING MR BOOLEY

On 12 May 1827 the members of the Pickwick Club in London unanimously approved several resolutions. They heard with 'feelings of unmingled satisfaction' Samuel Pickwick's paper entitled 'Speculations on the Source of the Hampstead Ponds, with Some Observations on the Theory of Tittlebats'. Pickwick and three others proposed that they form a new branch of United Pickwickians, to be called The Corresponding Society of the Pickwick Club, whose members would send back to London reports of their adventures and travels. The proposal was accepted and club members thought it a good idea that the 'learned man' Pickwick should travel more widely, 'enlarging his sphere of observation, to the advancement of knowledge, and the diffusion of learning'. The adventures of Pickwick and his friends were published as *The Posthumous Papers of the Pickwick Club* (later known simply as *The Pickwick Papers*) by Chapman and Hall, in 20 monthly instalments from March 1836 to October 1837. The first chapters weren't popular and only 500 copies of the second instalment were printed. But the story eventually captured the public's imagination and 40,000 copies of the final part were produced. Charles Dickens, in his mid-twenties, had completed his first novel and became famous.

On 12 May 1840 the members of The Pickwick Club of New Zealand met at Mr W. Elsdon's Commercial Inn and Tavern in Willis Street, Port Nicholson. It was just four months since the first New Zealand Company settlers arrived to establish what is now the capital city of New Zealand. The company purchased land from Maori at Port Nicholson, around Wellington Harbour, and the first shipload of emigrants arrived on the *Aurora* in

January 1840. At seven o'clock at Elsdon's establishment, what is believed to have been the first Dickens society founded outside Britain was officially formed. The rules and regulations were agreed upon and the health of the Queen, the New Zealand Company and its principal agent, and the settlement of Port Nicholson were all toasted. According to the colony's first newspaper, the *New Zealand Gazette*, the club, which charged a £25 entrance fee and a £5 annual subscription, had a 'considerable number' of members. 'To our friends in England this cannot fail to awaken the most pleasing sensations; as it tends to prove, that in this remote region of the globe — this land of savages — Englishmen relish the inimitable works of "Boz", and that they desire to spread the fame of the author in their adopted land.'

One English friend, the author of *The Pickwick Papers* himself, was indeed delighted to hear of the club's formation. In a letter in December 1840, 28-year-old Dickens wrote of a 'Port Nicholas Mens Paper' he'd received with an advertisement about Pickwick Club meetings. He derived 'great gratification ... from the circumstance of their meeting together for social purposes, under this name. To be associated with their pleasant recollections of home in their hours of relaxation, is to me a most proud and happy distinction. I really cannot tell you how very much it has interested and pleased me.' Details of the club's creation were discovered after one of the editors of the *Pilgrim Edition of the Letters of Charles Dickens*, Graham Storey, suspected 'Port Nicholas' was really 'Port Nicholson' and made enquiries in New Zealand.

The *New Zealand Gazette* explained the aims of the club. The colonists had successfully established Port Nicholson but they 'could not but perceive the necessity there existed for forming some bind of union which might still more closely unite the scattered elements of our society. This want has been supplied by the "Pickwick Club", and we rejoice to see that in the face of difficulties almost insurmountable it has succeeded in establishing for itself a character for unanimity and respectability second to no institution of its kind, and which, based as it is on the principles of mutual benefit and information, cannot fail to raise it to a still loftier station with the growing prosperity of the colony.' The club wasn't simply a place to socialise but it was an organisation 'destined to exert a great and salutary influence on the welfare of the land of our adoption'. It had a library of more than a hundred books, all donated by members.

On 12 May, every year at exactly seven o'clock, members of the Christchurch branch of the Dickens Fellowship remember the Wellington Pickwick Club by toasting the original settlers' club and Mr Pickwick. The Christchurch group is New Zealand's only remaining Dickens organisation.

The city of Wellington lies at the southwestern tip of New Zealand's North Island. The first settlement, 'Britannia', was located on the swampy land of Petone, near the mouth of the Hutt River in the middle of Wellington Harbour. But the direct southerlies that swept through the harbour mouth and the flooding of the Hutt River forced a move west around to the much more sheltered beach of the inner harbour and the steep hills behind it. Wellington Harbour was 'like a noble bowl among its surrounding mountains', and was 'the finest sight in the Antipodes' wrote British travel writer James Morris. James, who underwent a sex change operation in 1972, is now known as Jan. He described Wellington in his 1963 book *Cities*, a collection of articles, most of which first appeared in the *Guardian*, *The Times* and *Life* magazine. Morris worked for a decade as a foreign correspondent and from 1957 to 1962 he divided his time between working for the *Guardian* and writing books. He made several trips to the southern hemisphere. Morris described *Cities* as 'a view of the urban world as it looked, sounded and smelt to an Englishman in the fifties and sixties of the twentieth century'.

> On a spit of land at one end, between bay and sea, run the new runways of Wellington Airport. Further north, towards Kaiwharawhara, ships stand high and dry in the floating dock. Along the western shore run the quays and warehouse of the port, and neatly protected by the promontory of Seatoun runs the narrow outlet to the open sea. It might have been scooped out by a million bull-dozers, so exactly does it fulfil the functions of a port, but for the grand bare highlands that surround it.

The lights of the harbour at night reminded Morris of Monte Carlo, but the presence of the mountains gave the city 'its proper touch of the exotic'. The wooden buildings were reminiscent of the small seaports of Southern Chile.

'This is certainly a country I would like to live in,' Zane Grey said as he gazed at the hills surrounding Wellington. 'His eyes lingered awhile on the forested ranges looming against the eastern sky, all his sporting instincts aroused by the statement that deer, wild boar and goats roamed freely in their fastnesses,' wrote a correspondent. 'The hunter in him is expressed in the keen glance from half-closed lids born of his long sojourning in the wilderness he loves so well.' Grey had remarkable eyesight. He could see things under the water a long time before anyone else. Captain Mitchell, one of his companions in New Zealand, had hooked a swordfish off the Californian coast when Grey, who was peering into the water from another boat, suddenly shouted a warning to his friend that the fish was about to attack him. 'I sprang to my feet in an endeavour to see something of my antagonist, and next instant his sword was driven clean through the bottom of the boat and transfixed the thwart I had been sitting on,' said Mitchell.

It was still called Port Nicholson on the map when Anthony Trollope arrived in Wellington in August 1872. He thought it looked like St Thomas in the Virgin Islands, but the similarity was superficial. 'St Thomas is one of the most unhealthy places frequented by man, whereas there is perhaps no spot more healthy than Wellington.' Healthy but not wealthy thought Trollope who believed the town too closely hemmed in by the sea and too devoid of surrounding land to be prosperous. And then there were the earthquakes. Trollope saw that the town was 'built only of wood', and feared for its future.

⁂

Agatha Christie sailed to New Zealand as part of a promotional tour for the 1924 British Empire Exhibition in Wembley, designed to herald a great Imperial revival. Agatha's husband Archie was the British Empire Exhibition Mission's financial advisor. He was paid £1000 for his services and was allowed to have Agatha accompany him. She left their small daughter at home with her sister and travelled in first class luxury to South Africa, Australia, New Zealand and Canada. The ships and railways of the colonies provided most of the transport for free. Christie's first novel, *The Mysterious Affair at Styles*, had been published in 1920; she had completed her second, *The Secret Adversary*, and had almost finished her third, *The Murder on the Links*, when they set out on the Empire tour.

Christie arrived in Wellington in 1922 and was pleased to escape the attentions of a fellow passenger known as 'The Dehydrator'. She remembered the three-day voyage from Hobart to Wellington well for there was a passenger on board who had patented a dehydrating device. He proudly sent samples of his dehydrated food to the Christies and Major Belcher's table at every meal. Belcher, who was leading the mission, was also annoying Christie. 'He was rude, overbearing, bullying, inconsiderate, and mean in curiously small matters. For instance, he was always sending me out to buy him white cotton socks or other necessities of underwear, and never by any chance did he pay me back for what I bought.' She thought he behaved like a spoilt child who knew how to turn on enough charm to be forgiven for his bad behaviour.

The mission's report on New Zealand would prove controversial. It questioned the quality of the country's best land, the facilities for grading stock, its dairy production, its employers, the management of the railways and the 'wide gap' between the best New Zealand hotels and the average Canadian hotel. The New Zealand high commissioner in London claimed the mission went beyond its remit and cast 'grave and warranted reflections of the resources of New Zealand'. The country's prime minister supported the accusations. 'The Mission rushed through New Zealand in a time of depression and jumped to unwarranted conclusions,' reported one Wellington newspaper. 'It is admitted that the dairy output is susceptible of improvement and that land values can be reduced, but this does not justify misleading comments.'

⁂

We'll tak' one stretch — three weeks an' odd by any road ye steer —
Fra' Cape Town east to Wellington — ye need an engineer
RUDYARD KIPLING, 'McAndrew's Hymn'

Kipling describes a voyage he took from South Africa to New Zealand in 1891 aboard the SS *Doric* in a highly regarded poem that was first published in late 1894 in *Scribner's Magazine* and was included in the compilation *The Seven Seas*. He wrote that the *Doric* was the ship in the poem and according to the *New Zealand Marine News* Kipling based the engineer on the *Doric*'s Chief Engineer R. Reid.

... the auld Fleet Engineer,
That started as a boiler-whelp — when steam and he were low.
I mind the time we used to serve a broken pipe wi' tow.
Ten pound was all the pressure then — Eh! Eh! — a man wad drive;
An' here, our workin' gauges give one hunder' fifty-five!

A quintessential Englishman in his mid-sixties 'appeared, in the act of wiping his smoking head with his pocket-handkerchief, at the entrance to Port Nicholson'. Dickens wrote about Mr Booley in his 1850 story *Some Account of an Extraordinary Traveller*, for the weekly journal he edited, *Household Words*. The unmarried Mr Booley lived a routine, boring life before taking an impulsive decision. At one o'clock one afternoon he left his house without telling anyone and apparently set off on the first of many voyages to different parts of the world. After 'seeing' the United States, he 'set sail' for New Zealand. After arriving at Port Nicholson he was soon on his way into Wellington.

> After contemplating the swarms of cattle maintained on the hills in this neighbourhood, and always to be found by the stockmen when they are wanted, though nobody takes any care of them — which Mr Booley considered the more remarkable, as their natural objection to be killed might be supposed to be augmented by the beauty of the climate — Mr Booley proceeded to the town of Wellington.

'It is almost incredible that a man in Mr Booley's station of life,' wrote Dickens, 'however adventurous his nature, and however few his artificial wants, should cast himself on a voyage of thirteen thousand miles from Great Britain with no other outfit than his watch and purse, and no arms but his walking-stick.' Towards the end of the story, Dickens reveals the truth. Booley tells the Social Oysters Club 'all my modes of conveyance have been pictorial'. He had been visiting panoramas in London.

Like Booley, Dickens was interested in New Zealand but never saw the country in person. He edited several stories about the colony for *Household Words* and in the early 1840s he tried to help his brother Alfred get employment as an assistant engineer and surveyor with the New Zealand Company. In a despondent mid-winter moment in London after receiving a critical review in *The Times*, Dickens toyed with the idea of visiting New Zealand himself. 'Disposed to go to New Zealand and start a magazine,' he wrote in a letter in early 1847. Fifteen years later he considered an invitation for a reading tour of Australia. It was worth £10,000 and New Zealand would have been a likely addition to the itinerary, but the deal fell through. In *Charles Dickens and New Zealand* J.S. Ryan suggests he may have been alluding to New Zealand at the start of his short story *The Long Voyage*. 'When the wind is blowing and the sleet or rain is driving against the dark windows, I love to sit by the fire, thinking of what I have read in books of voyage and travel. Such books have had a strong fascination for my mind from my earliest childhood; and I wonder it should come to pass that I have never been round the world, never have been shipwrecked, ice-environed, tomahawked, or eaten.'

'I doubt whether Demosthenes often looked at his papers, or Cicero when he was speaking, or Pitt,' wrote Anthony Trollope, who declared he had never seen such a reliance on papers in a national debating assembly as he encountered in Wellington.

> The gentleman on his legs in the House, — when custom has made that position easy to him, — learns to take delight in delaying the House while he turns over one folio after another either of manuscript, which has been arranged for him, or of printed matter which he has marked for reference. And then, to show how very much at home he is, while gentlemen are gaping around him, he will look out for new references, muttering perhaps a word or two while his face is among the leaves, — perhaps repeating the last words of his last sentence, and absolutely revelling in the tyranny of his position. But while doing so, he is unconsciously losing the orator's power of persuasion.

Trollope attended a parliamentary debate in Wellington in 1872. It took place in the wooden Gothic Parliament Building that was destroyed by fire in 1907 and replaced with the current Parliament House. Wellington's government buildings have always stood near the northern end of The Terrace and Lambton Quay. Trollope stayed at Government House, a building that used to stand near what is now the distinctive round-shaped Beehive, the executive wing of the current complex of parliamentary buildings. The seat of government was transferred permanently from Auckland to Wellington in 1865 after much bad-tempered rivalry between the two cities. Auckland was too far north; Wellington was an earthquake risk. Eventually, Wellington prevailed.

Trollope wrote about Julius Vogel's policies in *Australia and New Zealand*. Vogel was then the colonial treasurer under the government of William Fox and he was borrowing heavily and raising loans on the London money market to fund massive building projects, assisted immigration and land purchase for settlement. Trollope wrote that while Vogel's plans were welcomed at first, there was a suspicion that he had grown reckless. 'Mr Vogel was playing a great experiment, at the expense of the community, and the colony began to ask who was Mr Vogel, that it should trust him? I am constrained to say ... that I think the colony trusted him too far.' Trollope witnessed Vogel's speech during the no confidence debate instigated by Edward Stafford against the Fox government. The government was defeated, although Vogel later returned to power.

Trollope impressed a *Daily Southern Cross* correspondent with his knowledge of social conditions and politics. 'A bright hazel eye looks at his interlocuter through spectacles, and a pleasant decided kind of voice is suggestive of being that of a man who has seen for himself, taken in all surrounding circumstances, weighed them, compared them, and drawn his conclusions according to the evidence.' The reporter announced that since Trollope's arrival all his novels had been taken out of the Assembly Library, 'so anxious are people to be "up" in the writings of the present hero of the hour'.

Kipling criticised the existence of New Zealand's upper house in an interview for the Melbourne newspaper, the *Age*.

> What does it want with an 'Upper House' and a 'Lower House'? Why doesn't it go ahead and do its work and make the country? Why, there is more machinery for running their little handful of people than we have for the whole of the 300,000,000 people of India ... down in New Zealand you would think that you couldn't go 300 yards from the beach without running into an elector or a member of Parliament, and on the other side of that you meet the bush.

'At home, a standing argument against woman [*sic*] suffrage has always been that women could not go to the polls without being insulted,' wrote Mark Twain, who considered the right of women to vote in New Zealand in *More Tramps Abroad*. New Zealand became the first country in the world to grant women the right to vote in parliamentary elections just two years before Twain's visit. He wrote that in the first election under the new law the turnout of women was high and that an official report claimed 'women were in no way molested'. He thought the United States could learn from the New Zealand experience.

> Men ought to begin to feel a sort of respect for their mothers and wives and

> sisters by this time. The women deserve a change of attitude like that, for they have wrought well. In forty-seven years they have swept an imposingly large number of unfair laws from the statute books of America. In that brief time these serfs have set themselves free essentially. Men could not have done so much for themselves in that time without bloodshed — at least they never have; and that is argument that they didn't know how. The women have accomplished a peaceful revolution, and a very beneficent one; and yet that has not convinced the average man that they are intelligent, and have courage and energy and perseverance and fortitude. It takes much to convince the average man of anything; and perhaps nothing can ever make him realize that he is the average woman's inferior — yet in several important details the evidences seems to show that that is what he is. Man has ruled the human race from the beginning — but he should remember that up to the middle of the present century it was a dull world, and ignorant and stupid; but it is not such a dull world now, and is growing less and less dull all the time. This is woman's opportunity — she has had none before. I wonder where man will be in another forty-seven years?

'New Zealand democracy is the talk of the world to-day' wrote Henry Demarest Lloyd, in *Newest England,* published in 1900. Lloyd, an American journalist and political activist, visited New Zealand to report on the country's reforms. Richard Seddon's Liberal Government, which had given women the vote, was introducing several measures that contributed to the creation of a welfare state. Lloyd believed there was a movement afoot for the middle class to absorb all other classes, so that the rich didn't become richer and the poor, poorer.

> The New Zealanders are not in any sense extraordinary. There is only one remarkable thing about them, and that is an accident. They are the most compact and homogenous, the most equal and manageable democracy in the world. This is luck — not intention but circumstance. The country was too far away from Europe and from the thousand-year-old stream of westward migration to become New Europe, as the United States has done. It became only Newest England — what the Puritans and Pilgrims planned; the kind of country those Englishmen, Washington, Jefferson and Adams, expected would carry on their constitution ... The tactful portrait painter would not say that the New Zealanders were the most civilised, the most happy, the most prosperous people in the world, but they certainly are the least uncivilised, the least unhappy, the least disinherited. Danton's political

> genius taught him to say of the laws and policies he proposed not that they were good, but that they were the 'least bad'. There are no absolutely good governments or peoples, but some are not so bad as others, and for New Zealand it may be claimed that its government and people are 'the least bad' this side of Mars.

'The queer thing is that [New Zealand has] got all the things in the Liberal or mild Fabian programme — eight hours' day (and less), bigger old age pensions, access to the land, minimum wage, insurance, etc.etc. — and yet it's not Paradise,' wrote Rupert Brooke in early 1914. 'The same troubles exist in much the same form (except that there's not much bad poverty). Cost of living is rising quicker than wages. There are the same troubles between unions and employers, and between rich and poor. I suppose there'll be no peace anywhere till the rich are curbed altogether.' Brooke spent a couple of days in Wellington while he waited for passage to Tahiti. He amused himself in a country he didn't find 'frightfully interesting' by reading the Wellington Club's newspapers. He devoured an entire month of *The Times* and he saw his own writing in the *Westminster Gazette*. 'I don't think the articles are *good* (except one or two). But they serve their purpose: and there's more in them than in most stuff of that kind.' The Wellington Club was founded in 1841. Now housed in a relatively new, seven-storey building on The Terrace, the club has no known record of Brooke's visit.

Brooke saw a specialist about his foot that had become infected in Fiji and was still troubling him. The illness-prone poet, soon to be soldier, spent much of his short time in New Zealand dealing with health problems. He died less than a year and a half later. Brooke thought his next port of call, Tahiti, was paradise. He met a beautiful Tahitian girl and stayed with her for several months. He had been back in England for two months when war was declared on 4 August 1914. He considered becoming a war correspondent but in September obtained a commission in the Naval Division and before long he was writing his five famous war sonnets. Brooke got sunstroke on a ship heading for the Aegean and while waiting for the Gallipoli attack, he developed blood poisoning from an insect bite and died on a hospital ship in April 1915. Critics claim Brooke is remembered more for what he symbolised than for the quality of his poetry. He became the symbol of a generation of hopeful young men lost in the bloody trenches of the Great War.

> If I should die, think only this of me:
> That there's some corner of a foreign field
> That is for ever England.

RUPERT BROOKE, 'The Soldier'

Wellington's cenotaph is graced by a verse from one of Brooke's war poems. The monument commemorates New Zealanders killed in both world wars and bears an inscription from 'The Dead'.

> These laid the world away; poured out the red
> Sweet wine of youth; gave up the years to be
> Of work and joy, and that unhoped serene,
> That men call age; and those who would have been,
> Their sons, they gave, their immortality.

Brooke wrote about the capture of the German colony, Western Samoa, in 'Some Niggers', which appeared in the *New Statesman* soon after the outbreak of war and was included with his *Westminster Gazette* articles in the posthumous 1916 book *Letters From America*.

> And now Samoa is ours. A New Zealand Expeditionary Force took it. Well, I know a princess who will have had the day of her life. Did they see Stevenson's tomb gleaming high up on the hill, as they made for that passage in the reef? Did Vasa, with his heavy-lidded eyes, and that infinitely adorable lady Fafaia, wander down to the beach to watch them land? They must have landed from boats; and at noon, I see. How hot they got! I know that Apia noon. Didn't they rush to the Tivoli bar — but I forget, New Zealanders are teetotalers. So, perhaps, the Samoans gave them the coolest of all drinks, — kava — ; and they scored. And what dances in their honour, that night! — but, again, I'm afraid the houla-houla would shock a New Zealander. I suppose they left a garrison, and went away. I can very vividly see them steaming out in the evening; and the crowd on shore would be singing them that sweetest and best-known of South Sea songs, which begins 'Good-bye, my Flenni' ('Friend,' you'd pronounce it), and goes on in Samoan, a very beautiful tongue. I hope they'll rule Samoa well.

The tragic poet became a literary phenomenon. New Zealand author E.H. McCormick claimed the emotion surrounding Brooke in the country 'both contributed to and expressed the strange Anglomania, which beset the country, almost like some medieval visitation, in the early decades of the twentieth century'.

*

A Wellington branch of the Fabian Society was ostensibly created for the arrival of George Bernard Shaw in 1934. Shaw lectured the society and denounced parliamentary democracy. The British House of Commons had become a 'House of Hypocrisy,' he said. He appealed to

New Zealand socialists to denounce the Westminster model of government and claimed the country needed a Cromwell to say 'Down with democracy!'

'Hullo, North Island, South Island, and all the places I haven't been to. Bernard Shaw talking to the Universe! But more directly to New Zealand.' Broadcasting regulations were waived for his radio broadcast 'Shaw Speaks to the Universe' and he spoke uncensored. So he criticised the country's trade policy and the existence of a 'large number' of needlessly unemployed, and said that if work and leisure time were distributed evenly no one should have to work more than four hours a day. He claimed New Zealand was 'leading the rest of the world in Communism' and was 'second only to Russia', even though it didn't know it was Communist. His half-hour address was very influential.

> You have in Wellington a remarkable milk supply, which is the envy of the whole world ... But your milk I think costs too much. I just want to ask, why not distribute milk freely? That is very important in New Zealand. A little loss on milk does not matter ... when you have distributed free milk, which is just as possible as free water, I would then suggest that you should go on from free milk to free bread ... [then] such a thing as a hungry child will be impossible in New Zealand.

New Zealand's first Labour Government came to power the following year. It introduced a policy to provide every child with half a pint of free milk on school days. The scheme lasted for 30 years and Shaw received several letters of thanks from New Zealand mothers. During the Second World War New Zealand children were also given free apples from orchard surpluses.

Margaret Atwood offered the New Zealand government advice in November 2003 when she urged it to approach genetic modification with caution. Atwood was in Wellington for a writers' event and 'engaged her audience with a ready mix of wit and irony edged with a stoic acceptance of the existence of issues such as genetic modification'. The Booker Prize winner who has written about human clones, mutant creatures and doomsday future scenarios advised the prime minister not to do anything too quickly. 'As long as you haven't made the decision you still have choices. Once it's in [New Zealand] it's game over.'

Bruce Mason met J.B. Priestley in London in 1944. Priestly advised the aspiring young writer to return to New Zealand where he was familiar with both people and places. By the time the two men were reunited in Wellington nearly thirty years later Mason had become a well-known writer and actor, performing *The End of the Golden Weather*, which was later adapted as a film. 'He sent me a copy of this piece, and I found it a nourishing mixture of close observation, humour and poetic feeling,' Priestley wrote.

Wellington regards itself as a capital of culture and art and Priestley was taken on a one-day odyssey around the city's many attractions. It began with a morning press conference, followed by lunch at the Woolshed ('Wellington restaurants like to pretend to be something else, as if a suggestion of a masque appeals to the city') with Denis Glover. Glover, a 'rumbustious stentorian character', was a poet, journalist, typographer and publisher. '"I tell you," he roared at me, "I want to go and tell the English people what I think about them." To which I replied, without asperity, "And I tell *you* — the English people wouldn't care a damn what you thought about them." And I liked him even more for the bellow of laughter this brought from him.'

Glover sent Priestley his collection of poems *Enter Without Knocking,* which the English author enjoyed. In his New Zealand travelogue Priestley quoted part of a short poem he thought both sardonic and sad, for British and American readers not familiar with Glover's work. Glover had had a drinking problem for many years.

> He saw himself with some surprise
> A sorry sod with headlamp eyes
> AFORE YE GO the slogan read,
> But he stayed on and stared ahead
>
> DENIS GLOVER, 'Solitary Drinker'

Priestley visited the Alexander Turnbull Library after lunch. He wanted to see the prints and watercolours by the early settlers to include some in his book. He chose two pictures to reproduce in *A Visit to New Zealand* and was gifted two portfolios of prints, *Six Views* by Sir William Fox and *Five Early Views of the Hutt and Wairarapa* by Captain William Mein Smith. He considered the pictures a nice reminder of his time in Wellington and the 'splendid' Alexander Turnbull Library.

At first Alexander Horsburgh Turnbull kept his collection of books and artworks at his home and by the turn of the century he presided over an impressive library and reference centre. In his latter days Turnbull moved himself and his collection into a nearby Victorian-Tudor brick building on Bowen Street, opposite Parliament House. He died in 1918, bequeathing the Crown around 55,000 volumes as well as manuscripts, paintings and sketches, to be kept together 'as the nucleus of a New Zealand National Collection'. The Crown bought his house to hold the works and 'The Alexander Turnbull Library' was born. In 1973 the burgeoning collection was moved again and it's now part of the National Library opposite the Wellington Cathedral in Molesworth Street. Turnbull House survived the threat of demolition and is now a conference and community centre run by the Department of Conservation.

'There's nothing in Canada to compare with the magnificent libraries little New Zealand can show,' Rupert Brooke wrote in one of his *Westminster Gazette* articles, 'The Prairies'. George Bernard Shaw compared the Alexander Turnbull Library to one of the great libraries of the world. It was a 'treasure house' that 'would even make the Bodleian sit up'. Shaw asked, much to the amusement of a library attendant, whether a visitor always got the book they requested. 'If he asks for Whitaker's Almanac, do you say "I'm afraid it is out, but here is a volume of plays by Bernard Shaw which is much more interesting?" Because, if you did, he would go away with it quite satisfied.'

Inaugural Turnbull librarian, poet and historian Johannes C. Andersen wrote an account of Shaw's visit in the *Evening Post*. Andersen showed the Shaws a copy of the first English translation of the *Decameron* printed three years before the First Folio of Shakespeare in 1623, and Kelmscott Press books including one about Godfrey of Boulogne, 'reckoned to be one of the best ornamented books of English typography'. Mrs Shaw asked what was considered to be the library's main treasure and Andersen said he would choose the copy of Domett's *Ranolf and Amohia*, autographed for his friend Robert Browning. Shaw made 'one of his characteristic remarks' shortly after arriving but Andersen wrote that he would not repeat it and 'one realised that after the hour or so spent in Mr Shaw's company that he had a solid love of good English literature and beautiful English printing and English natural beauty; and, except for one minute, the person a certain English critic called Bernard Pshaw [*sic*] was only a mask covering a very estimable character'.

'In a raw young land such a literary oasis is like a Gothic Cathedral in the midst of a suburb of modern villas,' enthused Arthur Conan Doyle. He passed 'a mellow hour' among the Turnbull's treasures and said that if he lived in Wellington he would spend a lot of time there. He saw the first edition of *Robinson Crusoe*, published in three volumes in 1719 with a 'delightful map of the island which would charm any boy'. Conan Doyle assumed it would have been drawn with Defoe's help. He also saw a first edition of Coleridge and Wordsworth's *Lyrical Ballads*; an original Hakluyt; Kelmscott's *Chaucer*; a Plutarch and Montaigne; Captain Cook's *Diary*, 'written in the stiff hand of a very methodical man'; and a rare edition of Swinburne's *Poems and Ballads*. Conan Doyle also found a description of what he termed a Maori séance that he read as a literal account. Even more proof of life after death, he thought.

After the Turnbull Priestley continued his odyssey at a New Zealand Symphony Orchestra rehearsal. He resumed acquaintance with Alec Lindsay, the leader of the orchestra, whom he had met and written about in his book *Trumpets Over the Sea* when the musician was leader of the second violins in the London Symphony Orchestra (LSO). The book chronicled the LSO's season in Florida in 1967.

Priestley lectured at Victoria University in the evening. His performance was called 'Duality in the Drama', a new title for an old lecture he'd published as 'The Art of the Dramatist'. The day was capped with a reception in his honour.

> On the way home I reflected, no doubt a trifle muzzily, on the wide scope of this Wellington day. Consider it! — all the media in the morning; a poet at lunch; early settlers and old watercolours, then music, in the afternoon; the nature of drama in the evening; and the night bringing a rollicking good party. And I remembered what I had been told when I had decided on paying this visit: 'A beautiful country but otherwise dull,' they had said, 'terribly dull people, old boy'.

An author's visit to New Zealand wasn't always widely publicised, especially back in the nineteenth century. But one Wellington bookseller discovered the great Rudyard Kipling was arriving for a holiday and was determined to meet the author in person. Cuba Street bookseller Herbert Baillie of Baillie Bros arranged with another Kipling enthusiast, *New Zealand Times* proofreader Tom L. Mills, to go down to the port to meet the *Doric.* Mills slept in, but Baillie got to the port, found Kipling and offered to show the famous author around the city. A shipping reporter, who had no idea who Kipling was but was intrigued by Baillie's interest in the visitor, trailed them. Kipling and Baillie got on so well that they remained in contact after the author's visit. As they walked along Lambton Quay, Baillie offered to take Kipling to the national museum, a small wooden building tucked behind the Parliament Buildings in what is now Museum Street.

After the museum Kipling made his way to the Wellington Club where he met R.A. Loughnan, the editor of the *New Zealand Times.* Kipling claimed that he had never willingly submitted to an interview in his life yet he gave Loughnan a 'whole column of it'. The editor sensed 'the scoop of a lifetime' and in an extraordinary coincidence he went to see Mills, the proofreader and admirer of Kipling who'd lost his opportunity to see the author after oversleeping that morning. At midnight Loughnan told Mills that he interviewed Kipling, who insisted on seeing a proof before the paper could print it. Kipling proclaimed the article 'Rotten!' and derided its lack of a proper beginning or ending. The editor pleaded with Kipling who took the proof-slip, saying he would 'round it off as a good interview should be rounded off'. He added to the article,

> He (that is R.K. talking to the editor) tells a story of having in India interviewed a dentist who had travelled into Afghanistan and there pulled the eye-tooth of His Highness the Amir of Afghanistan. The ceremony was performed in open court and the steadiness of the operator's hand was increased by the knowledge that His Highness had full power and might have had the inclination to decapitate him on the spot.

Tom Mills was given the proof-slip adorned with Kipling's handwriting. He cut off the handwritten part and put it in his scrapbook. Years later Mills read a statement made by Kipling to Sir Robertson Nicoll, the editor of the *Bookman* and the *British Weekly*. The author claimed never to have 'granted an interview to any newspaper as he abominated interviews for publication'. So Mills photographed the piece of paper from his scrapbook and submitted it along with his story to the *Bookman*. Mills wrote that Kipling was shown the slip and remarked 'New Zealand, eh? Ah, I had forgotten that!'

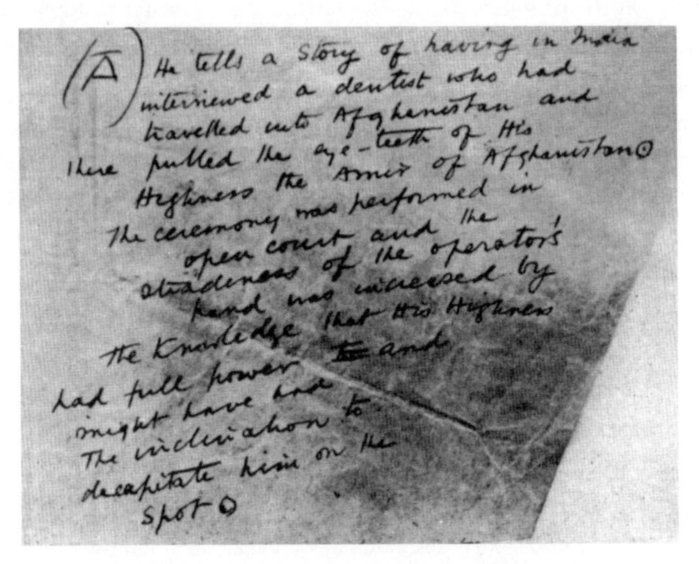

(A) He tells a story of having in India
interviewed a dentist who had
travelled into Afghanistan and
there pulled the eye-teeth of His
Highness the Amir of Afghanistan ⊙
The ceremony was performed in
open court and the
steadiness of the operator's
hand was increased by
the knowledge that His Highness
had full power ~~to~~ and
might have had
the inclination to
decapitate him on the
spot ⊙

THE PROOF-SLIP TOM L. MILLS KEPT FEATURING RUDYARD KIPLING'S HANDWRITING. Reproduced by permission of The Kipling Society from the Kipling Journal No.57, April 1941, p.15.

Kipling enjoyed a boating picnic in a calm Wellington Harbour with 'ten beautiful maidens' who took him 'for a row in a big canoe by moonlight'. Wellington reminded Kipling of Portland, Oregon. He liked the city and its people who were 'large, long-eyelashed, and extraordinarily good-looking'. Kipling had left his card at the club announcing himself to the 'station' as was the Anglo-Indian custom, and stayed at the Occidental Hotel at the corner of Lambton Quay and Johnston Street. The four-storey mostly brick building, with about fifty bedrooms and numerous 'elegantly appointed' rooms for eating and socialising, was popular with business travellers before it burned down. A special correspondent for the *Press* tracked Kipling to the Occidental and described meeting the 25-year-old:

> He is rather below middle height, youthful-looking, and slightly built, with a great air of briskness and activity, almost of restlessness as if always on springs. His hair is dark, but his eyes are blue, and the latter he has a way now and then of fixing on you with a peculiar intensity for a moment or two during

> conversation, this being always followed immediately by the utterance of some bright spontaneous idea felicitously and originally expressed.

Kipling wore bifocal glasses and had trimmed his famous moustache for an acting role on board ship. He suggested a walk and the two men discussed his books. The reporter asked Kipling which of his books was the favourite of New Zealanders. Kipling suggested *Soldiers Three* and *The Gadsbys* — which the reporter thought was the favourite among Wellingtonians — and Kipling was pleased to hear it. He was loathe to talk more about his books, saying, 'I have come out for a regular "loaf", and to get out of the reach of letters and telegrams and business generally, as well as for the sea voyage and to see those parts of the world I have not visited before. Of course I shall do a little work when I feel disposed, but not as a regular thing. As I do not mean to talk at all about my books, I am sure you will understand me this is to be simply "loaf".' But he didn't want to visit the South Island as it was too cold. The reporter suggested that surely he wanted to see the island's 'special features of interest'.

> 'Ah, but that's just where it is,' he replied. 'It is these features of interest I am afraid of, and I know just what it would be. I went through it all in America. They would be most timid in wanting to show me things, but they would insist on taking me to see all their new buildings, and factories, and freezing works, and corn, and stock, and so forth. Someone would point to a big building and say. "Look there, the foundation of that was only laid eighteen months ago, and by gad, sir, look at it now! What do you think of that?" No; I have gone through it all before. The South is too prosperous and go-ahead, and productive, and all that, and I don't want to see buildings and products.'

Kipling's health failed him in Wellington. He suffered a malaria relapse, an illness he'd contracted in India. He didn't show for a further meeting with the reporter scheduled for the following night. He sent a note saying, 'I find that yesterday's chill has started my old friend the fever upon the warpath anew, and unless I want a new set of chills I must get out of this place at once for something warmer. It's an annoying nuisance, because it stops my coming up tonight. However, I hope to be back in Wellington by Friday or Saturday week, after a run through the Hot Lakes. Very sincerely yours, Rudyard Kipling.'

Kipling wanted to travel up the North Island and leave Auckland for Samoa to visit Robert Louis Stevenson, before heading for Africa and India, possibly visiting Australia on the way. But he failed to get the steamer connection he needed to travel to Samoa, so he was forced to go to the South Island, to sail from Bluff to Melbourne.

Mark Twain's enduring problems on the railways delayed his arrival in Wellington. His first performance was cancelled but those already holding tickets were able to go the following night and that night's ticket holders were moved onto another night. There was no time to fit in an extra performance before he was due to sail for Sydney, however, so there were some disappointed customers. One Wellington reporter commented that the author was interested in 'colonial character, with a view to the inevitable book, but finds the urban population much like the urban population elsewhere, for travel is reducing the world to a terrible sameness'. It was written that Olivia Clemens hoped to find a 'quiet spot in Africa' where it was acceptable for 'interviewers and autograph hunters to be shot on sight', so that 'composition might go on undisturbed', even though her comment sounded very Twain-like.

Booker Prize-winner Salman Rushdie's visit in 1995 was surrounded by too much publicity. Rushdie had been in hiding since Iranian leader Ayatollah Khomeini issued a fatwa against him after the publication of his novel *The Satanic Verses* in 1989. The author was accused of blasphemy and a $2.5 million bounty was put on his head. He survived a few attempts on his life, including one that resulted in a would-be assassin's death as he was preparing a book bomb in a Paddington hotel room. Rushdie was appearing in public by 1995 but usually with only an hour or two's notice. The purpose of his New Zealand trip was to promote his first novel in seven years, *The Moor's Last Sigh*. But the Wellington *Evening Post* announced his visit the day before his arrival in Auckland on Friday, 1 December, and stated he would be appearing at the Parkroyal Hotel on the following Monday. The newspaper claimed the information came from his publisher, Random House. Security was stepped up and two armed diplomatic protection squad men met Rushdie when he arrived at Auckland International Airport. The New Zealand Muslim community publicly distanced itself from the death sentence and, despite the security concerns, Rushdie appeared in public as scheduled. The Iranian Embassy expressed its disappointment regarding 'arrangements made available for Salman Rushdie'.

Rushdie told the *Evening Post* in the early days of the fatwa he received offers of sanctuary from New Zealanders: 'I would get letters from people offering me their homes. "We live in the South Island, there's nobody anywhere for miles, please come and stay." I have so far not taken up any of their offers, but it was very nice to have them.' The man 'with a well-bred English accent', who was 'open and friendly, with a sense of humour and ease unexpected in a man whose life is constantly threatened', talked about the strain of the fatwa, including damage to his family life and the decision to protect his young son by staying away from him. In 1998 Iran's president announced that the death sentence would not be carried out, but hardliners in the country have periodically claimed the fatwa is still valid.

Wellington played host to a meeting between two intrepid explorer-writers at the turn of the century. Captain J.C. Voss circumnavigated the world in a Native American dugout canoe and wrote about his exploits in *The Venturesome Voyages of Captain Voss*. He exhibited his canoe, the *Tilikum*, in a large Wellington hall to some six hundred people. It was the first time Voss had addressed an audience from a stage and to overcome stage fright, he heeded some advice to imagine the sea of heads as a field of cabbages. After an hour's talk, his mate, Mr Buckridge, took over and lectured about his experiences with Captain Scott's South Pole expedition in the *Discovery*. He told a story about the crew taking whisky from the officer's stateroom, freezing it in the snow and eating it like ice cream. When he neared the end of the yarn 'his voice suddenly dropped, his eyes widened, and he looked very much bewildered,' wrote Voss. He whispered the rest of his speech, the crowd applauded and gathered around the *Tilikum*. Voss was about to ask his mate if he was sick when 'a handsome young gentleman stepped up to the stage and, shaking hands with Buckridge, said with a smile: "I could never understand what became of my whisky!" He was none other than Lieutenant Ernest Shackleton, of the *Discovery*.'

Sir Arthur Conan Doyle's visit caused all sorts of strange happenings according to the *New Zealand Freelance*. There was a rise in 'spook investigations', circles were formed all over the place, amateur mediums were in demand and 'tales of table-tiltings, table-knockings, and all sorts of uncanny messages are quite as common now at afternoon tea as the strawberries and cream, or as the waffles and maple syrup'.

Once known as the 'Empire City', Wellington's late Victorian character survived deep into the twentieth century. In the 1960s James Morris described the capital as an 'old-fashioned, genial provincial city'. He thought Wellington, like England, breathed an 'endearing but mystifying air of gameness', an attitude of getting through life by being cheerful.

> Nobody, you feel, is going to let you down or cheat you, slow though they may be in completing your commissions, and second-rate though the finished job may be. Some people find Wellington prim and stodgy, and prefer the sour ebullience of Sydney, or even Auckland's semi-American bustle. I much liked the taste of this little capital though, and found its character much more tart and stimulating than I expected — more varied in colour and more dramatic in posture, windier, woodener, more comically stiff of upper lip, and unexpectedly ennobled, like San Francisco, by that queen of the tramlines, the cable car.

Wellington was a 'cold, snobbish, lower middle-class colony of pretentious nobodies,' declared D.H. Lawrence. His acerbic opinion was formed when he and his wife Frieda stopped over in the city in 1922. They were en route to San Francisco from Australia and Lawrence had difficulty in obtaining a landing card for German-born Frieda. The couple were eventually allowed ashore and although the experience had put him in bad mood, Lawrence used his time in Wellington to heal a personal rift. He sent New Zealand's most famous author, Katherine Mansfield, a postcard bearing one word 'Ricordi' ('Remembrances'). The writers had a volatile relationship and in 1920 Lawrence severed the friendship by sending Mansfield a letter in which he wrote 'I loathe you. You revolt me stewing in your consumption …' According to Katherine's husband John Middleton Murry, Lawrence also said, 'You are a loathsome reptile — I hope you will die.' Katherine, who was suffering from the tuberculosis that would kill her, eventually forgave her friend, leaving him a book in her will.

(FROM LEFT) JOHN MIDDLETON MURRY, FRIEDA LAWERENCE AND D.H. (DAVID HERBERT) LAWRENCE IN LONDON, 1914 (PHOTOGRAPHER UNKNOWN). ALEXANDER TURNBULL LIBRARY, WELLINGTON, NEW ZEALAND. F-28642-1/2.

'Wellington is trim and neat and English; it reminds you of a seaport town on the South Coast,' wrote Somerset Maugham in his novel *The Moon and Sixpence*, based loosely on the life of artist Paul Gauguin. Maugham and his lover Gerald Haxton stayed at the Midland Hotel, a new Spanish Mission style building that used to stand in what is now Midland Park off Lambton Quay, on their way between Samoa and Tahiti in 1917. New Zealand was 'extraordinarily English', Maugham wrote to a friend. He had expected Wellington to resemble 'a city in the Western states', but it was 'much more like Bristol or Plymouth' and made him feel slightly homesick.

'In the winter [the winds] spring rasping out of the Antarctic, scurry and scour through the hilly streets of the capital, and so shake the frames of the suburban houses that you feel yourself to be actually at sea, in some stout old wooden-waller plugging down to Lyttelton,' wrote James Morris. To Morris, wind symbolised Wellington. 'If I wished to represent [Wellington] on a decorative map, I would inscribe there a zephyr-kiwi, perpetually puffing out its snout.' Morris visited the capital in winter and found a 'city of toasted sandwiches and steaming tea in shamelessly stuffy cafes, washed by the driving rains, dappled by splendid bursts of sun and cloud, always quaint and fragrant with wood'.

Agatha Christie also visited in winter but she was in the city on a 'perfect day'. Arthur Conan Doyle drove 'down the bay' to the summerhouse of Dr Morrice, an old friend and the husband of the daughter of the late Premier Richard Seddon, on a typically windy day. The hat belonging to Conan Doyle's agent, Smythe, 'disappeared with such velocity that no one was able to say what had become of it. It simply was, and then it was not,' wrote Conan Doyle. Despite the buffeting, the author noticed the prettiness of the harbour. 'The yellow of the foreshore, the green of the shallows, the blue mottled with purple of the deep, all fretted with lines of foam, made an exhilarating sight.'

'Oh — to be a Wellingtonian and to live, without going to an office, in one of those little houses!' wrote Priestley after surveying the city from Mt Victoria at the eastern edge of the city early in his visit. Wellington's 'distant clusters of little houses, brightly painted, ravished the eye and kindled the imagination'. But after a week in Wellington Priestley's affection for the capital waned, and he bemoaned the frighteningly steep hills and thought the city had an 'untidy unfinished look'. He was disapproving of weekenders sunning themselves at Makara Beach, 16 kilometres north of Wellington, as the grumpy old author thought beach-goers displayed an 'element of vanity'. Girls and women appeared to enjoy flaunting their figures and 'even some members of my own sterner and nobler sex have what we might call "a magnificent-torso complex"'. A nearby scene reminded him of his favourite place to paint, the west of Ireland. But he wrote that it lacked Ireland's 'curious magic', perhaps partly because he wasn't familiar with Maori myths and legends and because New Zealand didn't have a poet as great as Yeats.

Priestley grumbled about Wellington and at least one Wellingtonian grumbled back. In *A Visit To New Zealand* he quoted an article written after he had held a poorly attended press conference. 'He came in slowly and hesitantly, a bit like a sleepy old bulldog early disturbed. He was dressed informally; baggy grey slacks, black carpet slippers, badly stained unpressed jacket, stringy tie ...' In his defence Priestley claimed that 'only the first three words are strictly accurate: I did come in. The rest is on the wild side.' He critiqued each statement in turn.

> I was only dressed informally if a black cutaway morning coat, grey striped trousers, a stiff high collar and a silk cravat had been expected; and after all this was neither a wedding nor a funeral. The slacks I was wearing were not baggy but are in fact rather too tight. My slippers were neither black nor carpet. Certainly my jacket was unpressed, but then Wellington was leaving me barely time to shave, let alone sending clothes to be pressed. I think this reporter must have been sitting some distance away from me.

Priestley was hurt by the criticism and consoled himself with the memory of an adoring fan. 'The only person sitting very close was an extremely pretty girl, who never said a word but gazed and gazed at me, perhaps memorising those stains on my jacket. However, she cannot have thought I looked like a bulldog or she would have sat further away, well out of biting range.' Priestley was also impressed with New Zealand's broadcasters. 'There was less huffing and puffing and fussing in New Zealand studios than I had found anywhere else. Whatever else the New Zealander may be, he is no fusspot. This helped to confirm ... that behind the country's easy and casual manner and style there is an uncommon ability to organise things both efficiently and coolly.'

A 'hectic and crowded' Wellington awaited Noël Coward in 1941. There was controversy over whether some of his lyrics were suitable for broadcast to a New Zealand public. It 'flung me into a rage and I said firmly that either the concert must be broadcast in its entirety as arranged or not broadcast at all. The battle raged for several hours and I was ultimately victorious.' After the concert Coward had a 'slight set-to' with the Mayoress, who it seemed to him either 'suffered from delusions of grandeur' or from an attempt to overcompensate for extreme shyness.

> She said to me in ringing tones that I was never to dare to sing 'The Stately Homes of England' again as it was an insult to the homeland and that neither she nor anybody else liked it. I replied coldly that for many years it had been one of my greatest successes, whereupon she announced triumphantly to everyone within earshot: 'You see — he can't take criticism!' Irritated beyond endurance

I replied that I was perfectly prepared to take intelligent criticism at any time, but I was not prepared to tolerate bad manners. With this I bowed austerely and left the party.

NOËL COWARD SPEAKING AT THE WELLINGTON TRAVEL CLUB, FEBRUARY 1941
(PHOTOGRAPHER IRENE KOPPEL). IRENE KOPPEL COLLECTION, ALEXANDER TURNBULL LIBRARY, WELLINGTON, NEW ZEALAND. PACOLL-6497-16-4-1.

Afterwards Coward regretted losing his temper in public. He felt people in the public eye were sometimes unfairly attacked and wrote he had thought about establishing a society for the 'Prevention of Mental Cruelty to Celebrities'. 'The worst offenders are those women whose self-righteous egocentricity makes them wish to impress the celebrity than be impressed by him. These crusaders cherish the belief that forthright criticism, preferably in public, is more admirable than conventional politeness ... In this belief they are, alas, misguided ... They will be remembered, not for their moral courage, but for their lack of social grace.' Coward attended other functions without incident, including one jointly arranged by the Wellington Travel Club and other organisations. In his speech Coward claimed England was 'the only nation in the world that can support strength without abusing it'. He sang four songs, much to the delight of his audience.

After 'having minutely examined' Wellington and making himself the 'perfect master of the whole natural history and process of manufacture of the flax-plant, with its splendid yellow blossoms', Mr Booley journeyed to a 'Native Pa' — in his mind. He was surprised to find the pa was a town, not a parent. He was welcomed by a Maori chief with a long spear and saw Europeans and Maori rubbing noses. After getting involved in a fight between Maori and English soldiers, during which the Maori were woefully defeated, he 'plunged into the Bush, and there camped out for some months, until he had made a survey of the whole country'.

WITH A LOST SOUL AS MY GUIDE

'I AM AFRAID THAT THE average Britisher looks upon New Zealand as one solid island,' wrote Arthur Conan Doyle in *The Wanderings of a Spiritualist*. 'If he had to cross Cook's Strait to get from the northern to the southern half, he would never forget his lesson in geography.' Cook Strait separates the North and South islands and has a reputation for churning seas and wild southerlies. Travel writer James Morris described the waters as 'some of the choppiest and queasiest on earth'. The crossing is essentially east-west and twenty kilometres at its narrowest point it 'can be as nasty a bit of water as is to be found in the world, with ocean waves, mountain winds and marine currents all combining into a horrible chaos,' wrote Conan Doyle. He was in Cook Strait twice, firstly on a night boat from Wellington bound for Lyttelton and then when he left New Zealand for Australia. His first experience was a comfortable one. But as he departed on the *Paloona* he found himself 'steaming in a sharp wind' down its 'very turbulent waters'.

On 7 February 1770 Captain James Cook came close to shipwreck as he explored the strait that bears his name. Cook and the crew of the *Endeavour* narrowly escaped the rocks of what is now known as Brothers Island, after they left Queen Charlotte Sound and were navigating the strait. Cook avoided disaster by 'bringing the Ship to an Anchor in 73 fathoms water, with 150 fathoms of cable out. Even this would not have saved us had not the tide, which first set S. by E., by meeting with the island changed its direction to S.E. and carried us past the first point.' Almost a hundred and thirty years after Dutch explorer Abel Tasman reached New Zealand, Cook became the first

European commander to sail between the North and South Islands.

> A little before 12 o'clock the tide abated, and we began to heave; by 3 the anchor was at the bows, and having a light breeze at N.W., we made sail over for the eastern shore; but having the tide against us we made but little way. The wind afterwards freshened, and came to N. and N.E., with which and the tide of Ebb we were in a short time hurried thro' the narrowest part of the Strait, and then stood away for the southernmost land we had in sight, which bore us S. by W.

'The place is full of Cook's memory,' wrote Conan Doyle. He proudly declared that having seen Cook's work he would 'feel full of reverence' every time he passed the explorer's statue in front of London's Admiralty building.

> Everywhere the great man has left his traces … So coolly and deliberately did he do his work that even now his charting holds good, I understand, in many long stretches of coast. Tacking and wearing, he poked and pried into every estuary, naming capes, defining bays, plotting out positions, and yet all the while at the mercy of the winds, with a possible lee shore always before him, with no comrade within hail, and with swarms of cannibals eyeing his little ship from the beach.

Although there were 'several excellent harbours' in Cook Strait the ones on the North Island were dangerous because they were battered by southerly gales, wrote Joel Samuel Polack in *Manners and Customs of the New Zealanders*. 'The southerly gales commence with great force about ten o'clock in the morning, increasing in violence until they terminate in gales accompanied by squalls, raising heavy seas in the channel, which are further augmented as the opposing tide takes place, towards sunset,' he wrote. 'The violence of the gale then subsides, and within an hour after the disappearance of the great luminary a perfect calm prevails, which generally continues during the night and following morning, until about nine o'clock, when the same warring of the elements is repeated. During these gales the weather is pleasant overhead, a calm blue prevails in the sky, save those fleecy clouds termed by nautical men, as "Cats' paws and mares' tails", which but ill describe the strife of the elements.'

Captain Harry Neville 'experienced that vague and ancient delight of feeling the old boat pitch and toss upon the first waters he had ever sailed'. James Michener's creation crossed Cook Strait on his way to Christchurch in 1939 for his daughter Barbara's wedding in the short story *Until They Sail*, published in Michener's 1951 book *Return to Paradise*. Neville, a New Zealander, volunteered for the British Navy and often returned to his home country, crossing Cook Strait as he did so. He was on the ferry when he first decided to join the British Navy. Years later he was on the ferry when he heard about the birth of his first daughter Anne during the First World War. Neville's return this time, however, preceded a succession of tragic events.

Michener voyaged to around fifty islands during the Second World War with the US Navy and the experience inspired his Pulitzer Prize-winning first novel, *Tales of the South Pacific*. The best-selling American novelist was eager to revisit the Pacific and an assignment for *Holiday* allowed him to return to the places he'd seen during the war. The trip also produced *Return to Paradise,* a type of book Michener didn't think anyone else had attempted. He wrote a series of non-fiction essays and partnered each with a short story. 'Thus the reader could see from the essay what I thought about a given island; while from the fictional story he could determine what the island thought about itself.'

Approaching the South Island the 'wind was so strong that it pushed Véronique's blue bonnet off, and lifted the short fair curls that had taken the place of the lost ringlets right up from her head as though it had endowed each one with a joyful life of its own'. Her father William 'picked his little daughter up in his arms and pointed to the faint lovely coastline ahead of them. "Look, Véronique," he said. "There's *your* country, your own special country where you will grow up to be a happy woman. It is called the Country of the Green Pastures."' Crossing Cook Strait was a new start for Elizabeth Goudge's immigrant family in *Green Dolphin Country*. The epic nineteenth century tale tells of how William Ozanne, his wife Marianne and their young daughter, Véronique, are driven from the North Island by a series of hardships, including a violent earthquake and capture by Maori, and they move south intending to become sheep farmers. The seemingly implausible plot of *Green Dolphin Country* involves a bizarre misunderstanding. After settling in New Zealand, William proposes to the wrong woman by mixing up the names of two sisters in a letter home and only realises the mistake when his prospective bride arrives in Port Nicholson. But she has sailed halfway around the world, so he goes through with the marriage. Goudge claimed her novel was based on fact — that a man who had immigrated to the New World wrote home after many years and mixed up the name of his intended bride with that of her sister. Like Goudge's William, he kept quiet.

Goudge hadn't visited New Zealand when she wrote *Green Dolphin Country* and acknowledged her debt to F.E. Maning's *Old New Zealand*. Irish-born Frederick Edward Maning immigrated with his family to Australia in 1823 and settled in New Zealand as a young man. He was an adventurer who worked as a trader and later a Native Land Court judge. Maning lived with a Maori woman and had four children by her. In the mid-1840s he organised supplies for the government's Maori allies against Hone Heke and he began writing *A history of the war in the north of New Zealand against the chief Heke*. His *Old New Zealand* was a reference work for many early literary visitors. Since its release in 1944 *Green Dolphin*

Country (published as *Green Dolphin Street* in the United States) has sold more than a million copies. The 1947 movie of the novel grossed more than $5 million at the box office and won an Academy Award for special effects.

Anthony Trollope thought the land around Cook Strait suggested a mysterious and exciting world; even though it was just an illusion. He was travelling north from Wellington to Auckland, but his ship headed south first, crossing Cook Strait to touch at both Picton and Nelson at the top of the South Island.

> The headlands and broken bays, with the rough steep mountains coming sheer down into the blue waters, the closeness of the land, and the narrowness of the passages, all tend to create a mysterious charm, which he who gazes at them finds himself unable to analyze. He feels tempted to land at every gully which runs up among the mountains and to investigate the strange wild world which must be beyond them. He knows, in truth, that there is nothing there, — that one brown hill would lead only to another, that there is no life among the hills, and that the very spots on which his eyes rest really contain whatever there may be of loveliness in the place. But though he knows this as fact, his imagination will not allow him to trust his knowledge. There is always present to him a vague longing to investigate the mysteries of the valleys, and to penetrate into the bosoms of the distant hills. The sweetest charms of landscape are as those of life; — they consist of the anticipations of something beyond which never can be reached. I never felt this more strongly than when I was passing from one land-locked channel to another along the coast of Cook's Strait.

Picton is a small town on the shores of Queen Charlotte Sound and the arrival point for today's Cook Strait ferries. Trollope thought Picton a 'pretty, straggling, picturesque little town, lying as do all these New Zealand ports, pressed in between the mountains and the sea'. It had a fine climate, produced an abundance of English fruits and was framed by lush green fields. The only road out led to what was then a rival town, Blenheim. A couple of ships arrived at the port each week. But it had a 'general look of sleepy, well-fed prosperity' with 'good shops and tidy houses, and pretty gardens,' wrote Trollope.

Although he didn't visit the site, Trollope wrote of the 'Wairau Massacre', which was 'one of the beginnings of the rebellion of the Maoris against their English masters'. The battle of Wairau erupted in June 1843 after settlers arrived to survey the valley. Maori denied selling the land and when Ngati Toa chiefs Te Rauparaha and Te Rangihaeata disrupted the surveyors' work the settlers attempted to arrest them. A fight ensued and a stray shot killed Te Rangihaeata's wife, Te Rongo. Nine settlers surrendered, only to be killed to avenge Te Rongo's death. Twenty-two Pakeha were killed in the fighting, including Arthur Wakefield, the brother of Edward Gibbon Wakefield, the founder of the New Zealand Company. 'After the massacre Rauparaha and Rangihaeta were not taken,' wrote Trollope, 'and there arose a question, not only whether there was force enough in the country to apprehend them, but whether they were subject to English writs. It will easily be understood how such doings as this would shake the prestige of their British masters in the minds of these New Zealand savages.'

George Bernard Shaw arrived in Picton in April 1934 on the Union Steamship Company's *Tamahine*, a 2000-ton, 400-passenger vessel that plied the Cook Strait from 1925 to 1962. He spent a quiet night at his hotel and no ceremony surrounded his short visit. He continued to criticise New Zealand's dependency on Britain, however. Shaw pictured a 'Britain sick of being badgered, battered and kicked by her rapidly growing Dominions and withdrawing from the Empire'. In New Zealand's defence a reporter in Picton highlighted the Dominion's support of the 'Old Country' by sending troops to the Great War. 'You went into it out of pure devilment. You need not have sent those troops unless you had liked. You could have joined the Germans if you liked,' Shaw retaliated. In the early 1960s James Morris observed a tension between New Zealanders who distrusted Britain for strengthening its ties with Europe, and Englishmen living in New Zealand, who felt New Zealanders were being obstructive. He got the impression Australians thought it was 'high time' Britain entered the Common Market, but that across the Tasman there was concern and cynicism about Britain's new direction. New Zealand's independence was only political, he wrote in the *Guardian*. 'The Australian is becoming a new man, as Crèvecœur said of the American long ago: but the New Zealander's head is still the same shape as ours, and we unmistakably share a blood group.'

From Picton, Trollope sailed back up Queen Charlotte Sound, into Cook Strait and west towards D'Urville Island, named after the French explorer, en route to Nelson. Just before D'Urville Island the ship turned south again, entering Admiralty Bay, 'another of the wonderful land-locked harbours with which the coast is indented'.

It was around Admiralty Bay where Frank Bullen encountered 'the most interesting and extraordinary sight in the world connected with natural history'. Bullen was crossing Cook Strait from Nelson to Wellington. He had heard all the stories about the sightings of the mysterious 'Pelorus Jack' but wanted to see it with his own eyes. The author spent many years on a whaling ship and had a special interest in sea creatures. It was late afternoon, the ship had cleared the 'foaming, whirling' French Pass that separates the top of the South Island from the rugged D'Urville Island and the forecastle was crowded with passengers staring into the water. Pelorus Jack was at the starboard bow and easily kept pace with the vessel travelling at a swift 14 and a half knots. Only the slightest quiver of its tail was noticeable. Sometimes the creature darted from starboard to port by 'pausing for a few moments right ahead of the swiftly moving ship, then, dropping astern a few feet, he would cuddle up lovingly against her side, turning over as he did so, as if he enjoyed feeling her chafe against his body', Bullen wrote in *Advance Australasia.*

Pelorus Jack was a large grey dolphin that swam alongside ships travelling between Wellington and Nelson from 1888 to 1912. It was originally called 'the big white fish' before being named after Pelorus Sound to the south of Admiralty Bay. 'Jack' was added, probably in a whaling tradition (in *Moby Dick* there is a whale called 'New Zealand Jack'). The dolphin became the subject of a popular children's song and a chocolate fish.

It sought out steamers around the stretch of water across Admiralty Bay, north of French Pass, the narrow passage of water that ships journeyed through to reach Tasman Bay and the port of Nelson, and played around the bow, sometimes rubbing itself against the plates, for as long as twenty minutes. Locals claimed the dolphin preferred faster ships. But a sheep farmer who met the steamers twice a week to exchange mail said he had to push Pelorus Jack away from his dinghy in case the dolphin's vigorous rubbing capsized the boat.

There were various theories as to why the dolphin, whose sex was never discovered, was so friendly. Some thought the creature had lost its mother before being weaned. Others suggested it was isolated from its herd because it might have been an albino like Moby Dick. Some say it rubbed against ships to tear barnacles off its body. A more fanciful suggestion was that the dolphin was guiding ships through the dangerous waters of French Pass. Those who claimed the creature never entered the pass because it always stayed on the Wellington side disputed this notion. It may simply have enjoyed swimming in the ship's bow wave. There are several Maori legends about Pelorus Jack, or Kaikaiawaro, 'food of the deep'. The creature was believed to be an incarnation of a sea god that escorted Ngati Kuia descendants in the sounds hundreds of years ago.

The species of Risso's dolphins in Cook Strait were protected under an Order-in-Council of the New Zealand government after someone tried to shoot Pelorus Jack. This unprecedented act in 1904 brought Pelorus Jack international fame. Tourists crossed the Cook Strait just to see Jack and bought postcards of the dolphin on which it was written 'The only fish [*sic*] in the world to be protected by law.' It became so famous that an artist's impression graced the front page of the *London News* in December 1910. The picture accompanied a story that Pelorus Jack harboured the spirit of a Frenchman, Jacques Trégoulet, who drowned while trying to rescue a countryman. It was also written that Pelorus Jack always avoided one particular ship, because the vessel had hit it.

In his autobiography *Something of Myself* Kipling wrote that at Wellington he was met 'precisely where warned to expect him, by "Pelorus Jack", the big, white-marked dolphin, who held it his duty to escort shipping up the harbour'. But it's unlikely Kipling saw the creature and there is no report of the dolphin ever being sighted in Wellington Harbour. In the *Kipling Journal* in 1963 J.B. Primrose wrote, 'I have come to the conclusion that although

Kipling's memory of his long-past visit to New Zealand and Australia was hazy and often inaccurate, when he wrote *Something of Myself* about forty-five years later, there is usually a substratum of fact in what he remembers, and we shall have to leave it at that.'

Pelorus Jack was last seen around 1912. Speculation about the cause of the dolphin's disappearance continued for years. 'What has become of "Pelorus Jack"? Was he a lost soul?' asked a prominent newspaper advertisement in 1920. It had been placed by an 'ex-Spiritualist medium' publicising a show he was staging at the Town Hall in Auckland. It was scheduled to take place the night after Arthur Conan Doyle held a similar event at the same venue. Conan Doyle's rival promised 'terrifying revelations', including a solution to the mystery of Pelorus Jack. The creator of Sherlock Holmes was not impressed. 'Now, "Pelorus Jack" was a white dolphin, who at one time used to pilot vessels into a New Zealand harbour, gambolling under the bows,' wrote Conan Doyle, 'so that question really did raise curiosity. However, I learned afterwards that my successor did not reap the harvest which his ingenuity deserved, and that the audience was scanty and derisive. What the real psychic meaning of "Pelorus Jack" may have been was not recorded by the press.'

Mark Twain once worked as a licensed Mississippi riverboat pilot. His interest wasn't in legendary sea creatures but the practicalities of navigating a ship through the narrow and difficult French Pass. The author was sailing to Nelson from Lyttelton via Wellington and asked to be called on deck as the vessel approached the channel. He was roused at around 4 a.m. as the steamer was about to go through a rocky gap so narrow 'it seemed no wider than a street'.

> The current tore through there like a mill-race, and the boat darted through like a telegram. The passage was made in half a minute; then we were in a wide place where noble vast eddies swept grandly round and round in shoal water, and I wondered what they would do with the little boat. They did as they pleased with her. They picked her up and flung her around like nothing and landed her gently on the solid, smooth bottom of sand — so gently, indeed, that we barely felt her touch it, barely felt her quiver when she came to a standstill. The water was as clear as glass, the sand on the bottom was vividly distinct, and the fishes seemed to be swimming about in nothing. Fishing lines were brought out, but before we could bait the hooks the boat was off and away again.

Being grounded on a sandbank for half an hour was just a minor inconvenience for Twain who had endured a horrendous voyage to Nelson from Lyttelton. The author left the rainy southern port at midnight the previous day in the woefully overcrowded Union

Company's *Flora*. The boat was packed with people returning home from the Canterbury Agricultural and Pastoral Association show in Christchurch. Twain wrote there were around two hundred people on board while the first officer told him the boat was only allowed to carry 125. The cabins, the floor, even the table in the swill-room was covered with sleeping bodies and some people had to stand. 'The owners of that boat were not technically guilty of conspiracy to commit murder, but they were morally guilty of it.' It was dark, smelly, and many of the passengers were seasick. 'That boat was the foulest I was ever in; and the smell of the breakfast saloon when we threaded our way among the layers of steaming passengers stretched upon its floor and its tables was incomparable for efficiency.'

Twain's travelogue was published as *Following the Equator* in the United States and includes nearly two pages about his experience on the *Flora* that didn't appear in the Commonwealth and European edition, entitled *More Tramps Abroad*. In the missing text he is scathing of the Union Company's irresponsibility and claims the government turned a blind eye to the overcrowding because the shipping company was acting like a monopoly. This material may have been deleted for legal reasons.

Twain escaped the 'floating pig-sty' that was 'about the equivalent of a cattle-scow', by spending part of the night on the upper deck. He went ashore at Wellington, boarding the small but clean and comfortable *Mahinapua* a few hours later. Twain wrote of the *Flora*, 'I was praying with all my heart that she would sink at the dock.' The *Mahinapua* sustained no damage while grounded in the narrow French Pass and continued down the coast into Nelson Harbour on the eastern side of Tasman Bay. After Anthony Trollope sailed through the French Pass into the same harbour he noted that 'it is all very well now for steamers with charts and coal and all nautical appliances to thread their way in and out through these marvellously intricate passages; but one is lost in wonder at the audacity of the men when one thinks of the work which such sailors as Tasman and Cook were called on to perform'.

MURDERERS' ROCK AND THE QUEEN OF CRIME

THE WHOLE NELSON REGION WAS a 'garden', except for one place, Mark Twain wrote. 'That is a wild place — wild and lonely; an ideal place for a murder. It is at the base of a vast, rugged, densely timbered mountain.' Twain was gripped by the story of one of New Zealand's most notorious murder cases, in June 1866. Four men were on their way from the Wakamarina River west to Nelson. But James de Pontius, a miner, storekeepers James John Kempthorne and James Dudley and hotelkeeper Felix Mathieu suddenly disappeared. The men had been ambushed and killed by 'four desperate rascals', Twain wrote. The villains had already murdered another man. 'A harmless old labouring man came wandering along, and as his presence was an embarrassment, they choked him to death, they hid him, and then resumed their watch for those four. They had to wait awhile yet, but eventually everything turned out as they desired.'

Four strangers, Philip Levy, Richard Burgess, Thomas Kelly and Joseph Thomas Sullivan, were detained as suspects. They had criminal records in Britain and were known to have committed crimes on the Victoria and Central Otago goldfields. A search recovered a dead packhorse and the missing men's swags, but no bodies. The government offered money and a pardon to any accomplice who spoke out. Joseph Thomas Sullivan confessed he'd been the lookout and his information led to the discovery of the bodies of the four missing men. Several days later the body of Wakamarina farm labourer James Battle was found. In the course of the trial it was claimed that Sullivan had killed Battle but his death sentence was reduced to life imprisonment because he had confessed. He was later released and deported. His three companions were found guilty of murder and sentenced to hang.

Twain had a copy of a David M. Luckie's *Maungatapu Mountain Murders*, from which he quoted extensively in *More Tramps Abroad*. Newspaper editor Luckie became famous for chairing a meeting to raise funds to search for the missing men and later covered the trial.

For its 'brevity, succinctness, and concentration,' Twain wrote, Burgess' confession written in jail on 7 August 1866, 'is perhaps without its peer in the literature of murder'; the document was 'a business statement of murder'. Burgess described lying in wait for the four men, tying them up and marching them to a nearby creek. The villains robbed their victims and claimed they'd be taken away one by one over the steep range and freed. James Dudley was the first to be separated and led about fifty metres away through scrub and choked. The killers had decided guns would make too much noise, but choking took too long and they changed their minds.

> Sullivan took De Pontius to the left of where Kempthorne was sitting. I took Mathieu to the right. I tied a strap round his legs, and shot him with a revolver. He yelled. I ran from him with my gun in my hand, I sighted Kempthorne, who had risen to his feet. I presented the gun, and shot him behind the right ear; his life's blood welled from him, and he died instantaneously. Sullivan had shot De Pontius in the meantime, and then came to me. I said, 'Look to Mathieu,' indicating the spot where he lay. He shortly returned and said, 'I had to "chiv" that fellow, he was not dead,' a cant word, meaning that he had to stab him. Returning to the road we passed where De Pontius lay and was dead. Sullivan said, 'This is the digger, the others were all storekeepers; this is the digger, let's cover him up, for should the others be found, they'll think he done it and sloped,' meaning he had gone. So with that we threw all the stones on him, and then left him. This bloody work took nearly an hour and a half from the time we stopped the men.

Twain believed Burgess' confession revealed a man who cared nothing for the fate of his victims but cared a lot about his own. Burgess wrote: 'I lie under the imputation which says, "Come now and let us reason together, saith the Lord: though your sins be as scarlet, they shall be as white as snow; though they be red like crimson, they shall be as wool."' The judge dismissed this as 'scandalously blasphemous'. Twain wasn't so sure and believed Burgess faced the gallows untroubled. Murderers' Rock still bears the name it was given after the events of June 1866.

A young mother who'd go on to kill far more people than the Maungatapu murderers passed through the region in 1922. Hundreds of characters met their end by the pen of Agatha Christie whose elaborate murder plots made her one of the best-selling writers of the era. In her autobiography Christie writes about Nelson and driving through the Buller Gorge on her way down the South Island. The dark gorge with ferns and cabbage trees protruding from precipitous cliffs has been flooded, shaken by earthquakes and was home to hundreds of transient workers during the gold rush. Maori helped early European travellers and goldminers through the river's dangerous rapids and today the gorge attracts thrill-seeking water sports enthusiasts.

'I still think New Zealand is the most beautiful country I have ever seen. Its scenery is extraordinary,' Christie wrote. The British Empire Exhibition Mission, which Christie travelled with in New Zealand, enthused about the tourism potential of the upper South Island. In the Christchurch *Press* it was reported that the mission believed the 'stretch of country from the Buller Gorge to Hokitika, if only properly advertised, should attract thousands of tourists from all parts of the world. The members had seen nothing to equal the scenery of this district since leaving England.' It's possible Christie drew on her New Zealand memories when she wrote her 1976 story *Sleeping Murder*, as her character Gwenda says of New Zealand, 'It's the loveliest country in the world.'

'New Zealand is probably the most beautiful country on earth,' wrote James Michener. The American, who was thought to have seen more of the world than any other novelist, was one of a group of eminent authors including Saul Bellow, V.S. Pritchett, Frank O'Connor, William Faulkner and S.J. Perelman, who wrote for the lavishly illustrated monthly *Holiday* during the post-war travel boom and the new era of long-distance air travel. In the January 1951 edition of the magazine Michener wrote that New Zealand school children were taught that when Prime Minister Richard John Seddon died, 'he passed on to a better place even than God's Own Country'.

New Zealanders found it hard to believe in the existence of a better land than theirs. 'Consider what you could see in one day's travel,' Michener wrote, and beginning at the top of the North Island and working his way down the country he described a 'dazzling tropical beach', enormous game fish, kauri forests, desert, volcanoes, geysers and mud pools. A flight to the South Island, where the 'real beauty of New Zealand is found', would reveal majestic mountains, extraordinary limestone formations, and fiords including Milford Sound where 'high waterfalls plunge from mountain plateaus' and 'jagged bays probe dark forests' and where a trail called 'The World's Finest Walk' could be found.

It was an ambitious itinerary. Perhaps Michener fell briefly into the trap Aldous Huxley described in *Along the Road: Notes and Essays of a Tourist*, where he claimed people privileged enough to travel had a tendency to mythologise and over-hype places they'd seen in order to justify their trip and to make them feel superior to the 'stay-at-homes'. New Zealanders may be guilty of mythologising their own landscapes as well. Numerous tour operators boast that Kipling claimed Milford Sound was the 'eighth wonder of the world'. Yet Kipling travelled down the east coast of the South Island before sailing to

Australia, on a route that lay some distance from Milford Sound. If he did utter the words widely attributed to him, it's unlikely he was drawing on first hand experience.

Nevertheless, the importance of high praise from the likes of Michener and Christie shouldn't be underestimated. As Robert Louis Stevenson once wrote, 'I have often been tempted to put forth the paradox that any place is good enough to live a life in, while it is only in a few, and those highly favoured, that we can pass a few hours agreeably.' His essay was entitled 'On the Enjoyment of Unpleasant Places'. Stevenson's theory was that if we stay long enough anywhere we end up making ourselves at home. 'Reminiscences spring up, like flowers, about uninteresting corners. We forget to some degree the superior loveliness of other places, and fall into a tolerant and sympathetic spirit which is its own reward and justification.'

The *New Zealand Freelance* printed a story from Greymouth that support for spiritualism on the West Coast was so strong it was 'as if Conan Doyle had given them a personal visit'. According to the report, in the West Coast town with its treacherous sandbar, 'the daily question has ever been not what the weather's going to be, but "How's the Bar?"' Some of the 'local wiseacres' held a séance during which the medium claimed to have contacted a former harbour master. In the ensuing excitement the 'alleged spirit' was bombarded with questions. '"One at a time, gentlemen," pleaded the ancient salt. "Well, can you give us a message from the spirit world?" said the chairman. "Certainly," was the prompt answer: "How's the Bar?" That settled all their doubts. It must really be the old harbour-master's spirit.'

In the 1870s Greymouth was sandwiched to the north and south by two gold-mining districts. The discovery of gold had a dramatic effect on New Zealand's development. Earnings from gold doubled that of wool at one point. The precious metal was extracted by washing alluvial gravels, silts and sand and by crushing veins of gold infused quartz. The coastal gold-mining town of Hokitika, about forty kilometres southwest of Greymouth, was the setting for a little-known short story by Anthony Trollope. He wrote in the *Daily Telegraph* that Westland was 'essentially a goldfield', and that since 1860 the province had sent 'home' gold to the value of almost £6,500,500, and that the yield seemed to be increasing. It was to Trollope's 'infinite regret' that he didn't have time to cross the South Island from the east coast to see the 'glories of Hokitika'. The Westland region was also celebrated for stunning scenery, with its glaciers and the majestic Aoraki/Mt Cook. 'Of course to my dying day the conviction will haunt me that when in New Zealand I did not see the one thing best worth seeing in the colony,' he wrote. Noël Coward echoed Trollope's sentiments some seventy years later, and was 'very sad' he didn't have time to see the West Coast, as he particularly wanted to visit it.

Back in England Trollope could explore Hokitika in his imagination. His imaginary wanderings appear in *Catherine Carmichael; or Three Years Running*, published in the Christmas issue of the *Masonic Magazine* in 1878. Trollope's eponymous heroine, Catherine Carmichael, grows up in Hokitika. She's the oldest of nine children born to a rough gold-digger who emigrated from Scotland when Catherine was young. They live a difficult life moving from one shanty to the next. Catherine's mother gallantly tries to educate her children while her father drinks. But the mother passes away and her father drinks even more and eventually dies, penniless. Catherine's younger sisters return to Scotland, and the boys try to support themselves as diggers. Twenty-two-year-old Catherine meets and falls in love with a poor gold-digger, John Carmichael, who came to Hokitika after quarrelling with his cousin, Peter, with whom he had been living in Canterbury. Peter is wealthy, brutish, nearly fifty and had once been her father's partner in the gold mines. Peter then arrives in Hokitika to help arrange the younger girls' journey back to Scotland and he offers Catherine a home in Canterbury at his property 'Mount Warriwa' as his wife. He talks about the arrangement 'as he might have done of the purchase of a lot of sheep'. Catherine feels she has to accept.

> It was so evident that she could not be allowed to increase the weight of the burden to be imposed upon the aunt at home! It was so evident that her brothers were not able to find a home for her! It was so evident that she could not live alone in that wild country! And it seemed also to be quite evident that John Carmichael had no proposition of his own to make to her! Peter Carmichael was odious to her, but the time was such that she could not allow herself to think of her own dislikings.

Catherine and Peter travel for 'two days and two nights across the mountains to Christchurch'. The discovery of gold on the West Coast in the 1860s meant a direct route was needed from Canterbury to Westland across the middle of the South Island and the Southern Alps. Surveyor Arthur Dudley Dobson found a route, by travelling up a mountain valley on the eastern side, now known as Bealey Valley, and discovering a five-kilometre saddle at its head, which took him down a steep valley now called Otira Gorge and into the open country of Westland. The saddle joining the two valleys, Arthur's Pass, bears the surveyor's name.

Agatha Christie made special mention of the beauty of Otira Gorge. She spent three weeks in New Zealand in the middle of the winter and wrote: 'I vowed then that I would come back one day, in the spring — their spring, I mean, not ours — and see the *rata* in flower: all golden and red.' She never did return to see the blooming rata, one of the best-known New Zealand native trees which flowers between November and January and

OTIRA GORGE, WEST COAST ROAD BY CHARLES BARRAUD. ALEXANDER TURNBULL LIBRARY, WELLINGTON, NEW ZEALAND. PUBL-0016-40.

thrives on the rainy West Coast. The rata 'forms the staple forest' of the Otira Gorge, 'flushing its own dusk, in flower-time, with a rose-red diffused and mantling as that on the cheek of an apple,' Blanche Baughan wrote in her 1925 booklet *Arthur's Pass and the Otira Gorge*. The rata took the place 'on this moister side of the Alps, of the black-birch in Canterbury'. After immigrating to New Zealand around the age of thirty, English-born Baughan toured the country extensively. Her work was collected in *Studies of New Zealand Scenery* and *Glimpses of New Zealand Scenery*. Baughan, who was also a prison reformer, published poetry as well as prose. She described entering Otira Gorge and discovering the rata after leaving Arthur's Pass.

> And now, the Pass clean out of sight, the road enters upon a masterly cork-screw, known as the Zigzag, back to the river-side and down into the Gorge. The blessed company of the green things makes haste to gather over the rough stones and set the air again 'in spice', but there are some changes among them. The Snow-Grass is gone for good; daisy-flowered *Olearias* mingle with the Grass-tree and Cassinia; and so does another shrub, with pointed dark leaves like those of a myrtle, and, in late summer, a ruby crown above them of flower-stars made of stamens.

Rudyard Kipling also found literary inspiration in New Zealand's flora when he wrote his poem 'The Flowers', one of *The Seven Seas* collection published in 1896.

> Broom behind the windy town; pollen o' the pine —
> Bell-bird in the leafy deep where the *ratas* twine —

Fern above the saddle-bow, flax upon the plain —
Take the flower and turn the hour, and kiss your love again!

After continuing his imaginary travels around New Zealand, camping near streams and in whare, Dickens' Mr Booley met Miss Creeble, of The Misses Creeble's Boarding and Day Establishment for Young Ladies, Kennington Oval. Along with 'three of her young ladies' Miss Creeble and Mr Booley travelled together observing the 'Kaikatea [kahikatea], the Kauri, the Ruta [rata], the Pukatea, the Hinau, and the Tanakaka [tanekaha].' They saw the 'beautiful, aborescent, palm-like fern, abounding everywhere, and frequently exceeding thirty feet in height'.

J.B. Priestley's wife, writer and archaeologist Jacquetta Hawkes, pleaded with the prime minister not to let any more bush be destroyed. 'It is such beautiful bush, with trees and plants that are so interesting and ancient. There is nothing like this bush anywhere in the world and it helps to make such a lovely atmosphere if calm and quiet,' she told a Christchurch reporter.

'No human pen or pencil could do anything like justice to the sublimity, the changing grandeur and incomparable beauty of combined savage and sylvan scenery,' wrote Michael Davitt about Otira Gorge. 'It's not a ten minutes' nor an hour's enjoyment of some new and captivating landscape. You roll on, as it were, for a whole day, through an ever-varying panorama of timbered ranges with snow-clad peaks, with massive crags overhanging a track which often proceeds along the edges of precipitous ravines down which, a thousand feet below us, rushed the angriest of swollen torrents,' he wrote. A moment's lapse in concentration or a horse's stumble could send his coach and its passengers plunging several hundred feet Davitt thought, as the roads through the gorge that had been cut from the cliff face narrowed to just a few yards. To his relief, however, the horses and the driver navigated the treacherous roads as easily as if they were on the wide, flat Canterbury Plains.

Arthur's Pass cuts through the upper end of the Southern Alps, the mountain backbone of the South Island. Mark Twain saw pictures of the 'alpine and sound scenery', which he thought reminiscent of Norwegian fiords and Alaska. James Michener described the Alps as 'immense rows of jagged peaks beneath which nestle dozens of wonderful lakes, each serving as a mirror for some great range of mountains'. It was on these imposing peaks that Sir Edmund Hillary trained before his successful ascent of Mt Everest in 1953. During the Everest expedition Hillary met a British reporter who became one of the most well-known twentieth century travel writers. James Morris was the first to report the successful ascent of Everest when, at 26, and with no mountaineering experience, he devised a clever plan to get the news of the triumph back to London without being scooped. *Coronation Everest* details his adventure as climber and journalist. Since meeting on the expedition Morris remained friends with Tenzing and Hillary. It was reported in *The Times* in November 1971 that he visited Tenzing in Darjeeling in 1970 and had been in the New Zealand Alps with Hillary earlier that year. Morris praised the carefree nature of the 'leathery giant from the Antipodes'. The first thing Hillary said to his fellow climbers when he returned from the successful ascent of Everest was 'Well, we've knocked the bastard off', Morris wrote. 'This free and easy approach to great adventures, this swashbuckling rollick through life has made him, by an agreeable and improbable paradox, one of the most famous men alive.'

The end of the road from the gold gully on the South Island's West Coast, across the Southern Alps to Christchurch on the east, signifies the end of the tough single life of Trollope's Catherine Carmichael and the beginning of her unhappy marriage. She marries in Christchurch on Christmas Day and the couple sets off for Peter's home at 'Mount Warriwa'. It's the first of three dramatic Christmas Days for Catherine, each one a defining moment in her life.

A MAD DOG AND AN ENGLISHMAN OUT IN THE MIDDAY SUN

BAD NEWS AWAITED A *Lyttelton Times* reporter as he arrived at the railway station on the morning of Tuesday, 3 November 1891. He intended to catch the 7.55 a.m. train to the port to meet Rudyard Kipling. The famous author was due on the Union Steamship Company's SS *Talune* at Lyttelton Harbour, southeast of Christchurch, having sailed down the east coast of the South Island. The *Talune* had docked earlier that morning and some of her passengers were already in the city. Was Kipling one of them? The reporter gambled that he wasn't and took the train to the port. Knowing only that Kipling wore 'somewhat peculiar spectacles' he started his search by seeking out his newspaper's shipping reporter.

As he rounded the post office corner he met a well-known barrister. 'Do you want to see Mr Rudyard Kipling?' the lawyer asked, and offered to introduce the scribe to the author, who he knew to be at the port's railway station waiting for the next train to Christchurch. Kipling refused to be interviewed, according to his usual custom as a man who 'was once a newspaper man and does not care to undergo the operation'. But the reporter needed a story so he offered to escort the author around the city. The invitation was accepted and on the short journey into Christchurch Kipling, although he complained about the slow speed of the train, was generally chatty and interested in his surroundings. He enthused about the fertile lands and the Heathcote River that snakes around the outskirts of the city. It was a key transport link between Lyttelton and Christchurch in the early days of settlement.

Named after an Oxford college, Christchurch is often described as New Zealand's most anglicised city. It was established by a God-fearing English elite led by John Robert

Godley, known as the 'founding father of Canterbury'. 'There existed a feeling that something great might be done for a small portion of the British race, by establishing a settlement on an entirely new footing, in which the best of everything English should be retained, English habits of life, English principles, English local government, English freedom, and above all the Church of England,' wrote Anthony Trollope. The author stood in Cathedral Square admiring the bronze statue of his contemporary Godley, who he remembered from Harrow as a boy 'thoroughly respected by all his schoolfellows'. Thomas Woolner, working in England, sculpted Godley's statue from photographs and it was exhibited in London's South Kensington Museum. 'The statue itself, which was known to many Englishmen before it came out to New Zealand, is very noble. Among modern statues, I know no head that stands better on its shoulders,' Trollope wrote.

The statue stood in front of the foundations of an unfinished cathedral. Seven thousand pounds had already been spent on the building before they ran out of money. Selling the site was mooted as an option, and Trollope was told that the cathedral had been abandoned. Public offices would be more useful than an extravagant church. 'I could not but be melancholy as I learned that the honest high-toned idea of the honest high-toned founders of the colony would probably not be carried out.' But work resumed the following year. The cathedral was completed in 1904 and is now a popular city landmark dominating the central square. Godley's statue was moved to make way for a tram shelter and toilets in 1918, but these structures were later demolished and the statue returned to its original position in 1933.

The city's wooden houses and grand stone banks were certainly not magnificent, Trollope noted, but Christchurch was 'comfortable and thoroughly English'. The Gothic Provincial Council Buildings still stand on the banks of the river Avon. 'The buildings form a quadrangle, and look as though one of the smaller and prettier colleges had been transplanted thither bodily from the banks of the Cam. As I stood and looked at it I could not but think that some exiled member of the university may some day have consoled himself with the same feeling.' Arthur Conan Doyle also found the city reminiscent of a romantic Oxbridge scene. 'When you are on the green, sloping banks of the river Avon, with the low, artistic bridges, it would not be hard to imagine that you were in the Backs at Cambridge.' Noël Coward thought Christchurch a 'lovely town, gently reminiscent of an English cathedral city'.

A 'globe-trotting grumpy-guts' who suffered 'bilious attacks of self-pity in the wake of a marriage break-up' hated Christchurch. The newspapers castigated travel writer Paul Theroux for his opinion of New Zealanders and their country in *The Happy Isles of Oceania*. Christchurch 'looked prim and moribund, like the sort of South London suburb I had mocked in England on Sunday outings with the kids, driving through on the way to Brighton thinking: This is English death, the indescribable boredom that makes you desperate to leave. Life is elsewhere, I thought in Christchurch, but in this purgatory I began reliving my past.'

Christchurch was James Morris' first stop in New Zealand. He thought living in the city would be like living in an English country town forty or fifty years previously. Morris was upset by an unnecessarily grumpy innkeeper, he thought the State overbearing and his trips into the country were ruined by park rangers, marked routes and fences. 'But beneath this tight-laced exterior, New Zealand is more fun than it cares to admit,' Morris wrote. The innkeeper warmed up to the visiting writer, and Morris learned that the pioneering and self-sufficient spirit of the New Zealander prevented the State becoming too intrusive, park rangers were happy to leave tourists alone and the wild landscape still held plenty of challenges.

'It was Junior England all the way to Christchurch — in fact, just a garden,' wrote Mark Twain. 'And Christchurch is an English town, with an English-park annex, and a winding English brook just like the Avon — and named the Avon; but from a man, not from Shakespeare's river [it was actually named after the Avon River in Ayrshire, Scotland]. Its grassy banks are bordered by the stateliest and most impressive weeping willows to be found in the world, I suppose ... It is a settled old community, with all the serenities, the graces, the conveniences, and the comforts of the ideal home-life. If it had an established Church and social inequality it would be England over again with hardly a lack.'

Twain was guest of honour at a Christchurch Savage Club Supper, an event based on a quintessential English tradition. The Savage Club originated as a gentleman's club in London. Around fifty 'savages' sat around flower-adorned tables in the Provincial Council Chamber, reported a local newspaper. They were 'attired in full "war paint", a costume which by the uninitiated, unable to perceive the subtle distinctions between the costume of civilised man and that of this particular tribe of savages, might have been mistaken for the evening dress of present-day Englishmen'. The menu was designed to make the great humourist laugh. The dishes included 'consommé du vagabond en route', 'mayonnaise à Mons Thomas Sawyer', and 'Gelée au vin Finn Huckleberry'. The President, Dr Jennings, made the author the first honorary member of the club. 'It makes me feel as large as your great moa — (laughter) — and if I go on dissipating like this I shall be as extinct as your great moa. (Laughter.)' Twain also joked about the prohibition movement in New Zealand.

> If you get it you will find it will put you into most difficult straits. In our country several years ago there was a man came into a prohibition town, a man like you savages here, and they said to him, 'You can't get a drink anywhere except at the apothecary's.' So he went to the apothecary, who said 'You can't get a drink here without a prescription from a physician,' but the man said 'I'm perishing, I haven't time to get a prescription'. The apothecary replied: — 'Well, I haven't

> power to give you a drink except for snake bite.' The man said, 'Where's the snake?' (Laughter.) So the apothecary gave him the snake's address, and he went off. Soon after, however, he came back and said, 'For goodness' sake, give me a drink. That snake is engaged for six months ahead.' (Loud laughter.)

The old Theatre Royal still stands in Gloucester Street but is no longer used as a theatre. Twain filled the place. The *Star* reported that the English language had no word for 'an entertainment like that which Mark Twain gave to his audience' and that sometimes the crowd of men and women were 'swept clean off their gravity by an overwhelming joke'.

> Mark Twain rambles from one subject to another in delightfully inconsequential fashion, so from the story of how he stole his first watermelon ... he passed to the conversation between Tom Sawyer, Huck Finn and the negro Jem on the subject of crusades. This was repeated in inimitable style, and full effect was given to its keen satire on international morality, and on the 'voice of authority' in matters of religion and conscience. With happy disconnectedness he then brought in that classic of American humour, the famous 'Jumping Frog'. The mirth raised by his laughter-provoking recital of this historic 'yarn' had barely subsided when he was discoursing about his journalistic experiences in the silver-mining community where respectability was only attained by killing somebody.

Twain thought American audiences took longer to warm up than those in Australia, New Zealand and England. They demanded a certain standard of entertainment and were reluctant to show their appreciation until they knew what they were getting. Colonial audiences were encouraging and friendly as soon as the performer stepped on stage.

Agatha Christie was horrified when asked to give a speech in Christchurch. She was invited to speak at a 'delightful little impromptu morning tea', given by the Committee of the Canterbury Women's Club. Despite her concerns Christie relented and 'spoke most enthusiastically of the scenic beauties of New Zealand, most particularly of the West Coast'. She was presented with a lavish bouquet of orchids and maidenhair from the Botanic Gardens. One local reporter was particularly interested in her clothes. 'The guest of honour wore, over her mole coloured marocain frock, a charming loose Paisley wrap, with mole collar and a small mole hat of hatter's plush, with upturned brim trimmed with pastel tinted ribbons that toned with the wrap.' Agatha and Archie Christie stayed at Warner's Hotel in Cathedral Square. The building still stands and has welcomed the likes of Scott and Shackleton. After surviving several demolition threats it underwent a complete restoration.

'When we are fighting so grimly for the future of civilisation the desire to make some contribution is stronger in me than any other incentive I have ever known,' Noël Coward told a largely female Christchurch audience in January 1941. He was touring to make serious broadcasts and to provide light entertainment to generate funds for war charities. Coward admitted to not being an expert on the international situation, but he knew the spirit of the English people. 'Even here, so far away, you are strangely near in sympathy to those people. This has touched me profoundly.' He believed the future of civilisation depended on the union of all the world's English-speaking people. Coward sensed 'a little apathy' for the war among New Zealanders, although he qualified his criticism by the shortness of his stay. He thought the attitude of the country's soldiers was excellent, however.

James Michener's *Until They Sail* studies the impact of an influx of American servicemen ('never before had a strange army come to take the place of every available man') on Christchurch. The story, written to partner his essay on New Zealand in *Return to Paradise*, revolves around four sisters from Captain Harry Neville's family of Ferrymead, a Christchurch suburb that overlooks the large, salty estuary of the Avon and Heathcote rivers. 'When they were young, the children had gazed upon this arm of the sea, imagining that they were in contact with their father's ship.' After losing their father Harry and their brother, the four girls (the virtuous, prim Anne who becomes pregnant out of wedlock; the vibrant newly-wed Barbara whose husband is also killed; the beauty Delia, whose decision to ask her husband for a divorce has tragic consequences; and the bright and positive baby sister Evelyn) deal with the tragic effects of war on their family and the arrival of American servicemen in different ways.

Until They Sail was made into an MGM film, shot on location in New Zealand starring Sandra Dee in her debut role, Paul Newman, Jean Simmons, Joan Fontaine and Piper Laurie. The movie 'has a great deal of warmth and pathos, some humour, and a fairly deft portrayal of the inevitable social conflicts which were the result of an influx of foreign soldiers in countries all over the world,' wrote a reviewer in the *Chicago Daily Tribune* in October 1957.

A Christchurch resident trying to establish a marine solar salt works in the suburb of New Brighton claimed to have been inspired by the New Zealand visit of *King Solomon's Mines* and *She* author Sir Rider Haggard. Leslie W.A. MacArthur wanted the plant to provide light physical labour for semi-disabled soldiers. Haggard toured Australasia in the winter of 1916 on 'after war' matters. The author was researching a plan for British soldiers to settle empty lands in the Dominions, as a way of rewarding the troops and strengthening the Empire. He visited South Africa, Australia, New Zealand, and Canada and a scaled-down version of his strategy became the 1922 Empire Settlement Bill. In an interview in New Zealand he stressed the importance of British soldiers who wanted to emigrate after the war, settling within the boundaries of the Empire. Haggard predicted the next world war before the first had ended:

> The German population will be restored in 20 years, with every man imbued with one desire — revenge on England that has cleared their pitch and spoiled their game. Now this is the very reason I am here. There will be a certain movement of population after the war, and I suggest that New Zealand should get some of the overflow from the British Isles if it can.

According to his biographer Tom Pocock, Haggard's tour of New Zealand was undertaken 'in a temperate, comfortable country of rich lowlands and valleys and magnificent mountains with a placid, self-satisfied population'. No promise of land was forthcoming. Prime Minister William Massey supported Haggard's goals but said there was little good land available and members of the New Zealand Expeditionary Force and its reinforcements would take priority. After satisfying the needs of its own soldiers the government would, however, 'give favourable consideration' to would-be British Army settlers. Haggard had also visited New Zealand in 1913 as a member of the Dominion Royal Commission. He studied farming methods as part of a report on the health of the Empire. He approved of New Zealand's agricultural economy but was concerned about the future of Maori.

Kipling wanted two things when he arrived in Christchurch: a cigar and a shave. The reporter, who was still in tow, offered to organise both. They walked out of the railway station building on Moorhouse Avenue, crossed the road and started the five-minute walk up Manchester Street towards Cathedral Square. They had barely left the railway station when they noticed another passenger heading into Coker's Hotel. Kipling was 'evidently pleased' with the establishment once inside. He got a cigar, which he lit, and the two men continued their journey.

Mark Twain was an admirer of Kipling. He predicted to a reporter that his countrymen 'may one day get something from that writer's pen with a flash of New Zealand colour in it. Kipling is a man who gets material wherever he is and never misses anything, but it may have to simmer and foster a long time before he uses it.' It was an astute observation. The barmaid Kipling met briefly at Coker's Hotel simmered in his thoughts for more than a decade when it seems likely that she emerged in the short story *Mrs Bathurst*. Published in 1904, it was a popular yet complex, confusing, obscure, even 'uncrackable' story according to one critic. It's about a group of naval officers discussing the desertion of a sailor called Vickery.

He'd been obsessed with Mrs Bathurst, a young widow who ran a hotel. She wore black silk and opened her establishment to 'warrants and non-coms'. Her customers could settle their bills whenever they wanted and she once loaned a sailor her gold watch because he'd lost his and needed to catch his boat. Mrs Bathurst kept a couple of bottles of one sailor's favourite beer behind the bar for the five years before he returned to the hotel. But then the story gets really strange. Somehow Mrs Bathurst is captured on film getting off a train. Vickery sees the moving picture in Cape Town and becomes obsessed with the widow. He watches repeat showings and it eventually leads to his descent into insanity and death.

In his autobiography *Something of Myself*, published posthumously and without revision, Kipling wrote that an Auckland barmaid inspired the character of Mrs Bathurst. The author recalled how the face and voice of a woman who sold him beer at a small hotel in Auckland was in the back of his mind for a decade. She stayed there until he heard a petty officer on a Cape Town train talking about a New Zealand woman who 'never scrupled to help a lame duck or put her foot on a scorpion'.

> Then — precisely as the removal of the key-log in a timber jam starts the whole pile — those words gave me the key to the face and voice at Auckland, and a tale called 'Mrs Bathurst' slid into my mind, smoothly and orderly as floating timber on a bank-high river.

But Kipling's official biographer, Charles Edmund Carrington, believed his subject was mistaken and the woman who inspired the character of Mrs Bathurst came from Christchurch, not Auckland. The key to the story is Coker's Hotel. It was renowned for its high standards, prompting one Christchurch newspaper to gush 'wherever the white man has established civilization, one has heard of Coker's Hotel. All the celebrities have sojourned within its hospitable portals.' According to Carrington, Coker's Hotel employed the last barmaid in Christchurch before barmaids were prohibited under new legislation and she was a 'celebrated lady'. He claimed Kipling based *Mrs Bathurst* on the barmaid, who the author met when he stayed in the hotel in 1891. Kipling didn't spend a night at the hotel as Carrington suggested, as he was only in Christchurch for half a day, but he did meet a barmaid when he called in briefly with the reporter to get a cigar.

A LATE-NINETEENTH CENTURY PHOTO OF COKER'S HOTEL, CHRISTCHURCH. Aotearoa New Zealand Centre, Christchurch City Libraries, Photo CD 13 IMG0029.

The once lavish establishment where the 'real' Mrs Bathurst formerly worked is now a backpackers' hostel. But the Christchurch barmaid has left a lasting legacy. Not only was she the inspiration for one of Kipling's most mysterious characters, she was the original 'It girl'. Kipling wrote that Mrs Bathurst was the kind of woman that could make a man go insane. 'Tisn't beauty, so to speak, nor good talk necessarily. It's just It. Some women'll stay in a man's memory if they once walk down a street, but most of 'em you can live with a month on end, an' next commission you'd be put it to certify whether they talked in their sleep or not, as one might say.' The Coker's barmaid inspired Kipling to use the word 'It', a couple of decades before British romance novelist and screenwriter Elinor Glyn became famous for inventing the term 'It girl'.

A New South Wales detective tracked the notorious villain Captain Starlight, a character in Rolf Boldrewood's novel *Robbery Under Arms*, to a posh Christchurch hotel. Starlight was 'ruffling it among the "aristocratic" settlers' of the city. Regarded as an Australian classic, *Robbery Under Arms* was originally written as a serial in the early 1880s, has never been out of print and has been adapted for film on more than one occasion. A bushranger tells his own story from jail as he awaits execution. Rolf Boldrewood, the pseudonym of Thomas Alexander Browne, was a young boy when he arrived in Australia. He'd been a pioneer squatter, police magistrate and goldfields warden, and wrote much of the novel from his own experiences. Boldrewood had a large family to support and wrote while doing other work, sometimes getting up at three in the morning to do so.

The charm of Christchurch was immediately apparent to J.B. Priestley when he arrived in 1973, but he wondered if the city's Englishness had been overemphasised. It wasn't so much an English cathedral city as a city that represented 'a dream carried 13,000 miles, down into the Antipodes, and subtly changing as soon as it began to be realised'. Priestley read about Christchurch being sleepy, but he disagreed and thought it lively for a city of 170,000 and that it had achieved a lot. The city was accused of being smugly conservative; again Priestley disagreed. How could it be with a recently completed town hall that was 'bursting above the river like a Chinese-red-lacquer-bomb'?

Priestley was described in the *Press* as 'a little slow and heavy of movement' but authoritative on a wide variety of subjects. Beginning work at 9.30 in the morning, he took a break in the afternoon and worked from about 5.15 until 7.00 p.m. He needed a reasonable level of quiet and didn't understand how some writers couldn't work unless they were in a room full of people. He was much more concerned with the amount of violence than sex in the work of current writers who had become dependent on 'shock tactics'. The pipe-smoking 78-year-old claimed he had never considered retirement. 'People must retire, otherwise there would be no jobs for younger men to be promoted to,' he said.

'But people who look forward to their long-promised retirement often kill themselves because it is so boring.' Priestley sidestepped the perennial question of what he thought of New Zealanders by saying people could read about his opinions in the book he was writing. He hinted that his 'impressions have been very favourable — rather surprisingly so'. He dismissed a claim made some years previously by the BBC commentator, Wynford Vaughan-Thomas, that New Zealanders had tiny minds.

He almost missed the dinner. Priestley was scheduled to fly to Christchurch from Dunedin but the crash-firemen were on strike and his flight was cancelled. So the author chartered a light plane, 'a kind of three deck-chair job,' from the local Aero Club. He began the journey with a dry mouth, but then he relaxed and thoroughly enjoyed the flight. It was a sunny late afternoon and the plane flew smoothly at just 5000 feet above the Canterbury Plains. They looked like 'variegated squares of polished wood'. Priestley arrived at a near-deserted airport to be met by a *Press* photographer who 'insisted upon our posing for him', the author wrote. 'I never saw that photo — did we gleam or glitter with triumph or did we try to suggest blasé charterers' boredom?'

J.B. PRIESTLEY AND HIS WIFE ARRIVE AT CHRISTCHURCH AIRPORT ON 4 APRIL 1973. COURTESY THE PRESS, CHRISTCHURCH.

The dinner party that Priestley was so desperate to attend was at the home of Dame Ngaio Marsh, the famous New Zealand crime writer who had stayed with the Priestleys in England. Marsh's house in the Cashmere Hills, south of the city centre, was designed by Arts and Crafts architect Samuel Hurst Seager and is now a Christchurch tourist attraction. Priestley thought it 'delightful' and 'charming'. Marsh and her friend Helen Holmes organised a picnic for Priestley's last full day in Christchurch. Barring an amateur production of *The Winter's Tale* Priestley enjoyed Christchurch. But the town didn't seem to want to enjoy him. Relatively few invitations had been forthcoming and at a television interview he sensed the studio crew were so bored they were almost yawning. He also thought he disappointed the Christchurch branch of the Dickens Fellowship one evening by speaking too briefly. Priestley was a vice-president of the fellowship but didn't feel he had the time or motivation to go to meetings.

'They were nearly all very Dickensy people, almost as if they had been left over from some of his novels,' he wrote of the 50 members and friends at the Regal Lounge of the Clarendon Hotel. He didn't mean the comment in a pejorative way, he added, because they were 'amiable and sensible people'. But his 'Dickensy' comment hasn't been forgotten. Current fellowship secretary Esmé Richards says she can relate to the comment. 'When I joined the branch in 1989 and arrived at what I thought was the meeting venue, I saw a gentleman entering the building and I knew immediately I must be in the right place. He was dressed, ready for taking part in a sketch as part of that day's programme, with tails, a bright waistcoat and cravat and with his beard I thought it could have been Dickens himself.' Branch records show that a bunch of 'Charles Dickens roses' were delivered to Priestley's hotel, the Avon Motor Lodge (now the Holiday Inn On Avon, Christchurch) on Oxford Terrace, after the reception. It's believed that the locally grown roses were red, the same colour as Dickens' favourite flower, the red geranium. Priestley's wife Jacquetta sent a note on hotel paper thanking the fellowship for the reception and the flowers.

George Bernard Shaw didn't want to travel as far south as the Cathedral City. But then he read of Christchurch's claim to be the country's most intellectual city and changed his mind. There was also a practical reason for the revised schedule. A mix up over a ferry crossing left him with more time in the South Island than he expected. He consulted a map and saw that Christchurch was easily accessible by car. In the now demolished United Service Hotel on Cathedral Square, Shaw, 'his white head a candle which attracted many moths', treated a small crowd to an 'impromptu levee'. His 'beard and moustache curl with all the furious vigour of the caricatures, his eyes twinkle maliciously when he makes a point in conversation — a characteristic which even the films have not shown clearly — he talks with all the excitability of a young man,' one local scribe noted. 'He is full of gestures — continually thumping his knee to emphasise a point, throwing himself back in his chair to laugh, twirling his moustache

NOVELIST CHARLES DICKENS c.1860s (Photographer unknown). Alexander Turnbull Library, Wellington, New Zealand. F-106535-1/2.

or clapping his hands in the excitement of his own thoughts.'

'Of course the difficulty is these sheep,' Shaw replied. Dr H.T.J. Thacker had asked for his thoughts on vegetarianism. 'If only they would be content to take the wool off them and leave the meat it would be quite easy.'

'But you can't eat wool, sir,' remarked the questioner, to much laughter.

During Shaw's visit New Zealand hotels were issued with strict instructions regarding his diet.

> Mr George Bernard Shaw does not eat meat, game, fowl or fish, or take tea or coffee. Instead he will want one of the undermentioned dishes at lunch and dinner. He will eat green vegetables, puddings, pastry, etc., cheese and dessert like other people. He likes oranges and salads and nuts — especially walnuts.
>
> For Breakfast:
>
> Oatmeal porridge or other cereals and always grape-fruit.
> For drink: "Instant Postum".
>
> Other Meals:
>
> *One of the following dishes at lunch and dinner: —*
> Haricot Beans, dry, white; Butter Beans. May be plain boiled with a sauce; or curried or formed into cutlets.
> Lentils. As above.
> Macaroni. Au gratin; or with tomato, cheese, or other sauce, or curried.
> Spaghetti. As above.
> Welsh Rarebit.
> Yorkshire Pudding.
> Rice. Savoury, or Milanese (NO ham), or curried with haricots or eggs or nuts, raisins etc.
> Pease Pudding.
> Eggs (not too often). Curried, cutlets, mayonnaise, Espagnoli, en cocette a la crème, omelette, etc.
> Gnocchi.
> Sweet Corn.
> Curried Chestnuts.
> Minced Walnuts.
> Soups. Any thick vegetable soup, such as Lentil, Haricot, Pea (St. Germain), Barley (crème d'orge), Rice (crème de riz), Artichoke (Palestine), Celery, Onion, Tomato.

Henry Thomas Joynt Thacker was a colourful local figure. He was an outspoken wealthy doctor and was in the habit of being driven around Christchurch by a chauffeur. He also had the reputation for treating patients whether they could pay for it or not. He had been MP for Christchurch East and a mayor of the city. Thacker had sent Shaw a reply-paid telegram asking him for 12 words about his diet. He hoped to find out how the eminent author nourished his great brain.

Shaw replied 'Dr Thacker, Christchurch. Vegetarian fifty years. Tee-total always. Milk, butter, eggs. Shaw.'

According to Thacker, Shaw's reply showed that the playwright maintained 'great intellectual activity without the foods of heavy protein content which most men demand', and that 'his statement will give satisfaction to those who are interested in problems of diet'. Thacker recommended a diet of wholemeal bread, vegetables and fruit to others but it was probably a case of do as I say not do as I do. The doctor weighed 18 stone.

Thacker still suffered from an old football injury sustained at the University of Edinburgh, the same institution that Arthur Conan Doyle studied medicine. Both men also shared a love of sport. When they met up in Christchurch Thacker showed his guest a 'tumour of the exact size and shape of a boxing glove, thumb and all, which he cut out of the back of a boxer who had lost a glove fight and taken it greatly to heart'. The doctor offered Conan Doyle a huge moa bone as a present but the author had to decline the gift. He had never failed to impress upon his wife the 'extreme importance' of cutting down on luggage and he 'could not face the scandal of appearing with this monstrous impedimentum'.

Thacker's passion for the moa was enduring and he quizzed George Bernard Shaw on his knowledge of New Zealand's famous extinct creature. 'Do you know, sir, that we have in the museum here the largest moa skeleton in the world?' Dr Thacker asked. Looking surprised, Shaw admitted he didn't know what a moa was. 'It is the largest wingless bird in New Zealand, sir,' explained the doctor. 'A wingless bird! But I don't call a bird a bird unless it has wings. Wait a minute though! It sounds rather like a politician to me — one of those politicians who haven't the slightest knowledge of politics.'

It was once believed that the giant moa stood more than three metres tall, making it one of the largest birds ever discovered. However, evidence suggests that its neck was stooped and previous claims of the moa's height may have been exaggerated. 'It was a kicker, like the ostrich; in fight it did not use its beak, but its foot. It must have been a convincing kind of kick. If a person had his back to the bird and did not see who it was that did it, he would think he had been kicked by a wind-mill,' wrote Mark Twain after seeing the skeleton of the moa at the Canterbury Museum. Twain, of course, had his own theory on the plight of the moa. 'The natives used to ride it. It could make forty miles an hour, and keep it up for four hundred miles and come out reasonably fresh. It was still in existence when the railway was introduced into New Zealand; still in existence, and carrying the mails. The railroad began with the same schedule it has now: two expresses a week-time, twenty miles an hour. The company exterminated the moa to get the mails.'

Julius Haast explained to Anthony Trollope that New Zealand was once home to the 'Moa Hunters', a race of people that pre-dated Maori, but the author met several disbelievers and the theory has since been discredited. Haast was an explorer, geologist, writer and the founder of the Canterbury Museum. Trollope thought the huge flightless birds 'must be regarded as the most wonderful productions of New Zealand'.

Kaiapoi Pa was located on a peninsula between the modern-day Waikuku and Woodend townships, about twenty kilometres north of Christchurch. It was established as a Ngai Tahu tribe stronghold and was the South Island's largest fortified village. In 1831 Te Rauparaha, the famous Ngati Toa warrior from whom the All Black haka hails, attacked Kaiapoi Pa. Te Rauparaha and his men besieged the pa and the standoff lasted for three months. During a skirmish the wooden palisades caught fire, allowing Ngati Toa to enter the pa, capturing or killing most of those inside. The monument to the slain Ngai Tahu erected in 1898 intrigued Arthur Conan Doyle. 'You could still trace quite clearly the main lines of the battle which destroyed it. It lay on about five acres of ground, with deep swamp all round save for one frontage of some hundreds of yards.' He looked at the nearby Massacre Hill, where Ngati Toa celebrated their victory and where 'so many of the defenders were eaten that their gnawed bones covered the ground within the living memory of me' and was conscious, even on a sunny day 'of that heavy atmosphere within the enclosure which impresses itself upon me when I am on the scene of ancient violence'.

Anthony Trollope met Te Rauparaha's son at a dinner hosted by Governor Sir George Bowen and played battledore and shuttlecock with him in the governor's hall.

> It is said of him, the present man, that he has killed men, but never eaten them; of his father ... that he had killed and eaten men, — and he had no doubt eaten a great many; but of his grandfather, that he had killed men and eaten them, and had then himself been killed and eaten, like a true old Maori warrior as he was.

Conan Doyle's attempt to immerse himself in New Zealand's history turned into a 'fiasco'. He visited Tuahiwi School not far from Kaiapoi Pa. Tuahiwi, the centre of local Maori society then and now, is often referred to locally as 'the pa'. Tuahiwi School still exists but the 1920 buildings have since been replaced.

> As we approached the building, which was the village school room, there emerged an old lady — a very old lady — who uttered a series of shrill cries, which I was told meant welcome, though they sounded more like the other thing. I can only trust that my informants were right. Inside was a very fine assemblage of

> atmospheric air, and of nothing else. The explanation was that there had been a wedding the night before, and that the whole community had been — well, tired. Presently a large man in tweeds of the reach-me-down variety appeared upon the scene, and several furtive figures, including a row of children, materialised in corners of the big empty room. The visitors, who were more numerous than the visited, sat on a long bench and waited developments which refused to develop. My dreams of the dignified and befeathered savage were drifting away. Finally the large man, with his hands in his pockets, and looking hard at a corner of the rafters, made a speech of welcome, punctuated by long stops and gaps. He then, at our request, repeated it in Maori, and the children were asked to give a Maori shout which they sternly refused to do. I then made a few feeble bleats, uncertain whether to address my remarks to the level of the large man or to that of the row of children. I ended by handing over some books for their library, and we then escaped from this rather depressing scene.

Sir Joseph Kinsey was a well-known Christchurch figure. Kinsey was the agent, advisor and friend of Scott and Shackleton who was knighted for his services to Antarctic exploration. He told Conan Doyle the story of how he warned Scott that Amundsen was trying to beat him to the pole and presented the author with gifts of a didrachm of Alexander, a tetradrachm of an Armenian monarch, a sheet of rare Arctic stamps for his son, a lump of greenstone and a small gold nugget. Conan Doyle signed some books for Kinsey, giving the date as 'The Sacking of Woomeroo' (Kinsey's house in the northern Christchurch suburb of Papanui was called Warrimoo) because his host had been so generous. Kinsey had a copy of Conan Doyle's *The Coming of the Fairies* and several cards that the author had sent him were recovered from the book. These are now held at the National Library of New Zealand in Wellington and are testament to the men's friendship. 'A belated greeting from the old land,' wrote Conan Doyle on a Christmas card with the words 'A Psychic Greeting' printed on the cover. He also gave Kinsey one of the infamous 'Cottingley Fairies' photographs. On the back Conan Doyle had inscribed:

> Fairies photographed in a wood in the village of Cottingley near Bradford by two children, daughter and niece of the Electrician of a small factory there. Passed by experts and certified by Ed. L. Gardner of the Theosophical Society.
>
> A. CONAN DOYLE.

Sir Joseph Kinsey 'collects everything with appalling indiscriminateness,' wrote George Bernard Shaw. Kinsey welcomed the Shaws with 'shouting geniality' into his home when the playwright and his wife were on a whistle-stop tour of the city. Kinsey 'gave me an ornithorhynchus, and I am taming it,' said Mark Twain. The author didn't allow the huge stuffed platypus 'to leave his arms while are moving from boat to train and train to boat', wrote Olivia Clemens in a thank-you note to Kinsey. 'He says it is his most treasured possession. He does not think even his wife better surpasses it.' Olivia wrote Kinsey she had 'a most enviable collection of Maori things … I feel when I look at them almost as if I must be a chieftainess.' Kinsey 'made Christchurch a darling place and a charming memory for the Clemens family'.

Warrimoo, the large home where Kinsey entertained the likes of Conan Doyle and Shaw, is long gone. In July 2005 another of Kinsey's homes, at 14 Kinsey Terrace, Clifton Hill, was demolished despite the protest of heritage lobbyists. It was Kinsey's weekend cottage where Scott and Shackleton relaxed before setting off for the Antarctic from Lyttelton. The cottage, 'Te Hau', was designed by Samuel Hurst Seager, the same architect who designed Ngaio Marsh's house.

GEORGE BERNARD SHAW AND SIR JOSEPH KINSEY AT 'WARRIMOO', PAPANUI ROAD, CHRISTCHURCH, APRIL 1934 (PHOTOGRAPHER UNKNOWN). ALEXANDER TURNBULL LIBRARY, WELLINGTON, NEW ZEALAND. F-20830-1/2.

On Thursday 17 June 1920, Dr James Hervey Hyslop, former professor of ethics and logic at Columbia University and well-known psychical researcher, passed away. He'd been seriously ill for several months before thrombosis claimed his life at his summer home in Upper Montclair, New Jersey. At his funeral one friend confidently predicted Dr Hyslop's spirit would appear in time. Six months later Dr Hyslop made a reappearance of sorts.

A *Press* leader claimed Conan Doyle's spiritualistic mission was 'deplorable' from two perspectives. As 'a lay newspaper' it left the churches to fight the religious battle. The secular debate was another matter, and the *Press* took it upon itself to defend the 'intelligent layman — the man to whom slovenliness of thought is as offensive as dirt and untidiness in his material surroundings, and who sees in the spiritualist movement only a depressing combination of fraud and mental ill-health'.

> This point of view we feel bound to express at a time when a famous novelist, whose admirable tales have delighted millions of people, is drawing packed houses at the Theatre Royal as a witness to the existence of a spirit world of a most unattractive sort. That Sir Arthur Conan Doyle firmly believes in a spirit world with which one can get into touch almost as one can ring up a friend on the telephone is as certain as that he believes he is doing good by encouraging weak-minded people to fancy that they can hold communion, by ear and eye and touch, with loved ones who are dead. But success as a novelist, as a physician, as a physicist, or in any calling that makes its appeal to men of intellect, does not in the least degree guarantee that a man's delusions are different from, or more worthy of respect than, the delusions of the dull and uneducated.

That morning's newspaper had done little to dissuade Conan Doyle's supporters and a huge crowd showed up at the Theatre Royal. The author addressed the criticism in the *Press* and told the audience he didn't mind opposition, because argument helped to uncover the truth. At this juncture the six-months-dead Dr Hyslop returns to the fray. The *Press* quoted the psychical researcher's work to discredit Conan Doyle. According to the newspaper Hyslop had found many contradictions in descriptions of the afterlife as told by the spiritualists. Unfortunately for the *Press*, its attack was somewhat blunted by an unwitting resurrection. Hyslop was described as the current secretary of the American Society for Psychical Research and Conan Doyle seized upon the error. He made what he considered to be a 'mild and obvious retort' that as Professor Hyslop was dead, 'the *Press* went even further than I in saying that he *is* Professor at Columbia'. His joke sent his audience into fits of laughter. Conan Doyle also said that Hyslop had written a book called *Our Life After Death* and that he was a witness for the defence rather than the prosecution. The *Press* retaliated by suggesting the audience laughed at the Hyslop joke 'because, knowing nothing whatever about the facts, it was ready to believe anything Sir Arthur cared to say'.

The facts according to the *Press* were that Hyslop was listed as living in New York in the 1919 *Who's Who in America*, his book *Contact with the Other World* was published in 1919 and he was alive when *The World* compiled its 1920 Almanac, in which he appeared as the secretary of the American Society for Psychical Research. Yet in December 1920 Conan Doyle said he had been dead for 'some years'.

The editor of the *Press* was bombarded with letters from supporters and cynics. It published a variety of responses from church leaders under such headlines as 'A Blasphemy Nurtured In Fraud'; 'Spiritism The Abrogation Of Reason' and 'An Ancient Delusion'. Rev. W. Ready, of the Durham Street Methodist Church, wrote that spiritualism was popular because the Great War had changed the soul and the outlook of Europe.

> Today persons are only too glad to hear a whisper, or welcome a breeze from the invisible world to which their dear ones have gone in their thousands. Tide has turned. Materialism is bankrupt. Broken-hearted men and women have turned away from cold, comfortless materialism, and are now found clinging to some straw which may release the strain of their poor hearts, and the straws many are clinging to are crystals, table-rapping, séances, mediums, fairies, and last, but not least, the photographs, or what Conan Doyle calls 'psychic photography', where the medium loses from 20 to 30lb in the process of exhibition, really a fine remedy for anti-fat.

Annoyed that the *Press* had attacked his accuracy about Hyslop's death, Conan Doyle sent a letter to the editor.

> Sir, — I am amazed that the death of so well known a man as Professor Hyslop should be unknown in New Zealand, and still more that it should be imagined that I, who devote my life to this study, could possibly make a mistake upon so important a point. I had intended to say 'some time', and if I said 'some years' it was certainly a slip of the tongue. It may have been early in the present year, or it may have been late in the past one, but that he is dead is absolutely certain. It is difficult for me to give an exact date when I am away from all my means of reference.
>
> Yours faithfully,
> **ARTHUR CONAN DOYLE**

To this the *Press* responded that it was 'sorry that Sir Arthur did not do himself the justice of including in his letter the apology which we think was due from him'. The paper claimed that Conan Doyle had chosen to ignore the real point of the first editorial by focusing on the date of Mr Hyslop's death. Nevertheless, the paper couldn't drop the apparently trivial issue either.

> He ignored the crucial difficulty and rode off with a jeer at 'The Press' for not knowing that Mr Hyslop had been, as he alleged, 'dead for some years'. He obtained the 'laughter and applause' that he aimed at, and left the audience, as he intended, with the impression that there was nothing further to be said concerning our quotations, which the audience, as he intended, would imagine he had disposed of. Whether Mr Hyslop had been dead 10 or 20 years, as Sir Arthur's words suggested, did not, as a matter of fact, affect the point of our quotation [from Hyslop's book] at all. But Sir Arthur's statement was grossly opposed to fact. As we pointed out yesterday, Mr Hyslop, who issued a volume last year, was living when the 1920 almanacs were issued.
>
> Now Sir Arthur tells us that he is 'amazed' that we should imagine that he 'could possibly make a mistake upon so important a point'. After this, he admits that he did make a mistake. He 'intended' to say something else, and if he did say 'some years' — as he did — it was 'a slip of the tongue'. He does not even now know when Mr Hyslop died, but he thinks it may have been early in the present year or late in the past one. As a matter of fact, we had evidence that Mr Hyslop was alive until very recently, and so far as we were aware he was alive when we wrote. We have since ascertained that he did not die until June last, and it will therefore be clear to everyone that accuracy and candour were alike defied by Sir Arthur when he told his audience, in effect, that 'The Press' was ignorantly quoting a man of whose death many years ago it was unaware. It is difficult for Sir Arthur, as he says, to give exact dates when away from all his means of reference, but his reference books are surely not indispensable to the preparation of an apology when it is clearly due.

No apology was forthcoming, but another letter was.

> Sir, — I am collecting New Zealand curiosities, so I will take your leading article home with me. To get the full humour of it one has to remember the sequence of events. In a leading article you remarked that Professor Hyslop IS Professor of Logic. I answered with mild irony that he certainly is not, as he has been

> dead 'some years' or 'some time' – which of the two is perfectly immaterial, since I presume you will agree that in either case he had ceased to be Professor of Columbia. To this you were rash enough to reply with a challenging article with large headlines, declaring that I had blundered, and that this was typical of the inaccuracy of Spiritualists. I wrote a gentle remonstrance to show that I had not blundered, and that my assertion was essentially true, since the man was dead. This you now tacitly admit, but instead of expressing regret you ask for an apology from me. I have engaged in much newspaper controversy, but I can truly say that I can recall no such instance of effrontery as this. — Yours, etc.
>
> ARTHUR CONAN DOYLE

There was an appropriately disdainful response. It pointed out that Conan Doyle had made an error in claiming the *Press* stated Mr Hyslop *is* Professor of Logic instead of 'formerly' Professor of Logic. The newspaper predicted Conan Doyle would put the mistake down to another 'slip of the pen' and that if he was so careless with facts it was surely further evidence of the dubiousness of fairies and ectoplasm. The readers were made aware of a recent article Conan Doyle had written for the *Strand* magazine mentioning Professor Hyslop as if he were still alive.

> Of course he will have an explanation: it was merely a slip of the pen, or it does not mean what it appears to mean, or something else. We are sorry we have had occasion to complain of our distinguished visitor's lapse from candour, courtesy, and accuracy, but the result may be beneficial to him, since he will probably take care in the future, when opening hostilities, not again to use a gun that bursts in his hand.

Some correspondents supported Conan Doyle, including Dr John Guthrie, who the author never met but thanked in *The Wanderings of a Spiritualist*. 'I do think that Christchurch has some need to apologise for its controversialists — much more need than our distinguished visitor has to apologise for what we all know to be his honest convictions,' Guthrie wrote. Conan Doyle believed he had woken up a cathedral city with 'a disturbing inrush from the outer world'.

Twain told the *Press* he was very impressed with the standard of New Zealand newspapers. He was so busy he only read editorials because he believed they reflected the quality and character of a paper. He digested newspaper editorials in Melbourne, Sydney and New Zealand and he liked the 'vigour of their style, their scholarly language, and logical conclusions'. Christchurch was a small place with some forty thousand inhabitants, yet it could support two large daily papers, two evening papers, and two weekly journals. This was unprecedented in Twain's experience. 'It shows a real live intellectual community when so many journals are in full swing.'

The *North Canterbury Gazette* ran a very introspective editorial evaluating George Bernard Shaw's visit that lamented a deterioration of New Zealanders' development and attitude. That Shaw 'regards us generally as interesting half-grownups who are suffering from arrested development of individuality, with its accompanying deficiency in the sense of responsibility, is precisely what all visitors of distinguished intellect, before and after Lord Bryce, have said about us'. It was suggested that early settlers, because of their isolation from Britain, created a society free from many of the ills of the one they had left behind. But as communications, trade and financial indebtedness strengthened ties to the 'Old Country', New Zealanders became complacent and were at the stage of 'mooching along like remittance men, who have no opinions of their own, and no vigour of mind to create an individuality worthwhile'. Shaw claimed New Zealanders were too dependent on the mother country, still referring to it as 'Home', and the *North Canterbury Gazette* criticised those who had taken offence at the playwright's remarks.

> Mr Shaw, like all men of superior talent, combines two strongly opposing tendencies in the one personality. As a creative thinker he is, and has to be, strong for individuality and all its modes of expression. As a strongly socially-minded being, just as often he is a trenchant exposer of the pathetic and often maudlin weakness of individuals, whether single men, industries, or nations. It is only the duffers, the solemn persons who are now on platforms and in the newspapers airing their solemnities, who fail to understand this when it is pointed out to them. But duffers we must have, and duffers apparently we must always have, since otherwise the world would be all leaven and no lump.

Shaw read a newspaper report that the district radio inspector in Christchurch had banned the epilogue to his play *Androcles and the Lion* for being too controversial. He said the epilogue wasn't part of the play and had nothing to do with the play so it probably shouldn't have been broadcast anyway. 'Except for the time signals and the weather reports, everything on the wireless is controversial,' he added. *Androcles and the Lion,* written in 1912, was made up of a prologue and two sets, but no epilogue to be read by an actor on stage. Shaw added a long footnote to the published version about the play's purpose, and that was the target of the ban.

Shaw challenged the city's conservatism by supporting intermarriage between Maori and Pakeha even though 'several voices tried to persuade him to express his view on how the purely European population was likely to develop'. He thought Hitler's theories of a pure Aryan race were 'rubbish' and that the 'half-caste is a very remarkable person who possesses the standards of two races instead of one'.

There was a clairvoyant dog in Christchurch. It could bark out the number of coins in a man's pocket, or so Arthur Conan Doyle had been told by a stipendiary magistrate in Auckland. The author was told that there were 'four learned beasts in history: a marvellous horse in Shakespeare's time, which was burned with its master in Florence; the Boston skipper's dog; Hans, the Russian horse; and Darkie of Christchurch.' Inevitably, Conan Doyle visited the gifted dog's owner, Mrs McGibbon, and found the animal in question to be a 'dark, vivacious fox terrier, sixteen years old, blind and deaf, which obviously impaired his powers'. Mrs McGibbon's son had 'discovered' the dog's powers, which apparently included the ability to bark out the number of males (including himself in the total) and the number of human beings (excluding himself in the total) in the room. The animal barked constantly and pawed excitedly at Conan Doyle. 'When a half-crown was placed before him and he was asked how many sixpences were in it, he gave five barks, and four for a florin, but when a shilling was substituted he gave twelve, which looked as though he had pennies in his mind. On the whole the performance was a failure, but as he had raised by exhibiting his gifts, £138 for war charities, I took my hat off to him all the same.' Conan Doyle believed the dog once had incredible powers, but 'age and excitement' had impaired them.

A local spiritualist, Mr Michie, practised a type of self-hypnotism as a 'short cut to psychic power' that made him skeletally thin. His wife claimed the spirit of a man called Gordon Stanley spoke to her husband through her. Stanley warned Michie to fight the illness, saying his death happened in the same way. The 'spirit' was a clerk in Cole's Book Arcade in Melbourne and he gave Michie his widow's address. Michie wrote to her and got a reply that confirmed her husband had died two years previously from consumption and that he had been a clerk in Cole's Arcade. Conan Doyle wrote that although there were dangers in 'psychic research', death in pursuit of knowledge is sometimes acceptable. 'To meet death in conquering death is to die in victory.'

Samuel Butler earned a reputation in his lifetime as a crackpot philosopher but in death he came to be regarded as a significant Victorian writer. He arrived in the port of Lyttelton in 1860 and made the Canterbury high country his home until he returned to England four years later. He was originally booked on the ill-fated ship *Burmah*, which sank without trace on her way to New Zealand. Butler switched ships when it became apparent that passenger space on the *Burmah* was going to be reduced to make room for stock. He journeyed to New Zealand at the suggestion of his father, with whom he had argued over his refusal to enter the church and his desire to become an artist. The Cambridge-educated Butler, whose interests included classical literature, science, psychology, religion and ethics, resolved to become a farmer.

> The all-engrossing topics seemed to be sheep, horses, dogs, cattle, English grasses, paddocks, bush, and so forth. From about seven o'clock in the evening till about twelve at night I cannot say that I heard much else. These were the exact things I wanted to hear about, and I listened till they had been repeated so many times over that I almost grew tired of the subject, and wished the conversation would turn to something else. A few expressions were not familiar to me ... I was rather startled at hearing one gentleman ask another whether he meant to wash this year, and receive the answer 'No.' I soon discovered that a person's sheep are himself. If his sheep are clean, he is clean. He does not wash his sheep before shearing, but he washes; and, most marvellous of all, it is not his sheep which lamb, but he 'lambs down' himself.

Butler looked for a piece of land to establish a sheep station and from where he could explore the Canterbury high country. He was an inexperienced farmer and when he built a cob hut the thatches were put on upside down and the rain came in. But eventually his station was lucrative and his subsequent travels inspired one of his most famous works.

SAMUEL BUTLER IN 1862 (PHOTOGRAPHER UNKNOWN). ALEXANDER TURNBULL LIBRARY, WELLINGTON, NEW ZEALAND. F-3076-1/4.

✶

On the walk from Coker's Hotel to the centre of the city Kipling, with the *Lyttelton Times* reporter still in tow, complimented the horses, cabs, street verandahs, shops and the large glass windows he passed. He had a shave at Messrs Davis and Lamb's near Cathedral Square, an establishment he thought quite American in style. He admired Cathedral Square and although he'd been told Christchurch was like an English town he thought it more American. He looked inside the City Council Chamber, which he liked but thought far too extravagant for a place the size of Christchurch.

He called to see a friend at the Canterbury Club, which still stands on the corner of Worcester Boulevard and Cambridge Terrace. The friend wasn't there and Kipling left his card. He admired the black swans and their fluffy cygnets on the Avon River as he headed towards Canterbury College to meet his old sharp-tongued master from the English military college he attended a decade earlier. F.W. Haslam may have inspired Kipling's creation of the character 'King' in *Stalky and Co.* Kipling and Haslam reminisced for while, looked into College Hall where an exam was taking place, and then went to a classroom where Kipling was amused by the graffiti on the desks. Kipling was a scribbler himself. On board the *Doric* bound for New Zealand he covered the marble tables in the smoke room with pen and ink sketches and the stewards had to wash away his artwork in the morning. Canterbury College became the University of Canterbury and the site of the original university on Worcester Street is now an arts centre.

Kipling and Haslam, with the intrepid reporter for company, visited the museum, the Provincial Council Chamber (also too lavish according to Kipling) and the art gallery. The Canterbury Society of Arts' gallery on the corner of Armagh and Durham Streets, now used by the Law Courts, was the public gallery until 1932. The Armagh Street section opened in 1890, the year before Kipling's visit, but the Durham Street extension wouldn't open until 1895. While they were admiring paintings a fire bell rang nearby. Kipling was anxious to get to the blaze as speedily as possible and he betrayed his military training with a call to 'double'. Kipling watched the fire fighters extinguish the blaze in an old wooden stable and headed for the Christchurch Club, which can still be found on Worcester Street. From there he returned to the train station.

Kipling Street runs through Addington, a suburb to the southwest of the city centre. A statue of Kipling stands on the street that bears his name; it's one of a number of Christchurch streets named after famous authors. Dickens, Wordsworth, Byron, Tennyson, Shakespeare, Ruskin, Burke and Barrie all share the honour.

Kipling's statue is a bench on which the solitary author sits and waits for someone to join him. 'I always prefer to believe the best of everybody — it saves so much trouble' is inscribed on the back of the bench. There's also a plaque that commemorates his morning in the city and the encounter with the Coker's Hotel barmaid. The real Kipling travelled back to Lyttelton by train in time for the *Talune*'s 1 p.m. departure for Dunedin. Kipling was seen waving to Haslam and the reporter from the deck of the ship. He would never return.

CHASING THE GOLDEN FLEECE

AT TWENTY MINUTES TO TEN on a Thursday morning in the spring of 1860 Samuel Butler arrived at a wooden building on the corner of Worcester Street and Oxford Terrace. As he stepped into the Christchurch Land Office he braced himself for a confrontation. 'If it came to fists, I should get the worst of it — that was a moral certainty — and I really half-feared something of the kind.' Official business hours began at ten o'clock but the main door was open and Butler soon discovered the rooms inside were open as well. There was an application book on a table in whose pages was a list of names of those with a claim for land. The court settled the claims in the order they appeared in the list. 'I opened it with trembling fingers, and saw my adversary's name written in bold handwriting, defying me, as it were, to do my worst.'

The Land Office was the finishing post in a two-day horseback race packed with drama. The starting line was in a place Butler called Mesopotamia, a stretch of land along the Rangitata River at the foothills of the Southern Alps. He'd found it after several expeditions from Christchurch to the backcountry in search of unoccupied territory. But there was a problem. A large, rough, threatening run-holder called Caton had an application for 5000 acres of land close to the site Butler had earmarked and the boundaries were uncertain. What's more Caton had erected a hut on the disputed site believing the land was legally his and it was the very same spot as Butler intended to build his new home. Caton claimed to own the freehold on the land his hut stood on; Butler was sure Caton hadn't bought the freehold but suspected he was about to, so the race began.

Butler set off for Christchurch on a Tuesday afternoon, knowing the Land Office Board sat on Thursday. He stopped to eat at a shepherd's hut five kilometres down the road and intended to travel stealthily through the night. After crossing the swollen Ashburton River several times in complete darkness he became too afraid to continue, so he camped until dawn. He resumed his trek at sunrise and sensed he was being followed. Butler turned around and saw Caton a few hundred metres behind him. The two men rode together for a while, 'each of us of course well aware of the other's intentions, but too politic to squabble about them when squabbling was no manner of use'.

Whoever was first to record their name in the application book at the Land Office would be the first to have their case to purchase the 20 acres around the hut heard. Butler stopped for breakfast mid-morning but Caton rode on. Before noon, about a hundred kilometres from Christchurch, Butler's horse went lame. He obviously didn't have much faith in the animal because he had kept close to stations where he could get a replacement. Caton had no such concerns. He had a good horse so was able to leave the tracks and take short cuts over stony ground.

Caton managed to pull out a lead of a few hours and stopped at an inn about forty kilometres from Christchurch. Later that night Butler reached the same hostelry but left immediately on hearing his competitor was inside. The heavy rain stopped him setting up camp for the night so he was forced to keep moving. He eventually reached another guesthouse about twenty kilometres from Christchurch. He slept a few hours and made it into the city by seven in the morning, believing he could do nothing until ten when the office officially opened.

But Caton's name was already in the application book. Butler was ready to argue that it had been recorded before office hours and was therefore null and void, but on closer inspection, he noticed his own name already in the ledger. His solicitor had entered it into the book the previous day. But on even closer inspection he saw Caton's name *above* his own. How was this possible?

Caton had clearly and illegally inserted his name out of order. He could have faced legal action but his solicitor was Crown prosecutor. However, the commissioners took a dim view of the misdemeanour and Butler was allowed to purchase the disputed land. After winning the case Butler went to his solicitor's office in Oxford Terrace, sat down at the piano and worked off his tension by playing Bach fugues.

A First Year in Canterbury Settlement is a combination of letters home and articles Butler wrote for his Cambridge college journal. It tells of his story and explorations in his new home. Butler came to hate the book, which was published by his family in 1863, but it's a vivid and detailed account of settler life in Canterbury.

> The road from Christ Church to Main's [accommodation house] is metalled for about four and a half miles; there are fences and fields on both sides, either laid down in English grass or sown with grain; the fences are chiefly low ditch and

> bank planted with gorse, rarely with quick, the scarcity of which detracts from the resemblance to English scenery which would otherwise prevail.

His journey continued southward through the 'interminably monotonous' yellow tussock plains. To his left was Banks Peninsula, 'a system of submarine volcanoes culminating in a flattened dome, little more than 3000 feet high', and far away to the right rose the mountains of the 'Snowy Range', which Christchurch residents thought to be the backbone of the South Island. Beyond the range the land was mountainous, but the mountains themselves 'were seldom, if ever, until in immediate proximity to the West Coast range, abrupt like the descent from the top of Snowdon towards Capel Curig or the precipices of Clogwyn Du'r Arddu. The great range is truly Alpine, and the front-range occasionally reaches an altitude of nearly 7000 feet.'

Butler crossed the dry riverbed through which the Waimakariri once flowed to Lake Ellesmere, but had changed course north of Christchurch. The Waimakariri is a braided river, common in the South Island but not worldwide. Eroded pieces of the Southern Alps end up on riverbeds forcing an ever changing course.

'One sees Main's about six miles off, and it appears to be about six hours before one reaches it,' wrote Butler. More tussock-filled monotonous plains with cabbage trees lay in wait the following day, until he reached the Waikitty (the Selwyn River or Waikirikiri). 'It is wonderful how small an object gets a name in the great dearth of features. Cabbage-tree hill, half-way between Main's and the Waikitty, is an almost imperceptible rise some ten yards across and two or three feet high: the cabbage-trees have disappeared,' he wrote. He travelled on to the banks of the Rakaia, the second largest river in Canterbury. Butler thought the Rakaia looked more Italian than Swiss. It flowed through alternating patterns of calm and rapid water every few metres.

> The Rakaia sometimes comes down with a run — a wall of water two feet high, rolling over and over, rushes down with irresistible force. I know a gentleman who had been looking at some sheep upon an island in the Rakaia, and, after finishing his survey, was riding leisurely to the bank on which his house was situated. Suddenly, he saw the river coming down upon him in the manner I have described, and not more than two or three hundred yards off. By a forcible application of the spur, he was enabled to reach terra firma, just in time to see the water sweeping with an awful roar over the spot that he had been traversing not a second previously. This is not frequent: a fresh generally takes four or five hours to come down, and from two days to a week, ten days, or a fortnight, to subside again.

The dangerous rivers flowing from the Southern Alps to Canterbury's east coast intrigued Anthony Trollope and he wrote of them in both his fiction and non-fiction. He remembered the hazardous river crossings along the coast between Christchurch and Oamaru: the Rakaia, the Rangitata, the Waitaki; and they inspired parts of *Catherine Carmichael.* After getting married in Christchurch on Christmas Day, Catherine and her new husband travel two days and two nights down the east coast. As she crosses 'one great river after another on their passage down, Kate felt how well it would be that the waters should pass over her head.'

'The rivers here form the chief peculiarity of the country,' wrote Trollope.

> They are very broad, having generally two, three, or more courses, which when flooded by rains or by melting snow form one broad and rapid course. They are for the most part unbridged, and therefore at certain times impassable. Over one river with apparently endless different courses, called the Rangitata, we were preceded by a horseman who for his services charged us 2s. a piece. Over another, the Rakaia, the first elements of a railway bridge had been constructed, and we were taken over on a truck dragged by a horse who kept the bed of the river where it was dry or the water shallow, and ascended to the level of the frail-looking bridge where the stream was deep. The whole thing looked like sudden death, — but we reached the farther side of the Rakaia in safety, and were only charged 2s. a head for all that was done for us.

Catherine and Peter arrive at Mt Warriwa, a fictional sheep run on wide prairie land. Trollope wrote that the closest town for doing business was Timaru about forty miles away. 'There was not much there for a woman to love, but little as there was, she could have loved it for the man's sake, had the man been lovable.' But then John Carmichael returns to the sheep run. And he's the man Catherine loves. She resolves to tell her husband about her feelings. 'She must do that, or else she must become a false wife. As she thought of the possibility of being false, an ecstasy of sweetness for a moment pervaded her senses. To throw herself on his bosom and tell him that she loved him would be compensation almost sufficient to the misery of the last twelve months. Then the word wife crept into her ears ...' Catherine reveals her secret and insists John be sent away, so she can resist temptation. Peter agrees and takes John by horse and cart to Timaru.

Mark Twain arrived in Timaru in November 1895 and they had flocked from places like Temuka and Geraldine to hear the great man. But some people at the Theatre Royal didn't think he was funny enough. His humour was 'but the foam floating upon a deep stream of serious thought and of liquid wisdom,' reported the *Timaru Herald.* But not everybody understood the subtlety of Twain's wit. The editor of a Dunedin monthly literary magazine, the *Triad*, said Twain seemed 'to have conquered about ten percent of his hearers'. Someone heckled Twain as he spoke of Huck Finn's struggle with his conscience. Apparently it was 'all tommy-rot!'

> How is it that young men who have never been further than Waimate on the one side, and Temuka on the other, will persist in dogmatically opposing a crude opinion evolved from the 'idiotic area' of their puny little 'squinting brains', to the judgement of the cultivated world?
>
> *Triad*, 25 November 1895

Twain performed on a Saturday and there were no trains out of Timaru on a Sunday. So he relaxed and drove around the neighbouring countryside, noting in his journal 'folds of land with gullies between; green & trim & clean great fields (grain — wheat and oats) — big pastures full of sheep'.

Peter Carmichael drives out of Timaru. He crosses the 'two smaller rivers' in safety and reaches Trollope's creation, the Warriwa River. There is one ferryman. It is dark, the rivers are high and there is a strong current even though it is summer. The ferryman initially refuses to cross. He doesn't want to be drowned on Christmas Eve. But eventually he relents, and during the crossing Peter drowns. His body is taken back to Warriwa and Catherine's brothers go to the Queensland goldfield where John is told of his brother's death. He returns and the long-awaited reunion between the two sweethearts leads to an ending one critic described as 'perhaps the most perfunctory — and embarrassed? — ending in all [Trollope's] fictional works'.

Mark Twain visited Oamaru, where the fictional John begins the last leg of his journey back to Warriwa. The town still boasts impressive Victorian buildings made from the white limestone quarried nearby. The stone is soft enough to saw but hardens on exposure to the air. Twain performed at the Theatre Royal, a two-storey building on the corner of Thames and Coquet Streets near the waterfront. When the theatre was completed in March 1883 it was considered to be 'a measure of Oamaru's progress'. It later became the largest department store in town but burned down in 1969.

'The people of Oamaru were not slow to appreciate the opportunity of seeing and hearing the author whose books have been a potent restorative to many a drooping and despondent mind,' wrote a local correspondent. Those who didn't find American wit funny were 'too lugubrious to be tempted to smile even at the sight of a cork screw'. Twain came 'like a ray of sunshine into the troubled mind'. The town had 'seen the author of these delightful productions that range from "The Jumping Frog" to "The Tramp Abroad" and "Pudd'n-head Wilson", and his visit will linger long and lovingly in our memories'.

*

After crossing the Rakaia, Samuel Butler headed inland towards the Southern Alps along one branch of the Ashburton River, turning away from the Canterbury coast well before reaching Timaru and Oamaru. He had to cross the river repeatedly across featureless plains. 'We halted for the night at a shepherd's hut: awakening out of slumber I heard the fitful gusts of violent wind come puff, puff, buffet, and die away again; nor'-wester all over. I went out and saw the unmistakable north-west clouds tearing away in front of the moon.'

After unloading and greasing the dray, they set off with only half their load anticipating a bad road ahead. They would make a return journey for the remaining half.

> One dray had been over the ground before us. That took four days to do the first ten miles, and then was delayed several weeks on the bank of the Rangitata by a series of very heavy freshes, so we determined on trying a different route: we got farther on our first day than our predecessor had done in two, and then Possum, one of the bullocks, lay down (I am afraid he had had an awful hammering in a swampy creek where he had stuck for two hours), and would not stir an inch; so we turned them all adrift with their yokes on (had we taken them off we could not have yoked them up again), whereat Possum began feeding in a manner which plainly showed that there had not been much amiss with him. But during the interval that elapsed between our getting into the swampy creek and getting out of it a great change had come over the weather ... suddenly I felt a chill, and looking at the lake below saw that the white-headed waves had changed their direction, and that the wind had chopped round to sou'-west.

Butler's party left the dray behind. They found a hut with no roof but there was firewood and water. Then it started to snow. On the third evening Butler decided alcohol was in order and two men volunteered to trudge up to the steep terrace about forty-five metres above the hut. It took at least two hours before the men returned with the two-gallon keg, 'vowing that never in their lives before had they worked so hard'.

> Great excitement prevailed over drawing the cork. It was fast; it broke the point of someone's knife. 'Shove it in,' said I, breathless with impatience; no — no

> — it yielded, and shortly afterwards, giving up all opposition, came quickly out. A tin pannikin was produced. With a gurgling sound out flowed the precious liquid. 'Halloa!' said one; 'it's not brandy, it's port wine.' 'Port wine!' cried another; 'it smells more like rum.' I voted for its being claret; another moment, however, settled the question, and established the contents of the cask as being excellent vinegar. The two unfortunate men had brought the vinegar keg instead of the brandy.

At Mesopotamia, Butler read, explored, wrote and played Handel on his piano. The instrument had been transported by bullock dray from Christchurch. Handel and his music played a key part in his life and he always had music in his head. The years Butler spent there were lucrative: he almost doubled his capital, which enabled him to return to a comfortable life in England.

Blaise Cendrars wrote about a visit to New Zealand in the 1920s in 'Noël en Nouvelle-Zélande'. He described a farmhouse in which a glamorously dressed couple were sitting together at a piano playing *Pagliacci*. They were 'playing solely for each other, shoulder-to-shoulder, smiling radiantly. They were alone on the face of the earth ...' Cendrars, (the pseudonym of Frédéric Sauser) was a Swiss poet, novelist, soldier and merchant seaman who roamed the world living an adventurous, Bohemian-style existence. He lost his right arm in the First World War and then got into the movies. He worked in Europe and Hollywood before continuing his travels around the world. Cendrars portrayed New Zealand as a 'Land of Milk and Honey' where animals grazed peacefully on lush grass and a traveller could journey for days by car or weeks by horseback without seeing another human. Auckland-based poet Michael Jackson translated 'Noël en Nouvelle-Zélande' into English. He believed that Cendrars eulogised the environment he had deserted as a teenager and overlooked the 'violent dispossession that lay behind New Zealand's deforested hills and pioneer farms'.

The first chapters of Samuel Butler's much-revered novel, *Erewhon*, are largely based on his explorations in the Canterbury high country. Along with John Holland Baker in early 1861, he discovered a way through the Alps to the West Coast that would later be called the Whitcombe Pass. This expedition has been immortalised in *Erewhon* and is commemorated in landmarks like Butler Saddle, Mt Butler and the Butler Range. 'Exploring is delightful to look forward to and back upon, but it is not comfortable at the time, unless it be of such an easy nature as not to deserve the name,' Butler wrote in his novel. *Erewhon*, an anagram of Nowhere, satirises English social and economic injustices in an utopian setting. In the upside-down world of Erewhon, illnesses, including the common cold, are punished as crimes while lying and stealing are treated as unfortunate afflictions. Machines are banned so they can't take over the world. The narrator is a traveller, jailed by the Erewhonians, who eventually escapes with his fiancée in a large balloon. They crash in the Pacific but are rescued by an Italian ship and taken to England.

The first edition of *Erewhon* sold out in three weeks. Butler attributed its 'unlooked-for success' to complimentary reviews in the *Pall Mall Gazette* and the *Spectator*. 'It is obvious that we have amongst us a satirist of very remarkable literary power, as well as of a very cynical turn of mind. Since the days of Swift nothing has been written abler in its peculiar way, and certainly nothing more thoroughly bitter and contemptuous in its drift,' reported the *Spectator*. Butler would be remembered as 'the lord of irony, that master-spell,' predicted *The Times*.

Erewhon Revisited, published in 1901, was Butler's first book not published at his own expense. The traveller returns to find the Erewhonians, amazed by his disappearance, have made him the subject of a new religion. Some critics claimed the sequel surpassed the original, but *Erewhon* sold more copies.

Trollope is believed to have read *Erewhon* before writing one of his strangest novels, *The Fixed Period*. Both works are narrated in the first person by men who have returned to England from strange, fictional lands. Trollope's story is set on a futuristic (the late 1970s and early 1980s) island inhabited by an 'elite' group of New Zealanders who have gained peaceful independence from Britain. In Erewhon it is illegal to become ill or infirmed in any way before the age of 70; in Trollope's Britannula euthanasia is compulsory. The island is governed by the popular President Neverbend who introduces a law that every citizen should undergo compulsory euthanasia by having their veins cut in a warm bath while sedated with morphine just before their sixty-eighth birthday. Then they would be cremated. Neverbend offers to perform the first 'executions' and to dispel concerns about the smell of dead bodies he tests the furnaces. He 'supplied four immense hogs in order that the system might be fairly tested, and I had fattened them for the purpose, as old men are not unusually very stout.' A 'slight flavour of the pig' escaped after a trapdoor was left open by accident.

Citizens would prepare for death with a year in a special college in 'Necropolis'. People were promised an escape from the miseries of old age but Neverbend's motives were more economic than humane. 'It would keep us out of debt, make for us our railroads, render all our rivers navigable, construct our bridges, and leave us shortly the richest people on God's earth!'

Neverbend was looking to save £1 million each year by killing the 68-year-olds. Trollope reported in *Australia and New Zealand* that in 1871 the country's debt was £1.1 million. During his visit Trollope was very critical of the heavy borrowing of New Zealand's then Colonial Treasurer Julius Vogel. In his novel the elite New Zealanders rebel against the government's proposed level of public debt and it's one of the reasons they leave. Britannula's citizens ultimately revolt against Neverbend and his policies. Those nearing compulsory death ask England for assistance and a warship is sent to retake the colony. Trollope wrote *The Fixed Period* approaching an age at which, if he were living in Britannula, he would be preparing to face his death. Trollope died a couple of weeks after collapsing suddenly at the dinner table. He was a few months short of his sixty-eighth birthday. His attempt at satire and science fiction received a mixed response and critics panned it as 'essentially ghastly', 'a grim joke' and 'unfortunate'.

J.B. Priestley described Samuel Butler as 'in many ways the oddest and in the end the most distinguished of all New Zealand immigrants'. The playwright visited the type of Canterbury high country stations that his predecessor wrote so vividly about. Priestley was making his way down the South Island from Christchurch. He stayed at well-known sheep stations in the Canterbury high country: Mt Possession and Mt Peel, where Butler used to visit.

Priestley believed New Zealand to be the 'most fortunate' British colony, as the rough types had only streamed into the country for relatively short periods—during the whaling periods and the gold rush. 'There had been no constant importation of riffraff, boozy remittance men, desperate types a jump ahead of the police, and the like. The wild Irish had mostly gone to New York and Boston, there to corrupt local politics; or to Australia, where they succeeded in keeping warm an anti-English feeling. It was the industrious God-fearing Anglicans and cautious hard-working Scots who settled in New Zealand.'

The Priestleys headed further east, in the direction of Lake Tekapo, where something 'vaguely sinister, crept into the atmosphere' as the mountains lost their jewel-like colours at sundown. Priestley found New Zealanders unusually friendly because he believed they feared the isolated land they inhabited, with no pests or predators and where flora and fauna flourished, was too good to be true.

James Michener wrote about Lilybank, a station of 70,000 acres and 6000 sheep at the head of the 'superb' Lake Tekapo. It was typical of the sheep stations running merinos on mountainsides. Two large rivers east of Aoraki/Mt Cook, the Godley and the Macaulay, bordered the run while the Southern Alps provided the backdrop. From April to June the sheep were rounded up for 'eye clipping' and 'belly stripping' to prevent their shaggy wool freezing in the snow. Michener wrote that one man remained at 7000 feet above the sheep, tossing stones to keep the flock moving and keeping in touch with the other two by setting fires on the summits. The merino could eat wool off the backs of other sheep to survive, but during a bad winter Lilybank could still lose a quarter of its animals and in 1895 lost the entire flock.

The owner of Lilybank at the time of Michener's visit was Allan Dick. His wife, Betty, wrote a book about the two decades or so she spent there. Visitors came to Lilybank to learn about the geography, geology, flora, fauna and daily life on a high country station. Americans had a particular interest in the station. 'Situated as we are geographically we naturally appeal strongly to the "hunting" American visitor … These folk, complete with New Zealand guide, spend weeks on our mountains getting heads for their "trophy room" back in the States. Heads of deer, camois, and Himalayan thar shot in our mountains are greatly prized.'

During the 1990s Tommy Suharto, the disgraced son of the former Indonesian dictator, acquired Lilybank Station. He built a luxury hunting resort on the property then sold the property to a former Singaporean business associate Alan Poh for $1. It returned to New Zealand hands in 2002 when Lilybank was advertised at a little over $7 million.

Lilybank lies in the Mackenzie Country, a high inland basin beneath Aoraki/Mt Cook and the Southern Alps, named (although with different spelling) after the notorious James Mckenzie who was imprisoned in 1855 for driving a thousand stolen sheep from a South Canterbury station to the relatively unexplored region that now bears his name. Mckenzie denied the offence and was given a free pardon after his case was found to be flawed. He is thought to have left for Australia. Mckenzie became a folk hero to settlers wanting their own land in an area of rich landowners and conservative Canterbury society. Butler wrote of the notorious shepherd who was 'a man of great physical strength, and can be no common character; many stories are told about him, and his fame will be lasting'. Of Mckenzie's pardon Butler wrote: 'It was rather a strange proceeding, and I doubt how fair to the country which he may have chosen to honour with his presence, for I should suppose there is hardly a more daring and dangerous rascal going. However, his boldness and skill had won him sympathy and admiration, so that I believe the pardon was rather a popular act than otherwise.'

Priestley was driven through the small towns of Geraldine and Fairlie and into the Mackenzie Country. He thought it the 'most enchanting' countryside he had passed. If he were ten years younger, Priestley wrote, he'd return to the 'magical country of melting distant mountains' and emulate New Zealand's landscape painters and live in a caravan. Priestley was urged to see Aoraki/Mt Cook, Australasia's highest peak at 3755 metres, which he was told was on his way to Queenstown. It involved quite a detour. The road to Queenstown forks south at the bottom of Lake Pukaki but Priestley had to turn north to hug the western side of the lake 'which seemed to go on for ever', and further north again from the lake to the base of Aoraki/Mt Cook. Parts of the road were being repaired and it was a bumpy and uncomfortable journey that made Jacquetta feel sick. They eventually reached the luxurious Hermitage Hotel with windows looking out on the great mountain only to discover there were no free rooms. The famous author and his wife had to make do with less luxurious accommodation down the road. They returned to the Hermitage for dinner, 'where for the first time in New Zealand I felt I was surrounded by the rich and the grand'. The foundations of the 1884 Hermitage, which was destroyed in a flash flood in 1913, can still be seen about a kilometre from the current Hermitage.

The summit of Aoraki/Mt Cook appeared the following morning and Priestley painted a mountain he could see across the valley. On his way back down, the road alongside Lake Pukaki didn't seem as bad because he was in a better frame of mind. Everyone exists in an external and an internal place at once he explained. 'Many a man rich enough to own four beautiful houses cannot enjoy them because, in the interior country he carries around, he has chosen to exist in a slum or a miasmic swamp.'

Several travel writers have commented on the frustrating inability to leave ourselves behind when we travel. No matter how relaxing or beautiful an environment, work, stress, sickness, tiredness or preconceived notions about a place can all spoil the travel experience. 'We see places through our humours as though differently coloured glasses. We are ourselves a term in the equation, a note of the chord, and make discord or harmony almost at will,' Robert Louis Stevenson wrote in his essay 'On the Enjoyment of Unpleasant Places'. Stevenson thought it was possible for someone to think themselves into sympathy with their surroundings. 'We become thus, in some sense, a centre of beauty; we are provocative of beauty, much as a gentle and sincere character is provocative of sincerity and gentleness in others.' Priestley had a similar solution: moving away from the bad places in our minds would 'work in a rough-and-ready fashion and release us from much misery'.

Priestley couldn't remember the name of the place where they stopped for a lunch of sandwiches, scones with jam and cream and cold milk mixed with whisky, even after looking at two large maps. But it was somewhere on the road south from Lake Pukaki. He did remember the tearoom with a rose garden and a general store. The woman who ran the shop suggested to the author that it would be good for the local school children to meet someone so famous. A short time later around twenty children and their teacher appeared at the door.

He travelled through Lindis Pass and the rugged, dry plateau of Central Otago, where the mountains in earthy yellows and browns appeared inhospitable and threatening. The landscape reminded Priestley of some of the *Arabian Nights* tales he read as a boy. 'Now and again their slopes burst into fantastic out-croppings of rock, and these might have been all that was left of monstrous idols worshipped by some lost race of giants.' Central Otago was old gold-mining country and he thought the disfigured cliffs both depressing and ugly. Priestley followed the course of the Kawarau River on a road that passes through the spectacular Kawarau Gorge. It was remembered fondly by Agatha Christie in her autobiography and Priestley also recalled the 'green dusk of gorges' as well as seeming to 'hear the thunder of impatient rivers'.

The Priestleys were heading to Queenstown but made a detour to the historic gold-mining town of Arrowtown. The party 'glided' into an avenue of a quiet town that was lined with English trees planted during the gold rush. 'The gold that had once packed the place with miners, roaring in and out of its taverns, had vanished, but only to reappear in so many of its bright leaves.' Priestley complimented the local museum and its display of gold rush era vehicles. Arrowtown was a tourist attraction yet the town had retained its character, in the way Stratford-upon-Avon, close to Priestley's home-village of Alveston, served its own community and not just Shakespeare buffs. He thought Arrowtown looked like a deserted film set and wondered why there hadn't been a feature film about the Otago gold rush. He started thinking about a script entitled *A Stark and Spine-chilling Story of Robbery, Pursuit and Revenge in a Remote and Terrible Wasteland!!!* The story was of three men who were partners in the 1860s gold rush. They found gold and drew lots to decide who should look after the haul before the journey south to get it weighed. The man who won the lottery took the gold in the middle of the night and went north. The other two men pursued the thief, who headed for the mountains once he discovered his former partners were chasing him. It was a plot designed to exploit the breathtaking Otago scenery.

When gold 'broke out', it was like a disease. British novelist Rose Tremain visited Arrowtown on a tour with her husband and, like Priestley before her, she was fascinated by the museum and the landscape. She was inspired to set *The Colour* during the gold rush. Her 'first thought was that there was a wonderful novel to be written about gold, and the lure of gold', and her next was that it was a New Zealand story and she wasn't a New Zealander. So she created characters who came from Norfolk, where she lived, so that they could 'discover everything anew, as I discovered it'. She planned to return for further research but decided a trip might spoil her imagined landscape.

The Colour is the story of Joseph and Harriet Blackstone who emigrated, with Joseph's mother Lilian, from Norfolk to the Canterbury foothills. After finding grains of gold on his land Joseph became obsessed and abandoned his family for the West Coast goldfields. 'For gold is deceitful; this he was beginning to understand. It is as duplicitous as a girl. It shows itself and beckons. Within its first gleam lies the promise of more, much more, and so men go forward, cajoling the earth, breaking their backs and their hearts, but very often they're rewarded with nothing — or almost nothing: just the very little needed to keep hope and longing alive.' Harriet followed her husband only to find an unwelcoming Joseph working barren sites. She discovered the treasure eluding her husband and had an affair with Chinese gardener Pao Yi.

Chinese immigrants came to Otago and Westland to rework the goldfields after the rush had ended. Most came with the intention of returning to China after saving about £100. Jye Kang set his first novel, *Guests of the New Gold Hill*, in the Central Otago goldfields.

The story tells of three generations of the Oon family from the 1860s to 1940. Oon Ho and his son Oon Teh struggled to adapt to the hostile environment of their adopted country but later generations accepted the New Gold Hill as home. Jye Kang was born in China and moved to New Zealand in 1972.

An autumnal Queenstown was 'just beginning to retreat from being a resort into being a sensible little town again'. Priestley spent four nights there in 1973 and he thought Queenstown pleasant, but that its attractiveness came from its position among gorges, the Shotover and Arrow rivers, The Remarkables mountain range and Lake Wakatipu, 'which rises and falls several inches every few minutes as if a vast monster might somehow be still breathing down in its darkness'. He bought books in Wilkinsons Pharmacy, the old family store that has dispensed drugs — and until relatively recently, works of literature — on the corner of Rees Street and The Mall for generations. He'd bought tobacco in a hairdresser's elsewhere in New Zealand so it came as no surprise. Priestley was already laden with heavy luggage so his books were parcelled up and dispatched to England. They took two and a half months to arrive by which time the author had returned home; but it was worth the wait. After reading the first few chapters of F.W.G. Miller's *Golden Days of Lake Country*, he abandoned the idea of a film about the gold rush in favour of a movie about the early settlers around Lake Wakitipu. 'They were better men than the gold-miners, often greedy and dubious, and perhaps better men, only wanting to raise sheep in new country, than most of those we have known in this century.' Queenstown depended on supplies carried by boat from Kingston at the southern tip of Lake Wakitipu. If the supply line stopped for any reason the people went hungry and Priestley heard tales of crazed, starving miners being stopped at gunpoint from raiding newly arrived boats.

Anthony Trollope's point of arrival in New Zealand was Bluff at the bottom of the South Island. It was the middle of winter and the writer was moving north. He had been told that 'Lake Wakitip' was the place to see. The roads were muddy, slushy and snow-covered, but he was determined to see this wondrous scenery. The locals laughed.

The Commissioner of Crown Lands, Mr W.H. Pearson, met Trollope in Invercargill at the government's request. They took the train to Winton and Trollope had to endure 'a long and painful separation' from most of his luggage. It wasn't practical to carry it over the roads so the writer and his wife had to content themselves with a couple of leather bags while the remainder was sent by ship to Dunedin. But it would be some time before Trollope was reunited with his much-missed possessions. 'New Zealand steamboats are the most regularly irregular, and heart-breaking. If a would-be traveller should be informed that steamboats would start from a certain port to another, one on the 1st and another on the 15th of the month, his safest calculation would probably be to make his arrangements for the 8th,' he wrote.

They took a coach from Invercargill over a 'bush' road that passed through a broad valley with snow-capped mountains on either side. The coach was driven and owned by a Swedish innkeeper, in whose hostelry they stopped en route. He was married to a part-Pakeha, part-Maori woman who cooked Trollope delicious boiled turkey and plum pudding. 'I made a note that the mixture of the breed on the female side seemed to be favourable to cookery.' But the money-conscious author was suspicious that her husband had doubled the fare because he was a tourist. They spent the first night at a squatter's house. 'I perceived that the New Zealand squatter regarded himself as a thrice-shorn lamb, but was looked upon by anti-squatter as a very wolf.'

They reached Kingston at the southern point of Lake Wakatipu by noon on the second day. A steamer took the party about halfway up the lake to Queenstown. It was bitterly cold and raining and the scenery was obscured. 'We huddled down into a little cabin, and endeavoured to console ourselves with the reflection that, though all its beauties were hidden from our sight, we were in truth steaming across the most beautiful of the New Zealand lakes. They who cannot find some such consolation from their imagination for external sufferings had better stay at home.' Gold was discovered on the banks of the Shotover River, to the north of the settlement between Queenstown Hill and Bowen Peak. Queenstown was a prosperous goldfield town, its two thousand residents clustered close to the lake. Its location evoked memories of similar lakeside settlements in Italy and Switzerland but the town itself was 'unmistakably English'.

> The great drawback to New Zealand, — or I should more properly say to travelling in New Zealand, — comes from the feeling that after crossing the world and journeying over so many thousand miles, you have not at all succeeded in getting away from England. When you have arrived there you are, as it were, next door to your own house, and yet you have a two months' barrier between yourself and your home.

Trollope had already written extensively about goldfields in Australia and didn't feel the need to visit more around Queenstown. But after a night's rest he travelled to the top of Lake Wakatipu. A steamer that ran from Queenstown to the top of the lake usually went up the lake one day and down the next, once or twice a week. But there was an eminent visitor waiting so the *Jane Williams* steamed up and down in one day. It was cold but the skies were clear.

> I do not know that lake scenery can be finer than that of the upper ten miles

> of Wakatip; — although doubtless it can be very much prettier. The mountains for the most part are bare and steep. Here and there only are they wooded down to the water's edge, — and so much is the timber in request for fuel and building, that what there is of it close to the water will quickly disappear. As the steamer gradually winds round into the upper reach, which runs almost directly north and south, one set of peaks after another comes into view. They are sharp and broken, making the hill-tops look like a vast saw with irregular gaps in it. Perhaps no shape of mountain-top is more picturesque than this.

There were glaciers, lakes, fiords and sounds that were difficult to reach in the early 1870s, but Trollope predicted that the whole Queenstown district would become renowned for its stunning scenery. 'No doubt the time will come when these lakes and mountains, with passes through them which have never yet been trodden, will be as well known to the lovers of Nature as the Alps and Pyrenees,' he wrote in London's *Daily Telegraph.*

The journey from Queenstown to Dunedin, 280 kilometres away on the east coast, should have taken three days in 1872. It took Trollope six. The trip was tedious with forgettable stops at inns along the way. They passed through a succession of goldfield towns and Trollope was interested in the way the architecture in these places had developed. The 'canvas style' (tents) had gone and by the time of the writer's visit corrugated iron dominated, though more advanced wooden houses were being built.

> As I lay in bed in one of these metal inns on the road, I was constrained to hear the private conversation of my host and hostess who had retired for the night. 'So this is Mr Anthony Trollope,' said the host. The hostess assented, but I could gather clearly from her voice that she was thinking much more of her back hair than of her visitor. 'Well,' said the host, 'he must be a fool to come travelling in this country in such weather as this.' Perhaps, after all, the host was aware of the peculiarity of his house, and thought it well that I should know his opinion. He could not have spoken any words with which at that moment I should have been more prone to agree.

Priestley also travelled the road from Queenstown to Dunedin. It passes through Alexandra on the Clutha River, 'a pleasant little town, on a plain of its own, famous for its apricots and a Blossom Festival every September'. Sportspeople and tourists crowded into Alexandra in spring and winter but it was quiet when Priestley arrived. He noted the enormous clock on a cliff face above the town, easily visible during the day and illuminated at night. They lunched at a 'motel-cum-hotel', managed by a friend of his driver Pat Goode. After aperitifs and lunch they continued on to Dunedin.

The road shifts south, between the Old Man Range and the Knobby Range, and reaches the town of Beaumont. Trollope arrived there in deep August snow. It was so heavy the horses were unable to go on so the writer and his wife walked for five hours to Tuapeka (Lawrence), a distance of some twenty kilometres. The *Tuapeka Times* reported that Trollope, his wife and Mr W.H. Pearson arrived in Lawrence shortly after 1 p.m. on Monday, 12 August 1872.

They found an inn where they enjoyed a good meal and such was his enthusiasm for visiting local libraries, Trollope braved the bitter weather and walked around the town. He visited the local athenæum. 'In all these towns there are libraries, and the books are strongly bound and well thumbed. Carlyle, Macaulay, and Dickens are certainly better known to small communities in New Zealand than they are to similar congregations of men and women at home.' The *Tuapeka Times* wrote that Trollope 'was highly gratified ... that the inhabitants of this far corner of the earth read sometimes'.

There had been a rush to the athenæum in the days before the great man's arrival. The townsfolk had wanted to hold a dinner in Trollope's honour at the Commercial Hotel but because the author's schedule was so uncertain due to the inclement weather, it couldn't be organised in time. A letter in the local paper suggested that the recent interest in the library was caused by would-be attendees of the dinner browsing through Trollope's books so they didn't appear ignorant.

The newspaper also took a swipe at Trollope's companion, the Commissioner of Crown Lands Pearson. He 'must have been able to furnish Mr Trollope with valuable information regarding the goldfields, as he has never before visited them. However, the fact that he has existed for a number of years in that lively village Invercargill, without losing possession of his faculties, renders him peculiarly fitted to pilot a stranger through any country under the sun.'

Trollope's tortuous journey to Dunedin continued on an early morning coach. There were two roads out of Lawrence, a newer one, which was supposedly snow-bound, and an older track through the hills. The driver chose the old road, to Trollope's surprise.

> As we turned a corner, we found ourselves in a cutting, and we found also that the cutting was blocked with snow. The coach could not be turned, and the horses had plunged in so far that we could with difficulty extricate them from the traces and pole-straps. The driver, however, decided on going on. Shovels were procured, and for two hours we all worked up to our hips in snow, and did at last get the coach through the cutting. But it was not practicable to drive the horses down the hill we had ascended, and we therefore took them oat and brought it down by hand, — an operation which at any rate kept us warm. We had hardly settled into our seats after this performance, before one of the

> wheelers slipped into a miner's water-run, and pulled the other horse under the pole atop of him. The under horse was, as it were, packed into the gully and buried, with his brother over him, like a tombstone. So we went to work again with the shovels, and dug out first one animal and then the other.

They finally descended below the level of the snow and stopped for rest and sustenance in Milton, where Trollope's wife sat by a fire and was given dry stockings. They had dinner and some brandy and water. A good road lay ahead and a 'well-horsed' coach awaited. They arrived in Dunedin about eight in the evening, 'alive, in fair spirits, — but very tired, and more ready than ever to agree with that upcountry innkeeper who had thought but little of the wisdom of one who had come travelling by winter in Otago'.

THE LAST LAMPPOST

MARK TWAIN CONSIDERED THE CRUELTY of Nature. He saw a caterpillar with a shoot sprouting from the back of its neck. The creature had dutifully carried out what Nature demanded; it had burrowed a small trench where it lay partially buried in preparation for the big transition ahead. But it was all part of Nature's trap. Fungus spores blew though the air and lodged in a crease on the caterpillar's back. The spores began to sprout and grow.

> The roots forced themselves down into the worm's person, and rearward along through its body, sucking up the creature's juices for sap; the worm slowly died, and turned to wood. And here he was now, a wooden caterpillar, with every detail of his former physique delicately and exactly preserved and perpetuated, and with that stem standing up out of him for his monument — monument commemorative of his own loyalty and of Nature's unfair return for it.

Nature was cruel in other ways too, Twain observed. In *More Tramps Abroad* he wrote of a fish's eyes so covered with parasites it can't protect itself or eat; of a starfish that sheds its parasite-filled prongs to ease its suffering and regrows them only for the parasite to return. Eventually the starfish becomes too old to grow more prongs and starves to death. Twain learned about the 'unperfected tapeworm' in Australia that lays its eggs in offal. A dog eats the offal, bites a sheep, both animals drink from a stream and a man drinks the contaminated water and eats the sheep's flesh. 'Did the dog violate a law of Nature? Did the sheep? Did the man? I cannot see that any law was violated, except the one which says you must not lead any one into temptation — even a dog, or a sheep, or a man. But Nature is always doing that. It is her trade.'

The grisly lignified caterpillar that prompted Twain's diatribe against Nature was a gift from Dr Thomas Morland Hocken. A former ship's surgeon, Hocken was a well-known Dunedin figure who acquired a huge collection of literature, artworks and artefacts from New Zealand, Australia and the Pacific Islands. The treasures are now housed at the University of Otago's Hocken Library. Twain met Hocken at his home on what is now the corner of Burlington Street and Moray Place. As well as the caterpillar, Hocken gave the American a copy of 'his translation of Tasman's diary'. Hocken's wife Bessie had translated the Dutch explorer's 1642 journal. Twain admired the tattooed faces of Maori chiefs in his host's portrait collection. 'The designs are so flowing and graceful and beautiful that they are a most satisfactory decoration. It takes but fifteen minutes to get reconciled to the tattooing, and but fifteen more to perceive that it is just the thing. After that, the undecorated European face is unpleasant and ignoble.' In 1995, to mark the centenary of Twain's visit, the Friends of Hocken annual dinner was held on the same spot that Twain and the famous doctor met. Twain's countrymen living in Dunedin were invited to the event and there was American food and music.

'The people are Scotch. They stopped here on their way from home to heaven — thinking they had arrived,' Twain wrote of Dunedin. Scots settled Dunedin, a hilly city on the southeastern coast of the South Island, in 1848 and named their new home after the Scots Gaelic for Edinburgh. When gold was discovered in Otago the small settlement of Dunedin flourished. It was New Zealand's largest city once, filled with grand Victorian architecture. Michael Davitt found Dunedin a 'wealthy, healthy, and handsome city' that boasted an average death rate of 9.15 to 1000, making it the healthiest city in the world. Twain wrote that Davitt's opinions of the city were justified.

A 'stout, kindly woman, with a motherly manner, and a sensitive, expressive face', who never charged for her services, impressed Arthur Conan Doyle. He described Mrs Roberts as 'one of the most powerful clairvoyants and trance mediums' he had tested. She claimed to be in touch with a departed spirit Selina, the name of Conan Doyle's deceased mother-in-law, who wanted to pass her love to Jean, the name of Conan Doyle's wife. The author visited Mrs Roberts twice and on both occasions he believed the spirits were communicating through her. Conan Doyle received a warm welcome in Dunedin, which didn't surprise him given the Scottish heritage of the city and the fact that spiritualism was strong in Scotland.

'Dunedin is a remarkably handsome town,' wrote Anthony Trollope, 'and, when its age is considered, a town which may be said to be remarkable in every way.' At the time of Trollope's visit Dunedin had some twenty-one thousand residents, a sixth of today's population. The city's houses were well built and many of its civic and commercial buildings were 'large, commodious, and ornamental'. Trollope didn't think British colonists had ever succeeded more quickly or more thoroughly than they had in Otago. There was a good climate, good soil and mineral wealth. He'd recently been in Australia, where there were convicts and where land had 'been wasted by great grants'. New Zealand, in contrast, and for a country 'which forty years ago was still cursed with cannibalism' struck him with wonder that it should 'so quickly have possessed itself of many of the best fruits of civilisation'.

Trollope managed to offend the locals even though his stay in Dunedin was brief. It was announced he would be attending an evening function, but he didn't show. One theory is that his luggage had yet to catch up with him and he wasn't prepared to appear in front of a crowd in inappropriate attire. His lack of popularity was also partly the result of a story that his expenses in Otago were paid by the provincial government. Trollope had 'rushed through' the area so it was unlikely he could repay the kindness by adequately publicising the province in Britain. This was unfair. Although the authorities offered to pay the expenses, Trollope refused.

There was a story about a coachman who met Trollope in the wilds of Otago at a point in the road that was too narrow for the approaching vehicles to pass by each other. 'The novelist alighted from his trap, and with withering scorn addressed the coachman, ordering him to back his horses to let his own trap pass.' When threatened by the other driver, Trollope said, 'Do you know who I am?' The coachman didn't and was unimpressed on being told that he was in the presence of Anthony Trollope. The author's adversary warned Trollope that he would see his 'name on a tombstone' if he didn't move. Trollope did.

He departed Dunedin for Christchurch. 'We rose up a long wooded hill, with a view to the right over the land-locked arm of the sea down to Port Chalmers ... The scenery of the whole country round Dunedin is beautiful, and this is the most beautiful scene of it all.' The city is situated at the head of Otago Harbour, a long natural channel stretching northeast to meet the South Pacific Ocean. An eminent nineteenth century war reporter and author believed its position left it vulnerable to attack. Archibald Forbes had a reputation for brilliant dispatches from the field of battle and he was known in the newspaper industry for his ruthless pursuit of the 'scoop'. He'd made his name in the Franco-Prussian War and his reports from the front were so popular the *Daily News* tripled its circulation to 150,000 copies after he joined the newspaper. Forbes wrote 'The Present and Future of the Australian Colonies' after a year spent in Australasia. 'New Zealand seems to regard herself as absolved from the duty of self-defence, and, although Quakers do not abound among her people, to have adopted the imbecile dictum of a local pseudo-statesman that "in her defencelessness lies her truest protection".' He believed the location of several key cities offered natural protection, but that 'many others are clean naked; such as Oamaru, Timaru, Nelson, Gisborne, New Plymouth, Greymouth, Hokitika; while Dunedin, although the waterway to the face of that beautiful city is covered, is open to inshore cannon-fire across the neck of Ocean Beach'.

The Royal Albatross Colony at Taiaroa Head on the tip of Otago Peninsula is the only one of its kind. The birds arrive in September, court and mate in October and lay eggs in November and the chicks hatch in January and February. J.B. Priestley saw the albatrosses playing in the wind on a bitterly cold day but was left 'half in a dream' by the birds. He thought of the burden of Coleridge's 'Ancient Mariner'. An albatross can stand tall, with a 12 foot wingspan and weigh 25 pounds. A man would barely have been able to move with such a beast around his neck. It was the 'peak day of all our days in New Zealand' Priestley wrote. The albatross colony was part of an itinerary organised for Priestley by Dunedin journalist and artist Shona McFarlane. They toured the peninsula in miserable weather and visited the lavish Larnach Castle, architecturally 'a Scottish Baronial hotch-potch'. William Larnach built New Zealand's only castle in 1871, for his first wife Eliza.

It was a 'thrilling spectacle'. Soldiers came from camps as far as eighty kilometres away just to be there. They marched with the bands north up Princes Street, the main road, and through the Octagon. A troop concert for 1400 military men in the Town Hall was the 'high spot' of his tour wrote Noël Coward. The troops were 'quick-witted and wonderful; one of the most receptive all-male audiences I have ever performed to,' he thought. After an encore the playwright, actor and composer felt so 'exhilarated' he could have done it all again straight away. 'Mr Coward will be the first to admit he is not another Caruso, but he has a personality and a subtlety of manner which, combined with an easy and experienced stage presence, made his task of "putting it over" to the troops a simple one,' reported the *Otago Daily Times*. He sang his own songs as well as ones by Kearn and Gershwin and his most popular numbers on the night were two humorous works, 'Don't Put Your Daughter on the Stage Mrs Worthington' and 'Any Little Fish'. The songs were well known but some of the verses were not, 'nor are they ever likely to be published', it was reported. Coward's rendition of what was essentially thought of as his theme song, 'Mad Dogs and Englishmen', was also well received. Coward later gave a public concert with proceeds going to the Otago Provincial Patriotic Council and was honoured at a civic reception. The Beatles and the Rolling Stones followed Coward to the Town Hall over twenty years later.

'What *is* humour?' asked the *Evening Star*. The philosopher Aristotle defined humour as 'what is out of time and place without danger', yet his definition could apply to many unfunny things as well, the newspaper suggested. To make us laugh, 'the ordinary operations of the mind should be suddenly and unexpectedly broken with the sense of incongruity somewhere. If Mark Twain were to tell us that a room was as dark as midnight or as Erebus, we should receive the statement grave as judges. But when he tells us that the room was "as dark as the inside of an infidel" we undoubtedly laugh. Why? I really can't tell; but evidently the natural train of one's ideas has become suddenly broken and in the anarchy of the moment some distorted nervous current sets certain muscles in spasmodic motion — the motion we call laughter.' The *Evening Star* thought Twain was funny.

MARK TWAIN AT DUNEDIN CITY HALL, 1895
SKETCH BY WILLIAM HODGKINS. ALEXANDER TURNBULL LIBRARY, WELLINGTON, NEW ZEALAND. A-212-024.

He appeared on stage for the first of three performances at the City Hall in Dowling Street and was given 'the most cordial welcome, in short, which has ever been extended to a lecturer in Dunedin,' wrote one local scribe. The hall, which stood on a site that is now a carpark, was packed with professors, bankers, doctors, lawyers, businessmen, civil servants and young people. Another newspaper reported that the city was honoured to have such a great literary figure visit, and that while to many in the audience Twain 'came in the capacity of an old friend', there were others who knew his most popular books but weren't familiar with all his work. 'Such persons were to be seen amongst last night's audience. They could be detected sniggering prematurely and listening for what was coming. Happy and blest, indeed, were they, to be enjoying for the first time whimsicalities and satires and subtle humour that have set the world a-laughing.'

For nearly two hours the man with the thick, chaotic head of greying hair, bushy eyebrows and a 'slow Yankee drawl' recounted his own adventures and those of his characters while remaining 'solemn all the time as a wart on an undertaker's horse'. He had a habit of 'nursing his elbow and anxiously pressing his cheek with his hand as if suffering the agonies of an 80-horse power, stump-jumping toothache when on the point of slipping out some particularly excruciating absurdity', according to the *Otago Witness*.

Twain's other performances in Dunedin were as successful as his first, although the raconteur reached the platform on the second night breathless after claiming he got lost for three quarters of an hour looking for the hall. William Mathew Hodgkins drew Twain in mid-performance. The two sketches are among the few such illustrations known to exist. Dunedin resident Charles Umbers bravely penned an ode to the city's eminent visitor. Umbers, a Queen Street telegraphist, began his ode to Mark Twain with the verse,

> Silver-haired 'Pilgrim' from the western world,
> Wit of the inimitable and perennial joke,
> Though in our midst the subtle shaft be hurled
> Though in the ribs we feel the Twainian poke
> (Playful as old ladies in a crowd),
> With leathern lungs I shout aloud
> In a wildly enthusiastic manner —
> Hurray! Hurray!
> You're as welcome as the flowers in May;
> Bully for you and the Star-Spangled Banner!
>
> *Evening Star*, 6 November 1895

The first novel written, printed and published in New Zealand was penned by a Dunedinite. In 1865, 27-year-old journalist Benjamin Farjeon wrote a novel called *Shadows on the Snow* and dedicated it to Charles Dickens. Farjeon sent the great author a copy and enquired about contributing to Dickens' *All the Year Round*. He also asked his advice on whether he should move to London. Dickens replied that the dedication gave him 'great pleasure' and that he read the book with 'much satisfaction'. He couldn't guarantee to publish a piece from Farjeon in *All the Year Round* but he would read anything the young author wanted to submit. It is believed to be the only letter Charles Dickens sent to a New Zealander. Farjeon sailed for London in 1867 and became a successful novelist and the father of well-known children's writer Eleanor Farjeon.

It's not known where Jules Verne learned about Dunedin, yet the city features in *Les Frères Kip* (The Kip Brothers). The first five chapters of Verne's tale of mutiny and murder are set in New Zealand. The brothers arrive in Dunedin on the *James Cook* where they are delayed after the ship's crew desert to the goldfields. Although they didn't appear to be based on real pubs, 'The Three Magpies', 'The Old Brothers' and 'The Good Seaman' are mentioned as 'notorious Port Chalmers grog shops' from which a replacement crew is sought. A group of men on the run from the police join the schooner before it sails up the east coast and on to the Coral Sea northeast of Australia.

The Port Chalmers Museum has a mounted collection of small pieces of timber from the *Otago,* a ship once commanded by Joseph Conrad. The Polish born author of *Heart of Darkness* spent two decades sailing the world and his adventures inspired his works. Conrad captained the *Otago* on trips to Singapore, Australia and Mauritius in 1888 and 1889 and the ship became the subject of *The Shadow-Line*. Conrad's 1901 novel *Falk* was partly inspired by a bizarre disaster that befell a ship bound for New Zealand in 1899. The *Waikato* left London on 4 May and halfway between the Cape of Good Hope and New Zealand her tail shaft broke. The crew was unable to repair the ship, which drifted helplessly at the mercy of shifting winds and currents for four months. She was eventually discovered and towed to Fremantle, after cruising some four and a half thousand miles. In *Falk*, Conrad combined aspects of the *Waikato* story with his own experiences in Bangkok. It's the story of a man who divulges the dark secret of a ship that drifted many miles after her tail shaft broke between the Cape of Good Hope and New Zealand, her crew resorting to cannibalism.

New Zealand's first university was established in Dunedin in 1869, during the heady gold-rush era, and the University of Otago's neo-Gothic stone buildings remain an integral part of the city. American poet Robert Creeley began a tour of the six university cities of New Zealand in Dunedin in 1976 before heading north, at the invitation of the New Zealand Students' Art Council. It was in the city that he met his third wife Penelope Highton. He wrote of Dunedin:

> River wandering down
> below in the widening green
> fields between the hills—
> and the sea and the town

His poems, in the form of journal entries from tours and readings he had given in Fiji, New Zealand, Australia, Singapore, the Philippines, Malaysia, Hong Kong, Japan and Korea were compiled in his 1978 book *Hello: A Journal, February 29-May 3, 1976.* Creeley renewed his links with New Zealand when he became a Fulbright Scholar at the University of Auckland in 1995, where he wrote *The Dogs of Auckland*, an eight-part meditation.

The Hocken Library holds a letter Arthur Conan Doyle sent to a fellow doctor,

D.W. Carmalt Jones, Professor of Medicine at the University of Otago. He discusses the issue of life after death, writing 'surely it is better for you to know that love and an intellectual life carry on than that you end finally amid maggots in a box'.

J.B. Priestley left a dinner organised by the Otago University Vice Chancellor sooner than he wanted to. He spoke a little harshly to a guest who gushed about the advantages of living in New Zealand and how its people would largely escape the consequences of a northern hemisphere nuclear war. Priestley told her if she continued talking like that 'one morning half the country may blow up in your face'. He was 'genuinely afraid of complacent hubristic talking and thinking'. But he was thoroughly enjoying the party when he had to leave to honour another commitment. He promised to meet the amateur Little Theatre group, which turned out to be a noisy party of 'self important performers'. Priestley complained that the group had no serious interest in his opinions and it was the only engagement of his entire visit he considered a 'dead loss'.

Dunedin 'has a spirit, it has an atmosphere, of which the Octagon with its statue of Burns, the fine churches, the University's splendid original building, are the visible symbols,' Priestley wrote. 'The bracing air of the place helps to sustain life and breed character.' The city was architecturally modelled as a 'South Pacific Edinburgh' but Priestley believed American influences had resulted in some confusion. He guessed that the city 'must have been governed alternatively by wise men and blockheads'. But he thought the surroundings were 'magnificent', especially the Otago Peninsula and the ring of virgin bush like an English green belt. Dunedin was the place he would choose to live in exile, overtaking his previous favourite, an area just outside Vancouver.

✶

In 1891 an elderly Dunedin resident, William Ewing, received a telegraph from Rudyard Kipling that he would be coming to Dunedin on the *Talune.* Kipling had met Ewing on board the *Doric* from Cape Town to Wellington and despite a marked age difference the two got on well. The day Kipling arrived was a stormy one and he was seen on Queen's Wharf holding onto his bowler hat as he was buffeted by a vicious nor'wester. He stayed at Dunedin's Grand Hotel, the High Street building near the Octagon designed by the Italian architect Louis Boldini, but he spent most of his time at Ewing's house in Elm Row, a couple of blocks away. He drew a picture for one of Ewing's daughters of a quill pen with his head on it and the words, 'To ye memory of Rudyard Kipling, who came to see New Zealand, but didn't.'

Kipling didn't attract as much attention in the Dunedin press as he had elsewhere in New Zealand. There was a rival attraction in town, General William Booth, the founder of the Salvation Army, who travelled widely on evangelical missions and attracted large audiences and many column inches in New Zealand. They met on the way to Bluff from Melbourne on the *Mararoa.*

RUDYARD KIPLING [RIGHT] CHATS WITH WILLIAM EWING IN DUNEDIN, 1891. M.S. STEPHENSON COLLECTION, ALEXANDER TURNBULL LIBRARY, WELLINGTON, NEW ZEALAND. PAColl-0070.

Otago Witness reporter Malcolm Ross chatted to Mark Twain as the author smoked a pipe and cigars on breaks from his writing work in his cabin, on the upper deck of the ship. 'The stereotyped interview is distasteful to most literary men of any ability, so I discreetly kept pencil and note book out of view, and the gifted author never dreamt for a moment that he was being "drawn out" for an interview.' They met on the way to New Zealand from Melbourne to Bluff on the *Mararoa*. Ross gave Twain some books about New Zealand and asked him about his writing habits. Twain said that whenever he found writing a struggle he put the article or the book aside for a while and started on something else. He preferred a more relaxed style of writing to the laborious work undertaken by other authors. A friend of his 'overworked his brain to such an extent' while he was compiling an Arabic dictionary in Italy, that he deserted his work and wandered around the Continent until he was finally found in Belgium.

Ross found Twain 'deeply interested in details connected with the discovery and early history of New Zealand; also in the Maori race ... He marvelled at the work done by Tasman and Cook.' Asked which of his books he liked best, Twain said he wasn't sure because it had been so long since he had read them. Ross thought the author might slightly favour *The Innocents Abroad*. 'Yes, that was a splendid trip,' Twain commented. 'Everything was fresh and new then: everything is old now.'

Michael Davitt was also on board the *Mararoa* bound for Bluff. Twain entertained him in the smoke-room with stories, including one involving a remedy for insomnia. Twain tried a glass of beer before bed, but that only worked for a while. He tried two ounces of whisky, which he liked so much he increased it by another three. But the insomnia returned. Finally he stumbled across an 'infallible remedy', a children's book of German grammar. He could never get through a page before falling asleep.

In folklore Bluff is often thought of as the southernmost tip of New Zealand. The phrase 'From Cape Reinga to Bluff' is regularly used to describe the length of the country, but the most southerly point is actually further east, at Slope Point in the Catlins. Bluff is 27 kilometres south of the city of Invercargill and was established by Dunedin settlers who'd bought farming land in the deep south and needed to import stock from Australia.

Bluff is also the place where the rabbit plague began, or so wrote Mark Twain in *More Tramps Abroad*. The first rabbits were introduced in the early days of settlement, for sport, food and possibly to recreate a British environment. From 1873 to 1882 the number of exported rabbit skins rose from a few tens of thousands to over nine million. Plague-like numbers of rabbits swarmed over areas of the southern and eastern South Island and the southeast of the North Island. Despite the introduction of predators, rabbit control boards, poison, traps and bullets, the animals flourished. 'In England the natural enemy of the rabbit is detested and persecuted,' Twain wrote, but 'in the Bluff region the natural enemy of the rabbit is honoured, and his person is sacred.'

> In England any person below the Heir who is caught with a rabbit in his possession must satisfactorily explain how it got there, or he will suffer fine and imprisonment, together with extinction of his peerage; in Bluff, the cat found with a rabbit in its possession does not have to explain — everybody looks the other way; the person caught noticing would suffer fine and imprisonment, with extinction of peerage. This is a sure way to undermine the moral fabric of a cat. Thirty years from now there will not be a moral cat in New Zealand. Some think there is none there now.

A four-year study of New Zealand rabbits was an inspiration for Richard Adams' *Watership Down*. Naturalist Ronald Lockley wrote about sixty books but his 1964 work *The Private Life of the Rabbit: An Account of the Life History and Social Behaviour of the Wild Rabbit* was his most well-known publication. According to the *Times Literary Supplement* Lockley 'shows the rabbit to be a more complex fellow than one had thought'. Adams credited Lockley for his insight into rabbit behaviour. Welsh-born Lockley moved to New Zealand in 1977 with his third wife and died in Auckland in 2000 at the age of 96.

Bluff is the departure point to Stewart Island, the rocky outcrop 64 kilometres long and 40 kilometres wide off the tip of the South Island. Stewart Island is a couple of hours by ferry across the turbulent Foveaux Strait, a stretch of water famed for its annual crop of Bluff Oysters. Eric Linklater described the island in *A Year of Space: A Chapter in Autobiography*.

He found a diminishing island community in a densely bush-covered place of 'remarkable beauty'. But he also felt something 'sinister'. He enjoyed being in the bush only as long as he had companionship. Linklater spent a day at sea with two brothers and was taken up a 'curious, serpentine river that flowed, black and sluggish, through flat lands densely covered with high *manuka*, until, a long way up, the stream narrowed and we came to an almost imperceptible clearing and a half-ruined hut'. One brother went out deer hunting while the wife of the other brother, an Otago University lecturer and Linklater's travel companion, prepared food. The deer hunter returned empty-handed and the weather worsened. Linklater suspected the trio liked the idea of a night in the bush, but eventually they left and sailed back to their island base in 'half a gale'.

Bluff was the arrival and departure point for many visiting authors. On arriving from Melbourne on the *Albion* Anthony Trollope 'immediately asked to be shown some Maoris, but was told that they were very scarce in that part of the country. Indeed, I did not see one in the whole province, and it seemed as though I might as well have asked for a moa.' Bluff was then a small settlement framed by close hills and distant mountains. There was a quay, a railway, a post office and two inns. The scenery was 'wild and pretty' and reminded Trollope of the coast of County Cork in Ireland. He had heard about the cannibals of New Zealand and about the settlement of the colony that was 'the most absolutely Antipodean to Greenwich' and he wanted New Zealand to be mysterious, not simply another England. 'If I could find myself in a Maori pah, — then indeed the flavour of the dust of Pall Mall would for the time depart from me altogether. Most travellers have experienced the feeling, — have anticipated a certain strangeness which they have never quite achieved.' When Trollope reached Invercargill, now New Zealand's southernmost city, he felt exactly as he might have felt 'on getting out of a railway in some small English town'. By the time he arrived at the inn, and had 'gone through the customary battle as to bedrooms, a tub of cold water, and supper, all the feeling of mystery was gone'.

Invercargill is a sprawling, flat city, which has developed to service the farming industry. Trollope and his wife stayed two days in a place 'without any special attractions' but which was home to 'a brewer who was very anxious that I should take a barrel of his beer home to England in order that the people there might know what New Zealand could do in the way of brewing, and who generously offered to give me the barrel of beer for that purpose'.

Mark Twain's visit to Invercargill would 'live long in the recollection of the town, and his lecture will be among our most pleasant and treasured memories'. The author had 'one of the largest audiences that ever paid for admission to any entertainment in Invercargill'. Such was the demand to see Twain in Invercargill's Theatre Royal it was rumoured a speculator had bought all the tickets and tripled his money by reselling them. At the beginning of the twentieth century, the Theatre Royal on Dee Street, which a local reporter described as 'the old temple of art, sacred with a thousand memories', was converted into a shop and in the 1980s the building burned down and was replaced by the city's public library.

By sailing down the east coast of the South Island, Kipling missed the countryside others marvelled at. While he 'tackled' the South Island, 'mainly populated by Scots, their sheep, and the Devil's own high winds', in a small ship 'among colder and increasing seas', other writers had a more pleasant experience. Twain thought the scenery between Bluff and Christchurch the 'most charming' he had seen. It had a 'quiet beauty all of its own, and which makes it quite an Eden'. The land between Invercargill and Dunedin reminded Michael Davitt so much of home that he began to 'speculate about a possible line of terrestrial communication and influence right through Mother Earth, from Otago to the centre of Ireland. Once embarked on this line of thought, you are inclined to find everything as it ought to be in the best and brightest of New Zealand worlds.'

A procession marched to the sound of the Salvation Army Band. It stopped at a piece of vacant land beside the customhouse. After a short service the procession was reformed to accompany General William Booth to the *Talune*. A famous young author watched as General Booth boarded the ship. Rudyard Kipling saw him 'walking backward in the dusk over the uneven wharf, his cloak blown upwards, tulip-fashion, over his grey head, while he beat a tambourine in the face of the singing, weeping, praying crowd who had come to see him off'. Kipling had been in Bluff for 12 hours awaiting the *Talune*'s departure for Hobart and Melbourne. His visit to New Zealand was over. 'On a boisterous dark evening' Kipling departed 'the Last Lamp-post in the World'.

Departure

'FAREWELL, NEW ZEALAND! I SHALL NEVER see you again, but perhaps some memory of my visit may remain — or not, as God pleases,' wrote Arthur Conan Doyle, who left Wellington Harbour on Christmas Eve 1920. Behind him the sun was setting in 'a slur of scarlet above the olive green hills' and heavy fog was 'crawling up the valleys'. Ahead lay Melbourne and a family reunion. The small steamer *Paloona* was scheduled to leave at noon but the ship was missing a fireman and it was four in the afternoon when the vessel left port on a light northeasterly wind in fine but cloudy conditions. Whether or not New Zealand remembered him, the creator of Sherlock Holmes would remember New Zealand. 'It is a lovely place,' Conan Doyle wrote, 'and contains within its moderate limits the agricultural plains of England, the lakes and hills of Scotland, the glaciers of Switzerland, and the fiords of Norway, with a fine hearty people, who do not treat the British newcomer with ignorant contempt or hostility.'

Many authors who travelled to New Zealand knew a return was unlikely. Old age or indifference were factors; but it also took time, money and energy to travel many thousands of kilometres around the globe. On his voyage home George Bernard Shaw wrote to a friend that he hadn't seen any newspapers other than New Zealand titles for three months and all he had was 'a general impression that everybody's dead, and that I ought to be'. J.B. Priestley wrote of the dated opinions of actor friends who warned him New Zealand was dull. The 'long journey' was worthwhile. Distance was a particular problem for writers who lived before the advent of air travel, or before air travel became affordable. Agatha Christie was so taken by New Zealand's natural beauty that she vowed to return — but never did. For most of her life New Zealand was too far away and by the time it was possible to fly she had given up travelling.

Authors who couldn't or wouldn't return still had their memories and their notes and they took New Zealand with them. Nevil Shute, the best-selling author of post-apocalyptic novel *On The Beach*, visited in 1957. A reporter asked him if he was in the country to gather material for a new novel. 'Wherever you go you get to know things which eventually find their way into a book,' he replied.

Famous visitors often took home a collection of gifts and mementos to remind them of the land on the other side of the world. Shaw was given tiki, greenstone and a copy of John Lee's *Children of the Poor*, a largely autobiographical novel just published by the New Zealand criminal-turned-socialist politician and writer. Priestley collected New Zealand books and art works. The president of the New Zealand Association of Spiritualists gave Conan Doyle a woollen travelling rug for himself, a greenstone penholder for his wife and a small charm for his young daughter. Maori in Rotorua presented Noël Coward with a carved tobacco jar and inkstand and a Christchurch old age pensioner made him a violin. Janet Frame gave Salman Rushdie a signed copy of *Janet Frame: An Autobiography* and Rushdie returned the compliment by giving Frame a signed copy of *The Moor's Last Sigh*.

Agatha Christie was given a huge jar of meat extract. It proved to be a useful donation. By the time the Christies reached the last leg of the British Empire Exhibition Mission through Canada they had run short of money. They continued to stay in hotels but Agatha tried to economise on food. Breakfast was a set price, so she ate as much as she could. In the evening, when Major Belcher and her husband attended official dinners, she returned to her hotel room, complained of indigestion and asked for a large jug of boiling water, to which she added the meat extract. The jar from New Zealand fed her for about ten days.

By the beginning of 1898 Mark Twain had cleared his debts, but by the time he returned to the United States in 1900 he had been away for more than five years. Towards the end of his exile he opened the Kensal Rise Reading Room in London. Another speaker alluded to his nom de plume and the humourist made public a letter he had received from a little New Zealand girl. Her father told her the author's proper name was not Mark Twain but Samuel Clemens. The girl assured Twain that she knew better, because Clemens was the man who sold the patent medicine, and his name was not Mark. She wrote that she liked the name Mark, because Mark Anthony was in the Bible. Twain told his audience he had thanked the girl for her sentiments, and added that as Mark Anthony had got into the Bible 'I am not without hopes myself'.

A future New Zealand governor-general met a golden-haired poet on the Belgian Front and the two became good friends. Bernard Cyril Freyberg, whose parents immigrated to New Zealand when he was two, travelled to England at the outbreak of war to volunteer. Freyberg was heavily decorated for his battlefield exploits and was awarded the Victoria Cross. He would later distinguish himself in the Second World War. When Rupert Brooke died a few months after meeting Freyberg, the New Zealander helped carry his new friend to his final resting place in an olive grove on the island of Skyros.

But the most enduring legacy of New Zealand's relationship with its visiting scribes is the printed word. New Zealanders are renowned for pestering visitors for their opinion of the country and this need for reassurance is heightened when a famous author arrives. Early settlers displayed a painful insecurity. They knew that the United States, Canada and Australia were seen as superior locations for would-be emigrants. When Trollope left Auckland on the *Nebraksa* his book on Australia and New Zealand was about three quarters finished. The *Daily Southern Cross* speculated on what Trollope's pen had written.

> In time we shall doubtless have the pleasure of reading his matured opinions on the comparative futures to which the cluster of colonies usually known by the name of the Australasian colonies will severally attain. Love for our adopted country makes us hope, and its past history convinces us, that Mr Trollope will not assign to New Zealand the lowest position in that galaxy of nations which is springing up around us.

Trollope, whose son lived in Australia, was one of the few nineteenth century authors to visit New Zealand more than once. He returned to Auckland for a day in 1875, three years after his first visit. In a letter to the *Liverpool Mercury* he wrote of his interest in the colony and his pleasure at having the opportunity to learn more. When he left in 1872 he had written,

> New Zealand is over-governed, over-legislated for, over-provided with officials, and over-burdened with national debt. That it will have strength to struggle through with all the weight imposed upon it is not improbable. It has a magnificent climate, rich mineral gifts, good soil, — and among its people a resolution to succeed which is in itself equal to half a battle won.

On his return the pressing issues were the abolition of provincial governments and the £18 million pound debt created by Julius Vogel. Trollope suggested if Vogel continued borrowing he might create a situation in which Britain would have to rescue the colony from bankruptcy.

In *Tales of the Angler's Eldorado*, Zane Grey mused on whether he would ever see New Zealand again. He was writing of his departure in late April 1926. Grey claimed to have received hundreds of letters from New Zealanders, including schoolgirls and boys, welcoming him to the country. The messages continued, urging him to return. He published seven verses from one admiring fan, Constance Wheeler of Blockhouse Bay, Auckland, which he felt was 'singularly expressive of the friendliness of my youthful readers'. 'My Favourite Author' ends,

> Au revoir to you, Zane Grey;
> Luck be yours in every way.
> As you sail away from here,
> Guess you'll hear the fishes cheer,
> Till you come again next year.
> Then, by jove, they'll all feel queer.

Nola Luxford, a New Zealand actress and journalist, had approached Grey to help advance her film career before his first New Zealand trip. He was then the third biggest selling American author ever. The married Grey pursued her romantically and asked her to accompany him on his return to New Zealand as his 'secretary'. Luxford's refusal, and her insistence on a platonic relationship, ended the acquaintance. Throughout his life Grey cultivated a wholesome image which was recently shattered by Thomas H. Pauly's biography *Zane Grey: His Life, His Adventures, His Women.*

Without Nola and despite the controversy surrounding his first visit, the literary angler did return to his newly discovered fishing paradise on more than one occasion. His trips produced four books and numerous articles. As well as *Tales of the Angler's Eldorado* he wrote *Tales of Swordfish and Tuna* in 1927, *Tales of Tahitian Waters* in 1931 and *An American Angler in Australia* in 1937. He even wrote an article on New Zealand sheep farming for *Country Gentleman.*

Controversy also dogged Grey's subsequent visits. When he tried to return to Great Mercury Island he proposed to take a party of more than forty-five people. The Tourist Department wanted him back because of the money he spent in New Zealand and the publicity he generated. But much to the government's dismay a new owner of the island valued his privacy and disliked Grey. The writer had behaved badly and left the campsite in an appalling state during his previous visit to the island.

Some visitors to New Zealand were so famous many locals couldn't believe that such celebrity had touched their country, but occasionally a New Zealander has brushed against greatness without even knowing it. A man was reading a local newspaper in a smoking carriage with Kipling. The newspaper carried a telegram announcing that Kipling had caught a severe chill in Wellington and was heading south to recuperate.

> Probably he took the spectacled little man on the opposite seat for a foreigner, and for that reason conducted his conversation in the Morse Code, which, as everyone knows, is a series of dots and dashes. 'Look here,' he said, marking the offending item with a grimy finger-nail, 'look at this dash thing. Who the dot is Rudyard Kipling, and who the dash wants to know whether he's got a chill, and who the dot and dash cares whether he dies? No, sir, I want to know whether [the

> Australian racehorse] Carbine's dot and dot and dash hoof is sound.'
>
> *Argus*, 21 November 1891

Conan Doyle was departing from Lyttelton to begin his sea journey back to Australia. But a shipping strike had broken out. It was the festive season and it would probably be difficult to get as far as the North Island, let alone Australia. Conan Doyle and his agent Smythe managed to get passage on the *Maori*, but there would be no stewards or food on board. So they went to a Lyttelton hostel for supplies where they met a very drunk customer.

> 'Scuse me, sir!' said he, looking at me with a glassy stare, 'but you bear most 'straordinary resemblance Olver Lodge.'
>
> I said something amiable.
>
> 'Yes, sir —'straordinary! Have you ever seen Olver Lodge, sir?'
>
> 'Yes, I have.'
>
> 'Well, did you perceive resemblance?'
>
> 'Sir Oliver, as I remember him, was a tall man with a grey beard.'
>
> He shook his head at me sadly.
>
> 'No, sir — I heard him at Wellington last week. No beard. A moustache, sir, same as your own.'
>
> 'You're sure it was Sir Oliver?'
>
> A slow smile came over his face.
>
> 'Blesh my soul — Conan Doyle — that's the name. Yes sir, you bear truly remarkable resemblance Conan Doyle.'
>
> I did not say anything further so I daresay he has not discovered yet the true cause of the resemblance.

A large crowd gathered to farewell George Bernard Shaw in Wellington on Saturday, 14 April 1934. Bouquets of flowers were passed through one of the *Rangitane*'s portholes. As the ship pulled out of the harbour Shaw, buffeted by a brisk northerly wind in a zip-fastened jersey, pale pink flannel trousers and white canvas shoes, smiled and waved from high on deck. He looked relaxed. A couple of weeks before arriving at Plymouth he would write a letter in which he mentioned writing 'a play and a half'. These were *The Simpleton of the Unexpected Isles*, begun during his voyage out to New Zealand, and an unfinished draft of *The Millionairess*.

Journalists were keen to record the last utterances of a man who had filled column inches for a month. Asked whether he would return to New Zealand the 77-year-old replied, 'At my age I have no intentions at all, because I don't know whether I shall be alive.' He hinted that if he ever came back to the South Pacific he'd spend time in

GEORGE BERNARD SHAW, 1934. AUCKLAND WAR MEMORIAL MUSEUM, C18624.

Australia, which he bypassed on this trip. Shaw said he was 'extremely glad' he came to New Zealand and that 'it was rather too pleasing a place'. Perhaps the country should be presented in a less attractive way to stop the 'riffraff' of Europe flowing in, he suggested. In a letter of thanks to the Tourist Department the Shaws had written 'we quite agree that we never had such a tour in our lives'. Finally, after many goodbyes, a photographer on the deck of the *Rangitane* asked George Bernard Shaw for a departing smile. To which the playwright replied, 'If I showed my true feelings I would cry. It's the best country I've been in.'

BIBLIOGRAPHY

Alpers, A., *Katherine Mansfield*. Alfred A Knopf, New York, 1953.

———, *Dolphins*. Robin Clark, Milton Keynes, 1979.

Ausubel, D., *The Fern and the Tiki*. Angus and Robertson, Sydney, 1960.

Bornholdt, J., & O'Brien, G., *The Colour of Distance*. Victoria University Press, Wellington, 2005.

Baughan, B.E., *Arthur's Pass and the Otira Gorge*. Whitcombe & Tombs, Auckland, 1925.

Brooke, R., *The Letters of Rupert Brooke* (edited by Geoffrey Keynes). Faber and Faber, London, 1968.

Browne, J., *Charles Darwin: Voyaging*. Pimlico, London, 1995.

Bullen, F.T., *Advance Australasia*. Hodder and Stoughton, London, 1907.

———, *The Cruise of the Cachalot*. Macrae Smith Company, Philadelphia, 1925.

Butler, S., *A First Year in a Canterbury Settlement*. A.C. Fifield, London, 1914.

———, *Erewhon*, Printed by the Pynson printers for the members of the Limited Editions Club, New York, 1934.

Caldwell, E.N., *Last Witness for Robert Louis Stevenson*. University of Oklahoma Press, Norman, 1960.

Carrington, C.E., *Rudyard Kipling*. Penguin, Harmondsworth, 1970.

Christie, A., *An Autobiography*. Collins, London, 1977.

———, *Sleeping Murder*. Dodd, Mead, New York, 1976.

Cook, Captain J., *Captain Cook's Journal During His First Voyage Round the World Made in H.M. Bark "Endeavour" 1768-71*. Elliot Stock, London, 1893.

Coward, N., *Autobiography*. Methuen, London, 1986.

Cowan, J., *The story of Pelorus Jack, the white dolphin of French Pass, New Zealand, with Maori legends, by James Cowan*. Whitcombe & Tombs, Auckland, 1930.

Creeley, R., *Hello: A Journal, February 29-May 3, 1976*. New Directions, New York, 1978.

Darwin, C., *Charles Darwin's Letters: A selection 1825-1859* (edited by Frederick Burkhardt). Cambridge University Press, 1996.

———, *Journal of researches into the natural history and geology of the countries visited during the voyage of H.M.S. Beagle*. Harper & Brothers, New York, 1846.

Darwin, F., ed., *The Life and Letters of Charles Darwin*. D. Appleton, New York, 1887.

Davitt, M., *Life and Progress in Australasia*. Methuen, London, 1898.

Dick, B., *High Country Family*. A.H. & A.W. Reed, Wellington, 1964.

Dickens, C., *The Letters of Charles Dickens* (edited by Madeline House & Graham Storey). Clarendon Press, Oxford, 1969.

———, *The Pickwick Papers*. Penguin, London. 1994.

Dieffenbach, E., *Travels in New Zealand* (2 vols). John Murray, London, 1843.

Domett, A., *Ranolf and Amohia*. K. Paul, Trench, London, 1883.

Doyle, A.C., *The Coming of the Fairies*. Doran, New York, 1922.

———, *The History of Spiritualism* (2 vols). Cassel, London, 1926.

———, *The Wanderings of a Spiritualist*. Hodder and Stoughton, London, 1921.

Dumas, A., *Captain Marion* (translated by F.W. Reed). The Caxton Press, Christchurch, 1949.

———, *The Journal of Madame Giovanni* (translated by Marguerite E. Wilbur). Hammond, Hammond & Co, London, 1944.

Dumont d'Urville, J.S.C., *The New Zealanders* (translated by Carol Legge). Victoria University Press, Wellington, 1992.

Dupré, C., *John Galsworthy*. Collins, London, 1976.

Eisen, J. & Smith, K.J., eds., *Strangers in Paradise.* Vintage, Auckland, 1991.
Ellis, D., *D.H. Lawrence.* Cambridge University Press, Cambridge, 1998.
Ervine, St J., *Bernard Shaw.* Constable, London, 1956.
Froude, J.A., *Oceana; or, England and Her Colonies.* C. Scribner, New York, 1897.
Gentry, K., & McLean, G., eds., *Heartlands.* Penguin, Auckland, 2006.
Goodliffe, J., *These Fortunate Isles.* Canterbury University Press, Christchurch, 1992.
Goudge, E., *Green Dolphin Country.* Hodder and Stoughton, London, 1961.
Grey, Z., *Tales of the Angler's Eldorado, New Zealand.* Harper & Brothers, New York, 1926.
Hall, N.J., *Trollope.* Clarendon Press, Oxford, 1991.
Hammond, B., *The New Zealand Encyclopaedia of Fly Fishing.* The Halcyon Press, Auckland, 1988.
Hassall, C., *Rupert Brooke.* Faber and Faber, London, 1964.
Holroyd, M., *Bernard Shaw.* Chatto & Windus, London, 1991.
Huxley, A., *Along the Road.* Chatto & Windus, London, 1974.
———, *Ape and Essence.* Vintage, London, 2005.
Inglis, J., *Our New Zealand Cousins.* Sampson Low, Marston, Searle, and Rivingston, London, 1887.
Jackson, C., *Zane Grey.* Twayne, New York, 1989.
Kennedy, D., *Kennedy's Colonial Travel.* Edinburgh Publ. Co., Edinburgh, 1876.
Kennedy, R., *Kipling Down Under.* Xlibris, Philadelphia, 2000.
Kipling, R., *Kipling's India: Uncollected Sketches 1884-88* (edited by Thomas Pinney). Macmillan, Hampshire, 1986.
———, *Something of Myself for My Friends Known and Unknown.* Macmillan, London, 1937.
———, *The Best Short Stories.* Wordsworth Editions, Hertfordshire, 1997.
———, *The Seven Seas.* D. Appleton, New York, 1896.
Lawson, H., *Henry Lawson: Autobiographical and Other Writings 1887-1922* (edited by Colin Roderick). Angus and Robertson, Sydney, 1972.
Linklater, E., *A Year of Space: A Chapter in Autobiography.* Macmillan, London, 1953.
Lloyd, H.D., *Newest England.* Doubleday, Page, New York, 1900.
London, J., *The Cruise of the Snark.* Macmillan, New York, 1913.
———, *The Human Drift.* Macmillan, New York, 1917.
Lycett, A., *Rudyard Kipling.* Weidenfeld & Nicolson, London, 1999.
McClure, M., *The Wonder Country.* Auckland University Press, Auckland, 2004.
McCormick, E.H., *An Absurd Ambition.* Auckland University Press, Auckland, 1996.
McLynn, F., *Robert Louis Stevenson.* Hutchinson, London, 1993.
Mair, G., *Reminiscences and Maori Stories.* The Brett Printing and Publishing Co., Auckland, 1923.
Marrot, H. V., *The Life and Letters of John Galsworthy.* C. Scribner's sons, New York, 1936.
Maugham, W.S., *The Moon and Sixpence.* Grosset & Dunlap, New York, c1919.
Melville, H., *Moby Dick.* Random House, New York, 1930.
Michener, J., *Return to Paradise.* Random House, New York, 1951.
Moors, H. J., *With Stevenson in Samoa.* Small, Maynard & Company, Boston, 1910.
Morgan, J., *Agatha Christie.* Collins, London, 1984.
Morris, J., *Cities.* Faber and Faber, London, 1963.
Mullen, R., *Anthony Trollope.* Duckworth, London, 1990.
Osborne, C., *The Life and Crimes of Agatha Christie.* HarperCollins, London, 2000.
Parker, H., *Herman Melville.* The John Hopkins University Press, Baltimore, 2002.

Pearson, R., *The Fables of Reason.* Clarendon Press, Oxford, 1993.
Pocock, T., *Rider Haggard and the Lost Empire.* Weidenfeld and Nicholson, London, 1993.
Polack, J.S., *Manners and Customs of the New Zealanders* (2 vols). James Madden, London, 1840.
———, *New Zealand* (2 vols). R. Bentley, London, 1838.
Priestley, J.B., *A Visit to New Zealand.* Heinemann, London, 1974.
Raby, P., *Samuel Butler.* The Hogarth Press, London, 1991.
Reed, A.H., *With Anthony Trollope in New Zealand.* A.H. & A.W. Reed, Wellington, 1969.
Rhys, E., ed., *The Voyages of Captain Cook.* Wordsworth Editions, Hertfordshire, 1999.
Ryan, J.S., *Charles Dickens and New Zealand.* A.H. and A.W. Reed, Wellington, 1965.
Sala, G.A., *The Land of the Golden Fleece* (edited by Robert Dingley). Mulini Press, Canberra, 1995.
Sanborn, G., *The Sign of the Cannibal.* Duke University Press, Durham, 1998.
Sauter, R., *Galsworthy the Man.* Peter Owen, London, 1967.
Seymour-Smith, M., *Rudyard Kipling.* Queen Anne Press, London, 1989.
Shaw, G.B., *Bernard Shaw: Collected Letters 1926-1950* (edited by Dan H. Laurence). Max Reinhardt, London, 1988.
Shillingsburg, M. J., *At Home Abroad.* University Press of Mississippi, Jackson, 1988.
Stanley, H.M., *The Autobiography of Henry Morton Stanley.* Houghton Mifflin, New Boston, 1909.
Stevenson, F.V. de G., *The Cruise of the "Janet Nichol" Among the South Sea Islands.* C. Scribner's sons, New York, 1914.
Stevenson, R.L., *Essays of Robert Louis Stevenson.* C. Scribner's sons, New York, 1912.
———, *The Letters of Robert Louis Stevenson* (edited by Sidney Colvin). Scribner, New York, 1925.
Stone, R.C.J., *The Father and His Gift.* Auckland University Press, Auckland, 1987.
———, *Young Logan Campbell.* Auckland University Press, Auckland, 1982.
Straus, R., *Sala.* Constable, London, 1942.
Terry, R.C., ed., *Oxford Reader's Companion To Trollope.* Oxford University Press, Oxford, 1999.
Tremain, R., *The Colour.* Vintage, London, 2004.
Trollope, A., *An Autobiography.* J. W. Lovell, New York, 1883.
———, *Australia and New Zealand.* George Robertson, Melbourne, 1873.
———, *Later Short Stories.* Oxford University Press, Oxford, 1995.
———, *The Fixed Period.* University of Michigan Press, Michigan, 1990.
———, *The Letters of Anthony Trollope* (edited by N. John Hall). Stanford University Press, Stanford, 1983.
———, *The Tireless Traveler* (edited by Bradford Allen Booth). University of California Press, Berkeley, 1941.
Twain, M., *Following the Equator.* The American Publishing Company, Connecticut, 1897.
———, *Literary Essays.* Harper & Brothers, New York, 1897.
———, *More Tramps Abroad.* Chatto & Windus, London, 1897.
Verne, J., *A Voyage round the World* (3 vols). Routledge & Sons, London, 1876-77.
Voltaire, *Lord Chesterfield's Ears.* R. Carlile, London, 1826.
Wevers, L., *Country of Writing.* Auckland University Press, Auckland, 2002.
White, P., *Patrick White Speaks.* Jonathon Cape, London, 1989.
Wyndham, J., *The Chrysalids.* Penguin, London, 1958.
Yang, L., *Non-person Singular* (translated by Brian Holton). Wellsweep, London, 1994.

NEWSPAPERS AND PERIODICALS

Auckland Waikato Historical Journal
Auckland Weekly News
Bay of Plenty Times
Bookman
Century Illustrated Monthly Magazine
Chicago Daily Tribune
Cosmopolitan Magazine
Daily Southern Cross
Daily Telegraph
Dominion
Dominion Post
Evening Star
Guardian
Hawke's Bay Herald
Household Words
Islands
Kipling Journal
Landfall
Listener
London News
Los Angeles Times
Lyttelton Times
Manawatu Standard
Natural History
Nelson Evening Mail
New York Times
New Zealand Free Lance
New Zealand Gazette
New Zealand Geographer
New Zealand Geographic
New Zealand Herald
New Zealand Marine News
New Zealand Observer
New Zealand Observer and Free Lance
Nineteenth Century
North Otago Times
Notes and Queries
Observer Magazine
Otago Daily Times
Otago Witness
Pall Mall Gazette
Press
Quote Unquote
South African Christian Recorder
Southland Times
Spectator
Star
Stout Centre Review
Taranaki Herald
Times Literary Supplement
The Times
Timaru Herald
Tuapeka Times
Wanganui Chronicle
Wanganui Herald

INDEX

G

H

I

J

K

L

M